Media Theory

WITHDRAWN

2001

To *Jessie, Abby and Kate*
Media Theorists

Pintz Orum & Chopper

MEDIA THEORY

An Introduction

Fred Inglis

BLACKWELL
Oxford UK & Cambridge USA

Copyright © Fred Inglis 1990

First published 1990

Reprinted 1990, 1991

Basil Blackwell Ltd
108 Cowley Road, Oxford, OX4 1JF, UK

Basil Blackwell, Inc.
3 Cambridge Center
Cambridge, Massachusetts 02142, USA

British Library Cataloging in Publication Data

A CIP catalogue record for this book is available from the British Library.

Library of Congress Cataloging in Publication Data

Inglis, Fred.
  Media theory/Fred Inglis.
    p. cm.
    ISBN 0–631–15917–7   ISBN 0–631–15918–5 (pbk.)
    1. Mass media. I. Title.
  P90.I485   1990   89–17795
  302.23—dc20   CIP

Typeset in 10.5 on 12 pt Sabon
by Graphicraft Typesetters Ltd., Hong Kong
Printed and Bound in Great Britain by
T. J. Press (Padstow) Ltd, Padstow, Cornwall

Contents

Preface and Acknowledgements

If a book about the practice of a corner of intellectual life is to be any good, it must be grounded in an argument. That is to say, a book has its special authority in virtue simply of being that rather imposing object, a *book*, let alone what it may derive from its author. But especially in the case of a didactic (or a teacher's) book, its proper idiom should be discursive, interrogative, conversational. To catch that tone, I believe, it should begin from a sense of a living audience: friends, equals, sceptics.

This book starts and goes on with the specific picture in its author's mind of the members of the University of Bristol School of Education graduate seminar, 'Mass Media: Television, Film, Print', which ran for half-a-dozen or so years on Tuesday evenings, in 35 Berkeley Square and the various hangars of the University's hospitable audio-visual aid department. It had many members, and I cannot list them all here; it counted, as thought should, upon resourcefulness, good humour and improvization as much as upon intellectual severity.

In addition, it counted upon friendship, and several of the luminaries treated in the following pages not only taught me much out of hours, but themselves spoke to seminars of the famous course. I here salute the unremunerated contributions of Krishan Kumar, Nicholas Garnham, Phillip Whitehead and James Curran for their cheerful shaping of my mind and those of my students, for their plain, ready and knockabout way with difficult ideas, and for their tranquil acceptance of my making off with their best ideas.

A paragraph of his own must, however, go to my friend and student, Kieran Argo, who read the manuscript faithfully and promptly, as well as keeping it comprehensible and, as he and I both trust, *useful* to students in our common pursuit of a true and civic politics. Where the book is clear and terse, the doing is his.

Lastly, although its long genesis lay in my Master of Education seminars, the actual writing was conducted amid the extraordinary privileges and kindly munificence of the Institute for Advanced Study at Princeton while I was a member there in 1988–9. Not for the first time nor, I fondly hope, the last, I offer here my thanks to its staff and foundation for what are surely the most gracious and generous conditions ever made real for scholarship. In this connection also I should single out the two members of its faculty now, I am proud to say, my friends, who invited me there for that memorable year: Clifford Geertz and Michael Walzer.

Sean Magee at Basil Blackwell was always an encouragement, as well as a tipster and tolerant of my packed schedules. From here on, I'm happy to say, the problems of stocking and selling the thing are all his and those of his colleague, Simon Prosser, who reminds me to acknowledge the permission of the Controller of Her Majesty's Stationery Office to use Figures 1, 2 and 3 in chapter 3, as well as of Methuen and Co. Ltd. and Macmillan Ltd for the quotations from David Morley and Len Masterman respectively. All right, gentlemen; you can get on with it.

Fred Inglis

1

A Short History of Public Communication

I

'Theory' is a word which takes a lot upon itself these days. As often as not, to declare oneself a theorist is to be committed to the pleasures of complexity and abstraction for their own sake without any active concern as to whether such theory will explain anything. No doubt, the pleasures of theoreticism are real; they are the pleasures of mind itself, of turning the mere eventuality of experience – life seen as one damn thing after another – into patterns and configurations which have a *meaning*. No doubt such a process may turn to pattern-making for the joys of making those patterns as complicated or as inaccessible as one can. To be master of such a mystery is then to hold the power of new knowledge, useful or not. And in any case, the world really is a complicated place, and theories which either describe or explain it are likely to be complicated even when they strive, as they must, for the beauty of always simpler, more elegant theories.

So the delights of theory-for-theory's-sake, of which we shall see a certain amount in this book, are not necessarily trivial. But the point of theorizing is to understand: it is to gather the many bits and pieces of experience and events together in such a way that we see their pattern and, it may be, understand their sequence of causes, or, in another idiom, understand the reasons people had for acting as they did.

Putting things like that emphasizes the distinction just made between description and explanation, and this in turn finds a sort of parallel in the separation between the human and the natural sciences. The natural sciences, as one might put it in a slogan, seek theories which will explain the causes of things. The human sciences seek theories which will describe the reasons people have or (more usually) had for doing what they did. This isn't, of course, a hard and fast distinction: psychologists may seek cognitive theories with which to fix innate structures of mental processes, just as economists may characterize economic process in strictly mechanical, non-intentional forms. But, roughly speaking, the human sciences cannot treat their subjects as objects. For ethical as well as technical reasons, they can't treat the people they study as experimental integers, or handle social exchange as though it were a laboratory.

These well-known misgivings about the science of human affairs need only serve here to insist that a theory of media is necessarily mixed up in that everyday world of affairs, is an instance of what Aristotle famously distinguished as 'practical reasoning', and makes progress, on the whole, by devising ways of understanding human activity in terms which humans themselves must be able to recognize. On such terms, a theory may be thought of as a kind of lens which, once we look through it, makes it possible to see clearly what is going on; or it may be thought of as a frame within which things are brought into order and given relation one to another. Lastly, a theory may be used, less visually, as a sort of translating machine, which transforms a jumble of incomprehensible sentences into something slightly different no doubt (because translated), but both near enough to the original and intelligible to us.

To speak theoretically is, therefore, to speak with understanding as a goal. This is easier to take when we think, as we usually do, of understanding as something we look for when we are faced with the incomprehensible. The usual sequence is thought of as going through these three stages: puzzle – deliberation – understanding ('Oh, I *see*', as we typically say). But in the human sciences, it is at least as often the case that we think we know perfectly well what's going on; we already have a theory (or at least our common sense) which tells us that there is no puzzle here at all.

In these circumstances, the stranger with a new theory has to persuade us, the audience, that the descriptions or explanations yielded by the new theory are in some way better than what we have concluded for ourselves. That is to say, they may be larger and more inclusive, so we understand *more* than we did; they may, naturally, correct mistakes; they may, more trickily, simply free us from a way of looking at things which has become rigid just because it has become familiar:[1] a theory on this showing creates a new kind of understanding, and therefore a new kind of knowledge making possible, in turn, new action. It does this by turning the everyday into something strange. (By this token a good poem, say, is like a new theory.)

These are variously some of the modalities of theory, and we shall return, particularly in the final chapter, to the criteria we may need for distinguishing between types of theory. But I would stress here, at the beginning of the book, that I take 'theory' to be the tricky word in its title, rather than 'media'. Theory, as I said, has its daunting pretensions; to be told that such is the topic for a degree course is apt, quite understandably, to bring on catatonia amongst students. For theoreticism has had a high old time this past ten years or more, and its practitioners sit in high places telling their student audiences how they must learn to speak in the new sacred jargon. As we see, a special language is indeed necessary to frame and embody new ideas. But it need not be so *very* special, and nothing at all should be allowed to put down the lived connections between our practical experience and our theoretic knowledge of it.

A medium, as I shall repeat in chapter 2, is what transforms experience into knowledge. Or, as we might put it in other words, media (it is a plural word) provide the signs which give *meaning* to the events of everyday life.

'Media', the plural, naturally includes *all* such sign-systems; and semiotics – the subject-matter of the fifth chapter – is one popular attempt at a theory of how signs come to mean anything at all in the first place. How do we match blobs of coloured pigment on canvas to our expectation of a landscape? How do we learn to see runic squiggles as letters making sounds? Media are the instruments of this strange, taken-for-granted transformation. They give shape and focus, and therefore meaning, to the torrent of percepts and events which compose our experience. And this truth returns us to our ways of judging between the types of theory we need (and the types we don't). It recalls us to the fact that we are studying what really matters to us, as the messages pour out of the media with accelerating force. Such criteria cannot be separated from the human values, the distinctions of worth[2] and life-interests which impel us to puzzle out and seek to dominate the world and others in the world. In short, the facts we study are identified as such by the values which bring us to the field in the first place.

This homely truth comes out in the most basic kind of theoretic understanding (or practical reasoning) with which we are familiar in everyday life. For typically, when we are at a loss to comprehend (the origins of the word mean 'to fold around') a particular piece of human confusion, we ask how things got to be in such a mess in the first place. And the standard form of explanation in reply is then to compose an elementary historical narrative. Confusion then becomes intelligible in virtue of a narrative with characters, purposes, a plot, a beginning and a middle and if not an end, at least a bringing-up-to-date. Such a narrative is historical in that it begins in the past tense (the 'perfect') and comes up to the present tense ('present indicative'). The names of the tenses, moods and voices themselves give us a grasp on the kind of theory we have in front of us: 'active' and 'passive' voices imply a theory of action; the 'conditional' ('I should') and 'indicative' ('I do') parts of verbs refer plainly to what is conjecture and what is factual.

II

The best kind of media theory to begin with is a historical one. This is deceptive as a disciplinary claim, since history is, after all, a narrative made out of what once was life-in-earnest, and we cannot possibly get all of *that* in. But even when we have made bluff disclaimers about the inevitable selectivity of historical narratives, what is at stake is less the selection of the supposed facts, and much more the conceptual structure which organizes that selection. In other words, such leading characters in a historical narrative as the type of society described, or the form of its economy ('peasants', 'serfs', 'capitalists') are products, not of the bare facts but of ways of seeing the facts. At the same time, the deep-seated and pervasive sense of what a story is, which we take in as the earliest means of understanding the world (our first theory) shapes how we tell and hear a story, insisting that it have heroes and villains, dramatic conflict, progress towards resolution and so forth.[3] So it is that we each of us devise from a mixture of folklore, story-telling and such bits and pieces of disciplinary education as we carry around with us in the forms of sociology or history or political economy, a personal version of social theory, itself a broad, ecumenical term which covers most of what the human sciences seek to provide.

Social theory is a sign of the times, as any mode of thought must be. Somewhere towards the end of the nineteenth century in Europe, thinkers in the traditional modes of politics began to move out of that relatively circumscribed area, in which they dealt with its traditional subjects of power, distribution, status and privilege, and to grasp for a theory which would account for the pervasiveness of politics in all aspects of what was clearly an unprecedented form of life: the life of urban industrialization and the extraordinary new phenomenon of public opinion which it had produced. Nobody with aspiration to rule could do so without the behest of this public opinion; all those greedy for power sought ways to harness and instruct it.

The new social theory, as practised by men as diverse as Karl Marx, Max Weber, Emile Durkheim, John Stuart Mill, William James,[4] was expressive of a quite different and inclusive way of imagining society for which the novel is the type we know best. The very name of this latter is significant, 'novels' indicating that such stories bring with them what is new, the news. The great European novels of the 1840s and after, of Dickens, Stendhal, Turgenev, George Eliot, Mrs Gaskell and company moved grandly from place to place and across a whole society. Their massive architecture gave house-room to war and peace, to gaolbirds and bankers, to sex and death, and to the terrible clash of classes and generations, all within the covers of one book. They provided models of a total society and a way for their readers, the plentiful members of the educated public, to situate themselves within the emergent nation-state and in relation to masses of people they knew of but could not know, as we say, 'personally'.

This is surely the advent of what C. Wright Mills, the great American sociologist, was later to call, in a famous title, *The Sociological Imagination*.[5] There he contended that such an imagination, the historical product of urban, industrial and (more or less) democratic history, is our unique instrument for understanding the single, interdependent world in which we must live mutually and co-operatively, if we are not to blow it apart. That imagination has to work by casting as large a conceptual net as possible over the heaped, enormous territory of social facts and, acknowledging that many of the facts will escape through the wide meshes of the net, none the less try to grasp the contours and features of the landscape as best it may.

III

The sociological imagination, or the forms of social theory, are our instruments in this book. As I said, this means answering the question, 'How did things get into this mess in the first place?' If you look around the 1990s at the state of what is laughably called information technology, at the chaotic condition of the seething international markets in mass communications, at the sheer bulk of messages pouring down the airwaves into the heads of the roughly three billion people in the world who can see television or hear the radio, then the notion of providing one theory which will explain (or *re-describe* so that we understand it better) this babel is clearly monomaniac.

It is, however, important not to lose our nerve either. Let us start from the premise offered by Anthony Giddens[6] that the modern nation-state is defined by four 'institutional clusterings': capitalist enterprise, control of the means of violence, managerial systems of production, and hyperextensive surveillant and information channels. These clusters of power and institutions are not monolithic nor without mutual opposition and conflict; at the same time, however, they interlock, on our definition, as the quadrilateral of forces which create a state and set it in inevitable competition with rivals. If this is so, then to study public communications is to study one of the most important topics of the day. Such study should be a compulsory part of every citizen's liberal education.

So we must not, indeed, lose our nerve, or the nervous citizens will be trodden over by the tough eggs who see plainly that information and media are where the great aphrodisiacs, power and money, are boiling and pouring. The best way, then, to keep our nerve is to begin at the beginning, or at least at the moment at which the first enduring records of human speech, the alphabets, created several societies in which literacy enabled a new kind of thought, and writing created the material ground for entirely new relations between human beings. With the advent of the letter, the file, the archive, the bill, the list, the schoolbook, the history, the notebook, even when these were laboriously scratched upon a wax tablet, and in an alphabet with several thousand signs in it, we have a qualitatively different society.

Its predecessor was strictly oral. In oral society, the conditions of cultural continuity are very much more limited than in our own. They are necessarily face-to-face for a start, at least in so far as transmitting knowledge goes. And indeed all other forms of transmission have to start with the pupil (the next generation) being *shown* how to do things. No doubt this is still so. But the vast, book-based institution of education takes over in most nations at the very early age of five or six. In a wholly oral culture, meaning in language is highly specific and local: the categories of knowledge are those of everyday practical and particular concerns. In a famous instance, the Inuit (Eskimos) are said to have over a dozen words for different kinds of snow – snow you can walk on, that you sink in, that melts quickest, that drifts, that sears and scorches, and so forth – because finesses of distinction are of immediate, practical value.[7] On the other hand, they don't have (and do not need) what the linguists call 'signifiers' (i.e. words to refer to things) for what is not significant to them. But in addition, all languages have plenty of words they do not need at all, of course. No language is so tidy as to match its lexicon exactly to its needs.

In oral society,[8] now so extensively studied in the century-old history of anthropology as 'primitive' or 'pre-industrial' or, indeed, 'pre-literate', language is concrete and symbols are solid. There is for its members only a very short gap in cognition between 'signifier' and 'signified', or between word and object. Dictionaries, records of different usages in books of different generations, make, as we all know, the relation between word and object something much cloudier and more various.

The key context of oral culture is the memory. Memory is finite. Thus it is asked to store and keep accessible what is relevant. Anything else can be jettisoned. Of course, the process is not so simple nor so systematic. Oral poetry is the obvious storehouse of the pre-literate memory; rhyme and rhythm and other mnemonic devices hold things in the memory – as do narrative and repetition – at times arbitrarily. Not everything needed in the social memory of the oral culture is put into verse. None the less it makes sense to generalize the public communication system of pre-literates as like a broadish waveband of radio transmission constantly moving forward through time, picking up and making audible the conversation of its period, carrying with it some of the conversation of the past, but constantly leaving behind to become forgotten noise what is no longer needed for the present. One social exchange which highlights this process is when the representatives of literate cultures have arrived in pre-literate ones (generally in order to take them over as subjects of Empire) and have begun to write down what hitherto has been strictly but changeably remembered. There have then been fierce quarrels as to which record is correct: the one frozen in writing or the one changefully remembered. The pre-literate society, we may say, puts a higher value on the present tense: myth, proverb, law, belief, may all be adjusted to suit the present, *and then* represented as timeless (every generation does this to those who are younger – re-writing history – and thereby enrages its children). In such a society, Jack Goody tells us (p. 34),

> Myth and history merge into one: the elements in the cultural heritage
> which cease to have a contemporary relevance tend to be soon forgot-
> ten or transformed; and as the individuals of each generation acquire

their vocabulary, their genealogies, and their myths, they are unaware
that various words, proper names and stories have dropped out, or
that others have changed their meanings or been replaced.

As we shall see in chapter 9, this waveband movement recurs in
book-bound societies. They, too, invent and reinvent traditions to
suit the present. They largely do so, however, in competition with
other presents whose authors, going back to historical records, want
their new tradition to win over other ones precisely because it is
more faithful to what has been recorded. Although the accuracy of
all such records may be disputed, however, the fact of their existence
– the books are really there, and have been there, available for
consultation since they were published – cannot be. We have, then,
the type of our own society in which critical thought – the analysis
and criticism of the written thought of others – grounded in historical comparisons, becomes the general form of rationality, the criterion of the educated mind.

Writing, therefore, is indispensable to the creation of a historical
sensibility. After all is said and done (in chapter 4, for instance)
about how difficult it is to separate history and myth even today, it
is presumably true that for objective knowledge to be possible in
anything like the sense in which we use it when we speak of science
and rationalism, there must be the *idea* of the accurate, impartial
recording of events.

Such recording, however, will turn on the invention of a universal,
economic and phonetic alphabet, and such a remarkable cultural
creation is comparatively recent. The first alphabets were visual,
wherever they appeared. That is to say, the earliest representations –
carvings, cave-paintings – were stylized and made reproducible in
such a way that they could carry a message. The obvious problem is
that you need an enormous number of such signs or 'ideograms' to
carry all the messages a more complex society or group of societies
will want to communicate. Sometime before 3000 BC,[9] the great
urban cultures of China began to develop such an ideogrammatic
alphabet whose direct descendant, with more than 50,000 characters, is still in general use today. One important consequence of such
unwieldiness is the inevitable creation of an intensely specialized
elite who are sole masters of the mystery of the entire alphabet.[10]
The mandarinate, celebrated figures in all popular cultures for their
arcane knowledge, their book-bound scholarliness, their comically
bespectacled precision and absurd linguistic fastidiousness, were
brought into being by the gradual evolution of a writing system

which even now takes twenty years fully to command. The lesson as to how an intellectual elite arises in virtue of its handling of abstruse, protected knowledge should not be lost on readers of this book.

At about the same time, the Sumerian language speakers, developing in their turn the first internationally trading network to open up the Middle East and beyond from their rich base in the Fertile Crescent of Persia, began to run together some of the Egyptian hieroglyphics (which were all ideograms) and devices of their own capable of expressing phonetic transpositions. They were followed by various near-Eastern developments of syllable alphabets, which is to say signs for whole consonant and vowel sequences and still very cumbersome and prolix, as well as being incapable of representing the phoneme, or basic unit of meaningful sound. Thereafter, Hittite and other ancient Semitic civilizations (including the Jewish scribes) advanced the whole business considerably, though only with their own very ponderous alphabets requiring, as we noted, a sub-class to sustain and conserve the writing system, its reproduction (teaching it) and its technology. The class fraction of literates, then, is in a position to keep its own culture to itself, the more so as writing, in a commercial and bureaucractic state, is an indispensable source of power. Probably we can date the crucial division of labour between its mental and manual forms, overwhelmingly taken for granted today, from those uncertain centuries when Sumerian, Babylonian, Egyptain and Semitic[11] societies all set up their ruling bureaucracies.

The break, as one might put it, to a democratic, because easily learnable and clearly accessible, phonetic alphabet came in Greece. Not that there was anything inevitable about this. Writing, let us say, has been traceable in human societies for little more than 6,000 years; phonetic alphabets of a compact, familiar sort, for less than half that time. In a history of *Homo sapiens* now thought to be about a quarter of a million years old, it's not very long. As Goody says, 'The notion of representing a sound by a graphic symbol is itself so stupefying a leap of the imagination that what is remarkable is not so much that it happened relatively late in human history, but rather that it ever happened at all' (p. 38). The chances are that the Greek city-states developed their alphabets precisely because they had no trading empire and no elite class of literates, but were at the same time beginning to thrive on the trading routes between the Middle East and Mediterranean Europe.

However it was, the Greek alphabet developed quite rapidly from the eighth century BC onwards. All phonetic alphabets depend on

compression, and therefore facility, for their success. The wide range
of noises which human beings make can be successfully standardized
into only 40 symbols or less (this is true even of high-pitched,
vowel-based languages like Vietnamese, which uses the international
alphabet). Arguably the Greeks learned the new alphabet so quickly
because they were at the time devising a more broadly democratic
version of society in which the participation of their citizenry de-
pended on their being able to read and write. The new alphabet, no
doubt, would have been both cause and instrument in this process,
so that by 500 BC or so, the small, self-governing, prosperous Greek
and Ionian city-states were the first generally literate societies (even
counting in the slaves and the women). In 403 BC the official form of
the alphabet was fixed and ratified in Athens by its adoption as the
official script for the city archives.

IV

At this point, and in keeping with later arguments about the coming
of the book and then of electronic communication, it is worth
thinking aloud about the difference in consciousness – in modes of
thought, cognitive style, uses of image and icon, in logic, observation, deduction and so forth – brought about by writing and reading. As I suggested, critical history is only possible with written
records; it seems likely that a perfect and changeless set of thought
procedures like mathematics and its parent, logic, is impossible
without a script. Logic, an indisputable procedure for deriving conclusions, and empirics, a disciplined method of observation, are the
twin foundations of all scientific thought. Between the two, you can
devise systems of proof. Once you have written sources, you can
argue about their comparative truthfulness. Scepticism becomes a
necessity of mind, and so does chronology. If you are to sort
amongst the causes of things and tell a coherent history, then you
must space and time them accurately. The old timelessness of the
myths of oral culture is replaced by the classifications (biologists say
'taxonomies') of era and epoch, of point of view (thus Thucydides
sorted between the conflicting versions of whose fault it all was on
each side of the Peloponnesian war).

It is important not to let this account cast itself in the confident
accents of modernity. The changes from oral to literate forms of
thought are not fixed and are not always for the better. The important part of our lives to all of us is that lived in direct exchange with

others: a book is no substitute for a body. Much, therefore, of what I am about to say concerning the nature of oral cultures still holds – perhaps even more so – at a time when television obviously outstrips print as a source of general information, especially among those who rate books lower than intellectuals and students have to do.

In an essay called 'The Storyteller', the German cultural critic Walter Benjamin[12] (whose origins are more fully given in the next chapter) wrote sometime in the 1930s that 'the art of storytelling is coming to an end. Less and less frequently do we encounter people with the ability to tell a tale properly ... It is as if something that seemed inalienable to us, the securest among our possessions, were taken from us: the ability to exchange experiences' (p. 83). And he goes on, 'Experience which is passed on from mouth to mouth is the source from which all storytellers have drawn.'

For Benjamin, storytelling is a feature of oral culture which inherently differentiates such cultures from book-bound ones, but even more from *news*-bound cultures. He distinguishes on the one hand the *story*, which is deliberately enigmatic (you can't be sure of any single meaning) and is also a source of practical counsel as well as an everyday guide to conduct. On the other hand, he sees modern society as having replaced stories by *information*, and information (we might also say 'news') 'lays claim to prompt verifiability', is never miraculous but strictly plausible and above all is 'shot through with explanation' (p. 89). In other words, information deprives history of what Benjamin calls 'the epic side of truth [which is] wisdom'; it explains the causes of events rather than their meanings. It removes astonishment and thoughtfulness from the listener's response, and replaces them with the clarifications of a report.

He counterposes the novel as one villain of this tendency to the fairy tale, as *the* type of story-told-aloud. The novel, which, as we noted, invokes novelty as its essence, is born in the experience of the solitary individual. The story, told by one teller, is the product of many oral tellings which effect 'that slow piling one on top of the other of thin, transparent layers which constitutes the most appropriate picture of the way the perfect narrative is revealed through the layers of a variety of retellings' (p. 93). The novel, grandest of the art forms invented by the bourgeoisie of capitalism, expresses through its structure its sense of its novelty and the importance of the individual in all his or her individuality. The titles of some of Europe's most famous novels tell us this: *Tom Jones, David Copperfield, Emma, Jane Eyre, Anna Karenina, Père Goriot.* Personal moral psychology is at the very heart of the novel.

The fairy story does not individualize; it generalizes. Red Riding Hood, Kay and the Snow Queen, Rumpelstiltskin, Sir Percival, the Tin Soldier are all intent but mysterious, enigmatic figures in a much larger landscape. The stories contain good counsel, certainly – 'stick to the path through the forest', 'be as cunning as a cunning dwarf', 'placate big dogs', above all, be kind, be selfless, be good – but nothing is explained or 'plausible'. And thus, Benjamin says, 'the narrative achieves an amplitude that information lacks', a richness which partakes of the community of listeners among whom the story is shared.

Benjamin's compelling intuitions are borne out by anthropological reports in those societies where story-telling still thrives. In Ireland, Java, Morocco, Turkey and elsewhere story-tellers are widely said to be a dying breed, but there are still men who can tell stories for three days without repeating themselves. Clifford Geertz[13] describes two such men in Morocco, telling their tales to a genteel cacophony of tambourines, communal singing and chanting, whistles from the audience, and punctuating the tale with quotation, proverb and well-known jokes, the whole beano excellently fitting Benjamin's view of a good story, if in less stately guise.

> ... poetry, the performance of which is widespread and regular, most especially in the countryside and among the common classes in the towns, forms a kind of 'recitation' of its own, another collection, less exalted but not necessarily less valuable, of memorisable truths: lust is an incurable disease, women an illusory cure; contention is the found-ation of society, assertiveness the master virtue; pride is the spring of action, unworldliness moral hypocrisy; pleasure is the flower of life, death the end of pleasure. Indeed, the word for poetry, s‘ir, means 'knowledge', and though no Muslim would explicitly put it that way, it stands as a kind of secular counterpoise, a worldly footnote, to the Revelation itself. What man hears about God and the duties owed Him in the Quran, fix-worded facts, he hears about human beings and the consequences of being one in poetry. (pp. 113–14)

Such ribald ceremony is pretty well vanished in Britain and America, except in odd corners of the folk like the Amish or the Orcadians. But when in chapter 7 we consider the problem of the audience, we might remember the story-teller and wonder if the uses of the media even today do not include making up sources of counsel and enig-mas, the marvellous and the mysterious, out of titbits on the news and the puzzling behaviour of soap opera heroines.

V

Walter Benjamin serves to qualify the notion that there is an *absolute* difference between literate and oral cultures. Marshall McLuhan,[14] to whom we shall shortly return, sees the advent of print as the key to modern consciousness, the discipline which fixed men's minds along the straight, undeviating lines of print, and prevented their thinking and feeling in images, 'kinaesthetically' or in such a way as to bring hearing, seeing, tasting and touching all together as a lovely painting or music may. It is, however, a very long jump from the diffusion of the Greek alphabet in about 600 BC and the invention and diffusion of the printing press by Johann Gutenberg and William Caxton some time after 1460.

If we summarize the argument about the positive, radical consequences of the advent of literacy (i.e. writing) without print, we can say that even in societies where books are not printed but written out by hand, we have much greater openness of criticism and debate, much less likelihood of a sealed, clerical elite, much more reliability, methodicality and system in their modes of thought. In addition, with the help of as great a man as Aristotle, such a society will begin the classification and division of knowledge into its constituents – politics, ethics, physics, mathematics, logic, poetics, all according to Aristotle's grand scheme. In doing so, as Goody points out, it separates divinity from knowledge, natural life from human life, and begins the process of secularization. Lastly, it should be warningly remembered that, however good the gift of knowledge, its mere accumulation alienates scholars from the world. The more that is written down, the more impossible it is for any one person to master it all. New elites arise, created by the intensity of specialization in the different divisions of intellectual labour, each quite unable to comprehend the others. Above all, the historical proliferation of written documents, culminating in 500 years of printed books, indicates to all readers the infinite variety of individuals. The novel, arising from the happy combination of forces in 1700 or so which produced leisured social life, warm and well-lit rooms, newspapers and their workmanlike prose, and town gossip, is only the most familiar instance of the individualization of being to which the preservation of written records bears limitless witness.

It is important not to foreshorten the historical summary with which I begin. Writing develops over two and a half millennia, until the Greek alphabet emerges. But it is then another 2000 years before the invention of the printing press. In between, more people learned to read and write than could in Babylon, but mostly people didn't. There were still clerical and literate elites, as there still are. There were also those barbaric, nomadic societies, the Huns, Vandals, Tartars and the rest, who dedicated themselves to the destruction of the written 'word, and came pretty close to success. For a thousand years in Europe, darkness stood upon the face of the earth, and book culture barely survived. Much that was priceless was lost, utterly lost: almost all of Greek thought and literature, much of Roman literature. What remains, like the statues of the period, is in bits, and that little was preserved by chance and the monasteries, who stood in the ancient relation of literate elite to the unlettered, receptive and subordinate populace.

The coming of the book was the biggest change the world had ever seen. The book itself, this regular, neat box-like thing with its nicely cut and aligned pages, brings out very clearly the intersection, crucial to media theory, of what Raymond Williams[15] has called 'technology and cultural form'. Printing technology enabled that shape, but the culture at large gave it that form: a dust-jacket with that picture, those chapter headings, that story of such-and-such a length; above all, that anticipated market with its eager buyers.

The book arrived, as it was bound to do, held strictly within the cultural limits of the time. Pretty well the *only* book Johann Gutenberg would print in 1460 was the Bible, and that in Latin as the only common language of European literacy. Febvre and Martin[16] reckon that for the first 50 years of print, well over three-quarters of all books were in Latin. We may none the less still be surprised that nearly a quarter were already in local tongues – the so-called vernaculars – which is evidence for the independence of such tongues *in writing* and outside the elite and sacred language of Latin well before the coming of the book. However it was, by 1575, as Febvre and Martin tell us, a majority of titles published in Paris were in French. Thereafter, even though the intelligentsia – figures such as the English poets John Donne, John Milton, Andrew Marvell – corresponded in Latin until well into the seventeenth century, the vernacular tongues dominated print. In Anderson's words,[17] 'the fall of Latin exemplified a larger process in which the sacred communities integrated by old sacred languages [in Europe, Latin and Greek] were gradually fragmented, pluralised, and territorialised' (p. 25).

The explanation was simple enough. Print technology coincided with (*not* 'was caused by') the beginnings of capitalism. Capitalism is a weird enough historical figure, given its definition in chapter 6; here it will do to say that it was the first economic system to seek maximum profit as the sole source of its energy. This logic meant that once the Latin-reading elite had been sold all the books they would buy, and that market was saturated, print-capitalism would surge restlessly on its way, seeking new and of course much bigger potential markets, in the vernacular tongues of Europe. Febvre and Martin tell us that from Gutenberg's Bible just before 1460 to the end of the century, more than 20 million volumes (something like 35,000 editions) appeared in Europe, that Germany and Italy led the field, and that by the end of the sixteenth century, by which stage the anti-Catholic Reformation really had broken out of Latin into the vernacular, the total printed was already up towards 200 million. As McLuhan says in *The Gutenberg Galaxy* (p. 125), the book was the first commodity manufactured under conditions recognizable as modern mass production.

It has been much pointed out since Max Weber's classic essay *The Protestant Ethic and the Spirit of Capitalism*, how the movement of protesting, anti-Catholic, individualized religious feeling which was at the heart of the Reformation in the sixteenth century, and the surge of new economic life seeking individual profits wherever it could find them without regard to consequences for the soul or debts to rulers, urgently needed each other. Protestantism and capitalism did not *cause* one another; but they marched together across the continent. The first leader of Protestantism, Martin Luther, was the author of one-third of *all* books published in German between 1517, when he argued the heresy, and 1525. In 20 years, 430 editions of the biblical and theological translations came out.[18] Protestant literature spoke directly to the new middle class which read no Latin and which was the agent of the new capitalism. The languages which then emerged as modern English, German, French and so forth out of the chaos of dialects and spellings familiar to us from first editions of Shakespeare were shaped by the mixture of historical forces as I have described them: the new church languages, the new systems of economic production, and the classes which took for themselves the clerical, bureaucratic, legal and allocative power to make sure *their* kind of English (or French, or whatever it was) became the official kind, the kind with *power*.

My potted history shows that books changed the mind of Europe in the space of a century. They did so, it is trite to say, as a consequence both of their content and of their form. Their content was the new, heretical thought of the day in the newly established, non-specialist, everyday language of their linguistic community. Their form was, in the first place, literally that: the neat little box-shaped thing anyone could carry about (and which anyone, importantly, could hide). In the second place, it was the first embodiment of the commodity form: an easily made, mass produced, reproducible, profit-creating, obsolescent object.

This version of the first 5000 years of media perhaps emphasizes that to attempt media theory is to bring together the history of ideas and the history of economic production. Media theory, by this token, is political theory, as it is at the same time the latest arrival amongst the humanities. As we shall see, in my tale media theory offers itself as a key to historical development, especially in the present, and as the gently ecumenical heart of the good citizen's education.

Notes

1 This is the great German philosopher Hegel's view of the life of ideas: that they begin by making us free and slowly harden until we are imprisoned by them. Then yet new ideas arrive to free us, which age in their turn, and so on.

2 The phrase is Charles Taylor's, in his *Philosophical Papers* (2 vols, Cambridge University Press, 1985). Taylor contends that thought itself is necessarily grounded in such 'distinctions of worth' and must not try to get clear of them.

3 Compare Paul Ricoeur's essay, 'History and narrativity' in his *Hermeneutics and the Human Sciences* (Cambridge University Press, 1982), when he shows how fully history (in French, *histoire*) is grounded in the idea of a *story* (also *histoire*).

4 A list of their classic texts would be a list of the first classics in social theory, a 'great books' course in the five basic texts: by Marx, the so-called *Grundrisse,* Marx's notes for *Capital*; by Weber, *Theory of Social and Economic Organisations*; by Durkheim, *The Divisions of Labour in Society*; by Mill, *Principles of Political Economy* and his essays 'On liberty' and 'On the subjugation of women'; and by James, *The Varieties of Religious Experience.*

5 C. Wright Mills, *The Sociological Imagination* (Oxford University Press, 1962).

6 Anthony Giddens in his *The Nation–State and Violence* (Polity Press, 1985), p. 5.

7 Reported by Benjamin Whorf in his *Language, Thought and Reality* (MIT Press, 1956).

8 Much of the remainder of this section depends on the classic summary

of the relevant research by Jack Goody and Ian Watt, 'The consequences of literacy', collected in *Literacy in Traditional Societies*. ed. J.
Goody, (Cambridge University Press, 1972), and in many other places.

9 See the shortened selection from Joseph Needham's mammoth multi-
volume study, *Science and Civilisation in China* (Cambridge University
Press, 1980), chosen (under the same title) by Needham himself and J.
Ronan.

10 Max Weber spotted this, and wrote a sociology of such a bureaucracy
in the concluding part of his *Theory of Economic and Social Organisations* (New York Free Press, 1949).

11 For a full history, see D. Diringer, *Writing* (Thames & Hudson 1962).

12 Walter Benjamin, 'The storyteller', in his collection *Illuminations*, ed.
Hannah Arendt (Jonathan Cape, 1970).

13 Clifford Geertz, *Local Knowledge: Further Essays in Interpretive
Anthropology* (Basic Books, 1983). See especially the chapter, 'Art as a
cultural system'.

14 Marshall McLuhan, *The Gutenberg Galaxy* (Routledge & Kegan Paul,
1962). See especially the concluding chapter, 'The plight of mass man
in an individualist society'.

15 Raymond Williams, *Television: Technology and Cultural Form* (Fontana Collins, 1974).

16 Lucien Febvre and Henri-Jean Martin, *The Coming of the Book: the
Impact of Printing 1450–1800* (New Left Books, 1976, first published, Paris, 1958).

17 Benedict Anderson, *Imagined Communities: Reflections on the Origin
and Spread of Nationalism* (Verso, 1983), especially chapters 2 and 3.

18 *The Coming of the Book*, pp. 289–95 (see n. 16 above).

2

Mass Society Theory and the Impact of Technology

I

Media theory, according to the argument which closes chapter 1, is a version of political theory, and political theory is classically a matter of trying to work out how the world works *and* how it ought to work. At its heart, in other words, are the connections between theory and practice, thought and action, knowledge and virtue. As has been much pointed out, someone who says that he is just a practical man with no time for theory simply hasn't noticed what his theory is; when this is so, the chances are that it is bad theory. By the same token, the politican who roughly declares that the whole game is about power and that he has no time for bleeding-heart squeamishness about whether what he does is virtuous or not, has not cancelled virtue from politics, he has simply decided to operate a vicious, not a virtuous politics. The wrong end of power is oppression. To oppress someone is, among other things, to take away the virtue of freedom from their lives, and to do *that* is unmistakably to practise politics in relation to virtue, if only negatively.

The key word there is 'relation', but of course it is a very elastic and capacious word. When we speak conventionally of 'relating to' someone else, we usually have in mind more or less successful communication with them of a fairly positive, pleasurable kind. In other words, the definition of 'relate' would arise coherently, if at all, in our (historical) account of how we met the other person, what we did together, what our happinesses were, and so forth. Similarly, politics may be said to be the study of human relations, but so general a designation could be turned to *all* the human sciences (the humanities): psychology, history, literature, sociology and the rest. Each, however, has its typical approach – history, obviously, with the past as it really was, literature with the past and present as they might have been, sociology with the large structures of things and their social institutions. Politics has its central preoccupation with power indeed, but this is to say that its typical concern is with the conditions of duty, obligation, order and authority (and with their opposites, disobedience and disorder and liberty). These are the names of our relation to one another *in public*. Politics is the study of the public realm and doubtless it's hard to say where that stops: there's a politics in a family and a politics of the imagination. But if we stay with politics as the subject of public relations (as they say), then in modern times – say, since the invention of the telegraph in the 1830s – these relations have been, to use a technical verb, crucially *mediated* by public communication systems.

It is at this moment that politics and the mass media come together. While Karl Marx was battling during the 1850s to bring his theory of society together in terms of its economic system he proposed[1] as the central axis of social structure the determining connection between the 'mode of production' and the 'relations of production'. The mode of production, of which capitalism was and remains the dominant contemporary instance, signified the form in which the products of a society, whether manufactured, extracted or grown, were exchanged, consumed or used. In the subsistence economies of, for example, primitive peoples, all that was grown was shared and eaten. At its simplest, such a people does not trade or barter, but keeps itself steadily alive. (One example would be the Netsilik of Alaska until the early 1960s, another the Kalahari bushmen.) Under capitalism, the mode of production is driven by the twin, dynamic motors of investment and profit. Capital is not just another name for money: it is a name for a resource whose possessor invests it to produce 'surplus-value' or profit on the basis of commodities made and sold.

In Marxist theory, the mode of production and the social relations which express it are mutually embedded; that is, one brings about the other. The capitalist mode of production separates capital (which accumulates as profits) from labour (the costs of which capital must hold down as low as possible). This creates the two classes of capitalism, the owner and the wage slave, who are forever struggling against each other. Their relation-of-production is, according to Marx, *inherently* in conflict and exploitative of labour. The only way the forces of labour can win over capital is by socializing the means of production in a revolution. Marx saw this as the inevitable outcome of the drive of world history.

At this stage of our theory-building, there is no need to go further into Marxist theory. It is noteworthy that Marxism has been so important to media theory, as we shall see later, precisely because Marx understood first just how important masses of industrial workers would certainly become in the surge of historical change, as they became aware of their collective power in a self-conscious way impossible to the peasantry and serfs who preceded them in the world economy. Marx, we may say, put the 'mass' into 'mass media'.

His economic theory has been endlessly disputed and qualified. For our immediate purpose, however, it is his key idea of the *relations of production* which must come near the heart of media theory. As we saw, he distinguished between capitalist and wage slave, the man or woman who only has labour to sell, and a finite quantity of that (there are only 24 hours in a day, and a person must have some sleep). He also identifies this relation as one of bitter, necessary opposition, noting as he does so that people may be both capitalists as far as their employees are concerned, and employees themselves to bigger capitalists: most managers are in that position today. Lastly, he saw that capital must treat absolutely everything as a commodity if it is to follow its own, unstoppable drive for the maximization of profit. This means that people and spiritual values are all apprehended as abstract objects, potentially capable of being a source of profit. The whole social world is converted onto the single scale of exchange values, hence Marx's loathing of it.

I have cast my exposition of the relations of production very abstractly, as Marx himself does. But their precise form varies, as one would expect, according to the conditions of work itself. The relations of production in a traditional coal mine, for example, make for a high degree of solidarity among the miners; the work is killingly hard, sometimes dangerous, and much less divided into specialisms than some jobs. There is, therefore, not only strong mutual support but also strong egalitarianism among the men: each equally shares the work and counts on the others as they count on him. On the other hand, the relations of production between a team of long-distance truck drivers is much more remote, laconic, independent-minded. They are less likely to join together in collective action, but they are more likely to be alienated from their bosses who are a long way off and simply hand out the worksheet, than miners, who may defy their plant managers but know them on a direct, daily basis.

Some distance away from both is a VDU and database operator. Her relations of production are entirely mediated by the screen and the telephone, which never stops ringing. She too is a wage slave but in very different circumstances from the miner and the trucker. She is the creature of her machines, but sealed off by their demands and the headphones from any contact with her fellows. Miners hew out coal, truck drivers deliver freight. She handles information, in all likelihood figures whose meaning she doesn't know and doesn't care about.

She is a quite new product of industrial culture, so much so that some Marxists[2] have suggested that the determinant relation of modern society, if we share Marx's premise that everything starts from the economic, is less the relation of production and more the relation of *information*. What Anthony Smith calls 'the *geo*-politics of information'[3] is by this account our best way of grasping world movement. The media theorist, therefore, will divide inquiry into questions of hardware and software, a distinction which roughly corresponds to 'technology' and 'cultural form'. But in order to get at the qualitative heart of things, he should take as the first methodical instruction, always to analyse and understand the mode of information. To do so, we need to review a short history of rather more recent technology than the alphabet.

II

Perhaps we should start by reminding ourselves once again of the trickiness of the word 'medium' (though the Latin plural 'media' has pretty well taken over as a singular noun in everyday usage). A medium is any instrument of communication; it carries or 'mediates' the message. Thus the spiritualist medium, according to the crazy rituals of the ouija board, transmits the messages of the dead to the living; she is not speaking as self, she is spoken through. This is to use 'medium' correctly. The telephone, the radio, the film, the television are all equivalently media along with print and the human voice, to say nothing of painting or sculpture.

The trouble is, of course, that when we begin analysis of how each works, they are not at all equivalent, and 'mediation' begins to have a slippery feel as manipulation begins to find room to move. A telephone is fairly purely a medium; it is a mere extension to thousands of miles of the carrying power of the human voice; it enables conversation. Print is a pure medium, because although one cannot usually converse with the author of a book, and although print cannot readily carry the play of tone and gesture which give clarity, emphasis, and richness to the spoken word, the sparseness of the form – black marks on white paper – makes its operation plain to see and the act of reading easily contained.

Yet people are, as they say, carried away by books, made to laugh and cry by them, lost in them, absorbed by them. This being so, how much more is it likely to be the case with film and television, which offer so to 'naturalize' expression as to make it seem like nature itself? Such an offer is immediately deceitful. On films, in the cinema, the eye takes in features and faces, landscape and motion, as though they were all real life. But of course we do so not only in the isolation of the darkness (think how easily we are made to jump in the cinema) but also with a huge range of cinematic effects organizing the way we see the image according to the film-maker's intentions. So, too, with television, even in the cheerful concourse of the front room: it carries the power of production teams, and behind them of great corporations buying the attention of millions for the money and for the influence money will bring. These are just a few of the pressures around the frame of what we hear and watch which give such weight to the word 'mediation'.

The relations of production come right into the sitting room as we watch television or answer the telephone. 'Tele' itself comes from the Greek word meaning distant, and measuring the distance between the medium and the message[4] is the point of media theory.

The distance between two speaking voices is easy to see. However much is hidden in conversation and however people misunderstand each other, the basic speech act – you and I conversing – is the first model of communication. Print, as we have seen, enormously modified all that writing had done to complicate matters. It made possible conversation of a rather oblique sort with the past. It increased the competition between authorities: Holy Writ and the *Quran* may be the words of God; but who is Martin Luther? From Luther onwards, the author's authority becomes progressively harder to assert, the more so as markets pick up and depend on the ensuing competition and thereby win and lose their brief cultural authority.

Print, as we said, changed the basis of human self-understanding, gave huge energy to capitalism, formalized and ratified the linguistic communities which then emerged as nation-states.

In the second half of the nineteenth century, print itself began to be overtaken, first by electric and then by electronic communication. This is the third drastic discontinuity in the history of media and its triple movement: alphabet – print – screens.

To grasp the momentousness of this change requires a short

excursion into the astonishing activity in the field of communication which is part of the late nineteenth century industrial revolution. The telegraph, the telephone, the camera, the radio and the first devices on the way to electronic television were all more or less in place by 1900, and were, as one would expect, vigorously inter-dependent. The origins of the camera are fairly well known as part of the central history. Humphrey Davy was playing with the idea of 'writing in light' in 1800, and the projection of circular panoramas from a system of mirrors in a darkened observatory known as the camera obscura provided the template for the celebrated painting of urban panoramas of which the painter Canaletto is the best-known early exponent. The problem was not in making a lens capable of projection but in fixing the image on a suitably receptive surface. By 1839 Daguerre had solved it, and the photograph became a familiar feature of Victorian sitting rooms, the standard work of art of industrial popular culture.

The more difficult but just as relevant and dramatic developments were in electric telegraphy – the puzzling out of how to send instan-taneous messages over long distances. Electricity itself had been at the heart of the natural sciences (and therefore of technological change) since the early eighteenth century. A Frenchman, Lesage, had turned these inquiries towards the transmission of signals by interrupting impulses along a wire as early as 1774, and with others had speculated on ways to record these impulses at the right inter-vals on pieces of paper. With the demonstration of the magnetic needle confirmed by an Englishman, Sturgeon, in 1825, Samuel Morse, across the Atlantic, was in a position to devise his celebrated code in order to send readable messages in an alphabet composed entirely of long and short impulses. At first these messages had only a twenty-mile reach, but quickly Morse and company invented a message magnifier which pushed the message along the next stretch until Washington could reach Baltimore. By 1850 these systems were multiplex, which is to say that bundles of wires could carry many messages at once, and the enterprise went abruptly and suc-cessfully commercial. As the Western frontier opened up, what America needed above all, to control the movements of capital and production over its colossal distances, was long-range transmission. Morse provided it; it was economic, efficient, and very long-lasting – still in use during Second World War operations.

It was, however, one-way. The parallel search for telephone ex-change was successful soon afterwards: Bell made his invention workable by 1876, the Western Electrical Company took off and the rest, as they say, is history. The telephone is now the nervous system of the world. Moreover, its technology depends on a symmetry common to all electronic media and therefore crucial to our media education. Bell's predecessors had experimented with the make-and-break electric circuit as a means of transmitting voice impulses. Bell put a vibrating membrane, sensitive to voice and its variations of pitch, in front of an electromagnet. The electromagnet turned the vibrations into an undulating current which was transmitted. At the receiving end, the process was simply reversed to produce sound.

This is *the* model of all long-distance transmission and reception. Physical phenomena of a regularly punctuated sort (speech, visual images) are turned into geometrically analogous patterns of electric or electronic surges, transmitted, and by reversing the conversion-and-transmission process, reproduced as a copy of their first form (speech, visual images). Thus a radio receives from a transmitter on a given frequency of wave pattern which is identical with the speech signal. The frequency comes down the aerial into the receiver and is converted, nowadays by small transistor valves, back into intelligible sound. Magnetic tape records sound as varying disturbances of its surface which, when run along the receiver heads, are reproduced as the original sounds.

It is worth wondering at this juncture how practical the good media theorist ought to be. This is not a technology handbook, and the often difficult (but interesting) way in which media technology works cannot be explained, except glancingly, here. But there is a crux about theory itself in all this. To have even a schematic and elementary grasp of what is happening to the wires when you use the telephone, or to know roughly how the dots and lines on a television screen get there to make a picture in the first place is to shift the position of the theorist with regard to his theories, to his politics, and to his education.

Like the invention of the alphabet, these later instruments involve an astonishing leap of the imagination to conceive, let alone realize. To feel that truth right through you is part of what it is to be educated; it is, one hopes, to be inspired by the sense of possible good which these playthings might bring to the human world. In addition, the political, which is to say the public and civic, part of you is changed when you understand a little of the work someone else is doing. In the case of electronic furniture, one may be as respectful of the finicky knowledge and endless patience one technician has, as one may be sorry for the utter absence of knowledge, the imprisonment in minor movements of the fingertips in which this keyboard operator is held, and within which she is paid. It is the merest commonplace of experience that we all feel differently when we know a bit more about another person's work. In so far as media theory *is* a political inquiry, such knowledge inflects our politics.

Finally, this same truth holds for theory. A colourful thread in the texture of argument of this book is that it sets its readers exercises in practical reasoning. Theory in the human sciences must connect directly with practice. To be incompetent with the video camera, to know nothing of what happens in a fax machine, is likely to make me, out of nervousness at looking a fool, supercilious towards the machinery. Anyway, to be a manual worker, as we are all taught from the infant reception class upwards, is to be inferior to a mental worker. The theorist has the posh job. The only way to combat this arbitrary division is to try to learn a bit more about what is inside the box.

But, as is obvious, this is not a maintenance manual. All this book can do is indicate very general principles, the first of which is the conversion and reversion of light and sound phenomena along electric currents. The difficulty is to distinguish between the elementary and the superficial. Well, that's always hard. We know that molecules are compounded of atoms, mutually attracted and repelled by measurable and controllable forces. We can draw, perhaps, molecular structures. But such a definition has only a vague hold on the world as we move through it. Let us take, however, the advent of electronics as one of the decisive moments in this history, as it was decisive in the world at large, linked intimately to the extraordinary intellectual and literal power released by the new physics of Einstein and his collaborators after the publication of his theory of relativity in 1905.

An electronic tube is a great deal more powerful and flexible than an electric current. It is made up of an electric circuit with a vacuum enclosure containing two electrodes. Now an electric current is composed, in the first place, of electrons passing along the conductor. Each atom has a nucleus surrounded by electrons whirling in orbits which compose a cloud of charge. In the electron tube, now entirely superseded by the transistor and its semiconductors, the electrodes (or terminals) heat up and emit electron particles which, controlled technically, ionize or charge up the otherwise neutrally balanced atom with a positive charge. The resulting increase in velocity makes it possible to produce beams with a variety of light-giving and penetrative properties (X-rays, laser beams, television pictures).

The tube is the simplest way to grasp the process. Silicon transistors have notoriously miniaturized everything, producing current amplifications from negative charges resulting from the tiny shreds of so-called *n-p-n* semiconductors, whose algebra simply indicates the compressed passage of electrons from negative to positive and back. With no filament to glow, there are no warming-up or other heating problems.

This is the wide field within which television came to birth. Raymond Williams[5] points out that people were searching for it long before it came to actuality; it was imagined long before it was known, and must obviously be thought of in parallel to the development of the cine-camera. The cine-camera was, however, a much easier matter, once the fixed-image photograph, rapid-shot cameras and the invention of celluloid came together in the 1890s. Television demanded synthesis across the whole field of electronics, which began to blossom with Rutherford's Cavendish work from 1900 and Braun's cathode-ray tube (the earliest electron tube) of 1897. The celebrated Nipkow disc-scanner of 1884 first made scanning light fields conceivable. Nipkow's model is at the foundation of all scanning. Its disc is covered with tiny holes spiralling in wide loops towards the centre. It is suspended on a light-sensitive surface. As the disc turns under electric current, it 'scans' a loop of contiguous, concentric rings which cover the whole surface beneath. This light-sensitive surface responds to the electric scanning according to the strength of the current. A 'picture' can thereby be built up of its surface phenomena (just as the telephone turns electro-magnetic vibrations back into sounds).

Some more of the names, for piety's sake, should be repeated. In the 1920s, J. L. Baird and P. T. Farnsworth in Britain and V. K. Zworykin in the USSR were all working on Braun's cathode-ray tube, and credit is handed out to each of them according to national preferences. In the tube, as we saw, amplified current runs through the electrons to the cathode terminal which duly discharges electrons capable of converting light into currents (and the reverse). In television camera and receiver alike, a sensor element scans a picture as a series of discrete, finite elements (a normal TV picture has about 350,000 such elements). The sensor emits a signal corresponding to the brightness of the light-image. The sensor or electron scanner discharges its electrons at a mosaic of photoelectric caesium globules which turn electrons into light, amplify them, and produce an image.

When a television broadcast takes place, the picking-up operation from the light phenomena out there (real life) is, as in radio, simply reversed as electric signals are duly broadcast on wide wavelengths, sensed by television antennae at home, and beamed as electrons onto the photosensitive mosaic in the cathode ray tube, which is busily scanning the mosaic line for line (625 of them) in parallel with the television camera. (The mosaic is the retina of the TV set.) The fluorescent deposit glows when hit by the electrons and turns them back into light. We see the image, helped out by our persistence of vision, so that only a few static images are needed (as we know from the cinema) to create motion. The addition of colour to television was then a matter of refining the initial scanner so that it could break white light into the three primaries – red, blue, yellow.

Detours through the technology are always apt to sound anti-social. They tend towards the Great Inventor and Mad Scientist picture of history. In fact, these grand innovations were impelled by economic needs – the expansion west of the United States, the spread of the British Empire and its huge administrative superstructure; by market competition – Bell against Elisha Gray, Baird against the American Jenkins – and the plotting of future markets. So investment went into cinemas rather than home TV because cinemas were ready first, looked like theatres, and theatres were known to be popular when the movie industry began. Beyond these simple drives to development, there was also the largest and simplest of all, world war. The first one brought the telephone and the film to the point of take-off, the second did the same for radio (especially in domestic life) and electronic systems (especially television).

This is to anticipate. The general point stands: that technology is driven along by a complex, even baffling coalition of social and economic forces; it doesn't determine or fix us (the view known as 'technological determinism'); rather, we arrange for it to happen according to the mixed-up decisions of everyday life. Over the period of accelerated technological change we are considering – roughly, 1850 to the present – new communication systems were demanded by this unprecedented kind of society: one in which travel and therefore economic expansion had quickened out of recognition because of the steam engine in locomotives and ships; in which mass production had been formalized, and a mass proletarian workforce mustered and drilled to keep its hungry machines always turning; in which vast industrial cities were created in a few years. In those cities, colossal populations came together in new, mutually hostile social classes. They fashioned out of their new neighbourhoods, whether poor or rich, extraordinarily urgent and united instruments of class thought, opinion, fantasy, whose ebb and flow may thereafter be said to constitute the real source of progress and reaction.

The newspaper was the first site of public opinion, and electric printing combined with trains make it the first universal success story of communication technology in our period. But *all* printing boiled suddenly over in the industrial centres, and although the book, as we have seen, was already at the leading edge of capitalism's production, it moved onto a quite different scale with the coming of modern urban life.

III

Newspapers and novels were the two forms of print which expressed this life for the literate public, and literacy, it should be added, was not only confirmed by the installation of compulsory national education: in Britain, after the 1870 Forster Education Act, in the USA beginning more gradually but regularly, state by state from the middle of the century onwards. Even so, it was always more widespread than is usually believed before the vast education industry was founded by the nation-state.[6] Newspapers offered to the varying classes of their readership a way of situating oneself in this kaleidoscopic world. They could respond on a daily basis to its queasy changefulness. As Raymond Williams documents,[7] in the earlier part of this period in Britain – say from 1830 to about 1880 – hundreds of newspaper flowers bloomed, often in contravention of stamp duty, and giving voice to the very mixed experience of life in the new towns; the sudden money, the dreadful poverty, squalor and illness. But by the end of the century the big money had arrived to streamline and classify this diversity in the name of giant sales figures. The Lords of the Press, first Northcliffe and Rothermere, then Beaverbrook, finally Thomson (all ennobled by the British crown for services to falsehood), each anticipated the fearful incarnation of Rupert Murdoch and Robert Maxwell.[8] The *Daily Mail* and then The *Daily Express* bore down upon the busy scene with economies of scale (which means that the bigger you are, the easier it is to make production cheaper) and lower unit costs (which, in turn, means that the more units – in this case, copies of newspapers – you produce, the more you sell and the lower you can keep your profit on individual items, thus undercutting your competitors). They also directed their contents towards a specific social class and deliberately sought a stereotyped echo of its characteristic manner, vocabulary and tone. Finally, the new Lords hitched their news-papers to a politics, almost invariably to the politics of the capital they were in business to make lots of.

The First World War clinched their position and their success. The newspaper became a social institution, and reading the news a widely-felt and gratified need. The newspaper oriented its readers to the world and to the day. It gave (and gives) them an intelligible space and moment in relation to all that's going on amongst people one cannot know but can claim to understand. It gives an account, both defiant and obedient, of what the powerful are going to do to people (to us). And it keeps your chin up with a dose of briskness.

The newspaper, Benedict Anderson says, is a 'one-day bestseller'.[9] Nobody reads last week's newspaper, unless they find it wrapped round potatoes in the kitchen. But every day it sells out in millions, because it tells us an intelligible story, with a plot, heroes, villains, actions and direction, about the way of the world. It settles us in a sufficiently 'knowable community',[10] while placing those who are known in a believable nearness to those who are not. When it does this, the newspaper acts much like the novel. The novel puts us alongside a group of people we do not know, and invites us to share their lives. In so far as we heed the novelist's voice and sympathize with the characters, we do share them. The novelist arranges his characters (like the editor arranges his front page) so that we know which are the ones that matter to us, and how they connect with the others. With this structure he or she is able to catch in a net a whole area of society, even, if ambitious enough, the whole society. In *War and Peace*, Tolstoy's three great families in their numerousness are able to take in, at home and on the battlefield, all the vast experiences of the Napoleonic invasion as it bursts upon their class. In *Great Expectations*, Dickens places his orphan hero Pip, with scarcely even a name of his own (a pip is a dot) so that his life touches both well-to-do society and derelict convicts deported to Australia. Indeed Dickens's point about the 'knowable community' of Victorian life is that, once you really knew the social connections, the most pretentious people link up with the shadiest corners of the underworld.

This is the form of all novels as they seek to teach the frame of society and to find a clean and decent space within that frame on which to stand. So too, we may add, do newspapers, films and television. All narratives have a *moral* point to make, whatever else they may be doing, and that truism is one keystone in the arch of media theory.

It is a keystone built into our frame of mind by the first theorists of the mass media. I shall treat these groups rather briskly under two headings, the Liberals and the Marxists, because these are over-whelmingly the groups, so hard to reconcile, into which all media theory falls even at its most technical.

There are good reasons for this. Being a Marxist or a Liberal isn't something you first choose for fun and then live with. The commit-ment derives slowly from your disposition, upbringing and educa-tion in the first place, and then from the kind of questions you are putting to the historical experience and its intellectual difficulty in front of you. For the Liberal, a product of the great nineteenth-century emphasis upon the best values of Romanticism, the absolute measure, the origin and space of human value reposes in the indi-vidual person. This being so, the freedom of the individual is para-mount (hence the verbal root which liberalism has in common with liberty). No other person can tell that individual what to do, what to think or what to believe. Indeed liberalism, setting so much store by personal freedom, whose centrally defining act is the act of *choice* (moral choice, consumer choice, electoral choice), is largely a doc-trine of what *not* to do. You must not bully people to think in certain ways; nor should you act in ways which limit other people's freedom less drastically. They have their space and you have yours, and both of you have rights to the uninterrupted occupation of that space. But by definition, no one shares a picture of virtue with anyone else; there is no common arena of action nor mutual picture of the good life.

This is a rather brutal cartoon of liberalism. It is a doctrine of great subtlety and is still vigorously alive. But its limitations are clear. It cannot tell people what they *ought* to do, and is indeed hard put to it to name evil for what it is, as opposed to its just being a limit on freedom. (Rather like saying of nuclear weapons that mass extermination takes away our freedom. Hardly the strong way to put it.) It does have a very attractive and compelling view of indi-viduality, its necessary colour, strength of passion, its self-assertion and, most of all, the creativity which is compounded of all these attributes.

It is out of this last, rich tradition that one of the first and best-known media theories emerged, a theory which was at the same time a theory of mass society, a theory about the heritage of mod-ernity and the meaning of historical progress. Like any other theory it is bedded in a social class position, the historical nature of which is its strength and its weakness. It's often hard to tell which is which.

It begins, naturally, in the Victorian moment at which the intellectuals of the day suddenly realized that in urban capitalism they were dealing with an entirely new, rough beast of a civilization, and nobody was sure what it would do. John Stuart Mill, the ancestor and first codifier of Liberalism, had little to say about what this political economy would do for culture, and his famous ally Matthew Arnold[11] committed his life (he became a schools inspector) to the view that traditional culture, especially poetry, could, as religion faded, tame and make sensitive and humanly responsible the weird social monster whose three parts he named 'Barbarians' (landowners), 'Philistines' (middle class), and 'Populace' (proletariat).

IV

By the aftermath of the First World War when newspapers, radio, cinema and books had all benefited from that great surge of productive destruction which a huge war causes, it was hard to hold on to Arnold's convictions so ingenuously. There was, however, no shortage of fighting energy with which to resist, even overcome the beast of modern culture. And it was in these terms that the most intellectually thorough-going and convincing of British critics conceived the task. Modern culture was largely hideous because mass-produced for strictly commercial ends, and it was the vocation of those who cherished the true heart and beauty of English culture, in which what was best of England herself was kept healthy and vital, to use its strengths against the monster. If enough people could join this 'armed and conscious minority' – and such people, in the nature of the cause, would be teachers and students of English art and literature – then although commercialization could not be routed, its deathliness could be held back.

It is easy to sound ironic about this militant programme, its declarative language a mixture of the guerrilla and the evangelist. But it propounds an argument at the heart of this book in particular, and media studies in general. What is one to say before the horribleness of a newspaper such as *The Sun*, a novel like *The Rats*, a movie like *The Terminator*? F. R. Leavis and his wife Q. D. Leavis were in no doubt. Faced with the awful novels of a much more innocent age – her targets included the inventor of *Tarzan*, Edgar Rice Burroughs, and the harmless fantasist about devil-worship, Dennis Wheatley – Queenie Leavis came up with a closely analysed, fiercely condemnatory account.

In her classic study[12] she offered a comprehensive and comprehensible theory of both production and effects in modern culture. The unattractive part of the theory, which she embraced eagerly, was its inescapable conclusion that those who agreed with its premises and arguments were themselves of necessity superior in taste and discrimination to those who didn't. Those who didn't were, it followed, either ignorant (in which case, they could be taught to do, see and talk better), or irredeemable in virtue of their stupidity, sentimentality or worse. For Mrs Leavis started from a historical model in which an elite centre of a unified society produced a rich and satisfying culture. This art and culture were, in broad outline, intelligible, pleasurable and morally significant to a populace outside the elite but, held within its language and dominant assumptions, still able to share its narrative life. Such a society was, in her theory, impossible without a unified and religious view of history and nature, one in which man was bound into a coherent universe with an allotted, non-exploitative space and a common language capable of saying so.

Nor was this a ruthlessly supercilious theory. For it also followed from the model that the elite needed the people just as much as the people needed the elite. The life of popular culture gave energy, colour, and humanity to the art of the court whose rarefied world would otherwise have become precious and anaemic. The prototype of this society was, of course, Elizabethan, and Shakespeare and the metaphysical poets its greatest glories.

Mrs Leavis then projected her model into a long historical future, and found that as the unified society broke up under the various impacts of the late seventeenth century – the execution of the king, the advent of science, the coming of capitalism itself[13] – entirely new forms of cultural life and expression appeared. The new elite wasn't at a court, it was in the metropolis of London. It had no courtly duties to perform, and few responsibilities to the larger society, the 'populace' of old. Its medium was, as suggested in chapter 1 (more cheerfully than Mrs Leavis would have liked) prose not poetry; its typical subject-matter the life of an illegitimate, lovable rogue called Tom Jones, not great kings and princes like Lear and Hamlet. Its form was the novel.

Such a society, Mrs Leavis reckoned, took gradually but greedily to a commercial culture. The old unity held long enough to produce Jane Austen, whose novels spoke for a little corner of Surrey and Hampshire where cultivated men and women maintained a code of manners and a formal language which together upheld a code of moral conduct, conscientiously responsive to public duty as to private longing. After Jane Austen, however, Queenie Leavis saw a commercial culture arise and dominate the best inclinations of society, to the financial benefit of the producers. Through the course of the nineteenth century she saw, correctly, that the book became one of the leading commodity forms. To be mass-producible, it had to become capable of being written at high speed, with low unit costs (pay the writer as little as possible, keep the book as cheap as possible, hit the mass market), simple inter-changeability of parts (publish sequels with very few changes in the formula), and easy emulation by a range of other producers and products addressed to different levels of the market (thrillers by Raymond Chandler for me but by Jack Higgins for you). She analysed a range of contemporary thrillers and tales of erotic fantasy and manly adventure (Edgar Wallace, Elinor Glyn, Edgar Rice Burroughs, Marie Corelli) in order to show how simple their inner machinery was. She did so briefly, cuttingly, and with an unforgivingly precise distaste for her subjects.

It was not enough for her cultural theory, however, merely to demolish the producers and the product. For it to be complete and not one-legged, her theory had to include the consumer and the mode of consumption. For a satisfactory theory, she had to cover both sides of the cultural transaction, producer and consumer, and show how the purposes of each were reciprocal. To match the producer of cheap fiction (the novelist and his publishers), she provided an image of the typical member of the reading public. The typical man looked for fantasies which would restore the excitement, significant action and fulfilment which the dreadful tedium and alienation of his job so fatally lacked. The typical woman looked for parallel fantasies of emotional satisfaction, romantic transports, and delirious dependence on male heroism which the desperate smallness of her domestic space made to seem desirable. (Queenie Leavis was, after all, writing at one of the peaks of feminist activity.) Both wanted urgently to live their emotional lives 'at the novelist's expense' in one of her key phrases, because modern urban and industrial life cut them off from the strong language and belief of their agrarian grandparents. It starved them of creative work, and left them without community in the wasteland of their factories and mean, repetitive houses. The novelists who wrote to 'gratify' these wants were, Queenie Leavis would have it, themselves crippled by the same life-failures, and to prove it she quoted extensively and with their permission from their unguarded replies to her letters and questionnaires.

It remains a remarkable book, and essential reading for media students. Its shortcomings are severe, however, as I noted: it leaves the theorist cut off from sympathy for what is theorized about; it neglects the *structures* of production and looks only at the intentions and motives of producers; it rests its whole case on being right about its value judgements.

Queenie Leavis's husband, F. R. Leavis, built her project into a whole politics of culture (though he would have hated the phrase), and he too needs to be understood by media students as part of the foundation of our subject. In a famous early pamphlet (1930) called 'Mass Civilisation and Minority Culture'[14] he repeated (because they worked it out together) his wife's contention that modern society traduced the individual; made work deadly and repetitive, private life drearily acquisitive, and creative life greedily commercial. The only salvation from this vicious circle was the narrow, intense energy coursing through a carefully chosen sequence of writers, together composing a tradition which would energize those who were capable of hearing it to fight off the worst effects of modern life. If you really responded to Shakespeare, John Donne, Wordsworth and Keats, Dickens and George Eliot, you could pick up through D. H. Lawrence the life they made possible according to domestic and suburban terms in the 1930s. You could recruit a minority of vital, serious, anti-commercial, sensitive and, above all, independent individuals to keep culture going.

This is the classic doctrine of liberalism, and it continues to inspire the best teachers. For Leavis, the heart of the matter was education: good teaching of the best students (regardless of their class or colour or anything else) would keep tradition and the spirit alive. Accordingly he devised with his schoolteacher colleague and great friend, Denys Thompson, a teachers' and pupils' guidebook to the argument. *Culture and Environment*[15] came out in 1932 for sixth-formers. It counterposed a picture of pre-industrial life taken from a first-hand report written by a man in the business, and called *The Wheelwright's Shop*, to an American sociologist's description of the awful dreariness of contemporary life in a small American town.[16] It is sometimes ridiculed for sentimentalizing the skilled knowledge of wood, iron tempering, weathering and whittling celebrated by the ex-wheelwright, and no doubt there's justice in the charge. But Leavis and Thompson needed an example of wholesomely creative work with which to castigate what everyone agrees is the brutal boringness of most people's jobs today, 'deskilled' and dehumanized as they all are,[17] whether at the supermarket checkout or the VDU, at the packing factory or on the assembly line. In such a contrast,

simply made for classroom discussion, the wheelwright has a lot
going for him.

The register and measure of creative life was for Leavis the quality
of language. Pre-industrial society, so his argument went, spoke a
muscular, specific, *and* spiritual tongue which held together body
and soul, thought and feeling, as good poetry should. Sometime in
the late seventeenth century there took place what T. S. Eliot called
'a dissociation of sensibility', so that the language split into separate
functions with prose for reason and poetry for feeling. The split in
language split people's identities with it. By the present day, so the
contention goes, language had become either deadly prosaic, or
sentimentally poetic. Prose was in the service of the heartless quan-
tification of the frame of mind Leavis called 'scientism', poetry was
then hired to sell (literally) vacuously emotional fantasies. Their
standard modern form was the advertisement.

Culture and Environment invited students to study the language
of advertisements and the newspaper discussion of culture with the
same closeness as Leavis inaugurated in his innovating study of
poetry – the intellectual procedures he followed I. A. Richards in
calling 'practical criticism'.[18] The study of the 1930s had brought
home with great force the connection between mass culture and
commercial production. There, Leavis invincibly demonstrated the
snobbery, emotionality, the fantasy-gratification and plain silliness
with which the producers sold either novels or cigarettes.

There is an agreeably comic footnote to this. Thompson tells us
that the texts of the advertisements were written by Leavis himself
to avoid copyright problems. They are wickedly convincing; so
much so that it is hard not to feel the pleasure taken in the parody,
and to catch something of the ambivalence we all know when we see
those irresistibly gorgeous girls, gleaming silver cars and moon-
drenched silver beaches teasing us to buy something as banal as a
bacardi.

But his main critical premises stand four-square. Modern culture
is unstoppably commercial. Modern media systems are permeated
by lies and deceit: the word 'propaganda' was coined about them.
Individuals cannot just be naturally educated *into* their own culture,
they must be also educated *against* it.

V

This theory is reassembled here from a straightforward textbook.
Leavis's work proceeded, of course, to much larger and subtler

formulations beyond the reach of this straightforward textbook.[19] Always, however, he studied the conditions of creative culture and the social forms which make for good lives, at once vividly individual *and* expressive of community. He found them in places as dissimilar as D. H. Lawrence's coal-mining village, Joseph Conrad's training ship for the Merchant Navy, Mark Twain's landing station on the Mississippi, John Bunyan's Baptist congregation in Bedford. All these provide examples of a good *polity*, the word from the Greek which means civic community.

Modern public communications, for Leavis and Thompson or any other rational citizen, ought to work for the creation of such a polity, at once local and global. Thompson went on, in two excellent studies,[20] to show, respectively, how newspapers in their newsiness and in their advertising alike destroy the polity in order to gain crude wealth and power. It is a reiterated conclusion of all media theory, and it is searchingly documented by the two most impressive heirs to Leavis and Thompson, Raymond Williams and Richard Hoggart.

Williams we have met already and shall return to several times. Hoggart's classic *The Uses of Literacy*[21] is another on the shortish list I name in my last chapter, 'Question Time', as essential reading for all media theorists. Hoggart indeed agrees with Leavis that things are bad: that modern industrial culture has produced an imaginative life whose typical fantasies are brutal or saccharine or both, and whose public language as expressed in its official conversation in newspapers is phoney, truthless, trivial and crass. Writing up to 1957, Hoggart also compiles his own imitations of samples from the tabloid press, the sex-and-violence novel, the girlie magazine, and does so with killing accuracy. But although with Leavis he concludes that such stuff is indeed 'unbending the springs of action' in individuals, he also insists on the strongly resistant energies of ordinary people in the face of the debilitating effects of mass media, *and* he insists on the clear fact that a lot of material in this dismal culture has exactly the life which Leavis wanted. He showed by the sort of analysis asked for by practical criticism that the songs of Vera Lynn, the radio comedy of Al Read, the jokes and homely advice of the Yorkshire working class in which he grew up himself, were all capable of the poetic force, the spiritual energy, the human richness and vitality which were supposed to have gone for good, long before.

Hoggart does two exemplary things which entirely prevent his book from going out-of-date. He shows us how to value and to discriminate amongst the torrent of stories coming from the mass media, and he gives us plenty of hope for the future. Indeed, in his hardly less classic contribution to the British Government's report on broadcasting known as *The Pilkington Report* of 1963, he provided a description of how a decently democratic broadcasting system should work. *The Uses of Literacy* teaches us to see how good some television is, as well as how awful the rest remains. It shows us what, for our self-respect and our intelligent life in the future, we should want for ourselves.

VI

Neither Hoggart nor Williams can be classified as a pure liberal. Williams, indeed, gave his life's work to the establishment of a specifically socialist politics of culture. Hoggart also, working, as anyone serious about the human sciences must, from his truthfulness about the truths he found in his lived experience, is intent upon the understanding and knowledge needed to found a democratic and, in the long run, socialist culture. When he wrote his great book the conditions for such a venture were more propitious than they look now. He and Williams had to start, as we all do, from the tradition of thought there to hand, which was Leavis's and Thompson's. Contemporary with F. R. and Q. D. Leavis and Thompson, however, a group of German intellectuals in a privately funded research institute began work in Frankfurt on lines parallel to the English studies, but starting from a very different tradition.

The Frankfurt Institute[22] was funded in the 1920s from the fortune of a radical German businessman, Felix Weil, who wanted to see independent inquiry of a Marxist persuasion pursued against the grain of what he judged to be the dangers and conformism of average academic study in Germany. The membership of the Institute (for *Sozialforschung*, or social inquiry) was, as we now know, immensely distinguished, and a roll-call of those who interest us and were involved from its beginning includes some of the most important names in social, political and media theory: Max Horkheimer, Theodor Adorno, Leo Lowenthal, Herbert Marcuse, and, recurrently, Walter Benjamin.

These men were, naturally, writing in the first place in German. When Hitler came to power in 1933 the last thing he wanted and one of the first targets of his cultural hatred would be an intellectual research establishment with Jewish members and Marxist beliefs.

Gradually, and only just in time, the Institute emigrated to the USA, was re-established near Columbia University on West 117th Street in New York in 1934, and went home again to the smashed desolation of occupied West Germany in 1949.

In exile, and with their vision turned to the longed-for defeat of Fascism, the Institute's writers went on writing largely in German. This meant, of course, that it has taken time for their books to be translated and their ideas to come through. Leavis and Hoggart are immediately clear because we stand today in the same modes of thought and speech. The Frankfurt exiles, only available in translation since the 1970s and thinking in a very different idiom, are harder to sort out and to situate in their merited, necessary place in media theory.

For a start they were Marxists, and very heretical Marxists at that. They studied what Marx called 'the ideological superstructure' of cultural life built on top of the economic 'base' in which the mode-and-relations-of-production drove everything else along. They insisted, with Marx, on the material, not spiritual content of what they studied. And they saw cultural production as an industry like any other in most respects, whose function was to sedate the masses and keep them quiet so that the real beneficiaries of capitalism, the male bourgeoisie, could go on drawing the profits and kidding themselves that they were the civilized ones. In a biting passage, Herbert Marcuse wrote:[23]

> By affirmative culture ... is meant that culture of the bourgeois epoch which led in the course of its own development to the segregation from civilisation of the mental and spiritual world as an independent realm of value that is also considered superior to civilisation. Its decisive characteristic is the assertion of a universally obligatory, eternally better, and more valuable world that must be unconditionally affirmed: a world essentially different from the factual world of the daily struggle for existence, yet realisable by every individual for himself 'from within', without any transformation of the state of fact ...

He meant, as I put it, that the male bourgeoisie could kid itself that as long as there was a transcendental world of art-that-is-good-for-you which you can visit at school or on holiday or in the evenings, no one need do anything about the everyday facts of capitalist exploitation, cruelty and wretchedness. As Max Horkheimer, his director at the Institute, also wrote, 'the struggle against mass cul-

ture can consist only in pointing out its connection with the persist-
ence of social injustice.'[24]

'*Against* mass culture'. The Institute group broke with conventional Marxism in seeing mass culture as invariably deleterious
because invariably commercial. In sharing this conclusion with the
Leavises, they drew a very different moral. The only escape from a
corrupt mass culture would be a transformation of the means of
production. Individuals could not do it alone; there had to be class
struggle and class victory.

They were not at all dewy-eyed about this prospect. The German
and Italian experiences made it clear that there was nothing inevitable about socialist victory. In any case they were pungently critical
of Leninism, and committed to a view of art as always holding out
the golden promise of happiness, of the world as it might yet be,
replete, serene, joyful. At the same time, they would have no truck
with art which gratified fantasy, which was merely a consolation for
the disappointments of life, or which made itself easy to digest and
was no trouble to anyone. Adorno wrote:[25]

> A successful work of art ... is not one which resolves contradictions
> in a spurious harmony, but one which expresses the idea of harmony
> negatively by embodying the contradictions, pure and uncomprom-
> ised, in its innermost structure ... Art ... always was, and is, a force
> of protest of the humane against the pressure of domineering institu-
> tions ... no less than it reflects their substance.

The view of art he shared with his colleagues and with the Leavises
was of a process whose created products would be difficult and
intransigent precisely in order to prevent commercialization and to
hold onto truthfulness. High art by this token remains high, even
austere, not in order to preserve in those who know about it their
sense of their own superiority, but in order to maintain an un-
answerable and compelling criticism of the way things are, a picture
of how they might be better, a call to humanity and its guardian
intelligentsia never to fall into conformity and resignation.

There are three contributions to the work of the Institute which
all beginning media theorists should read. The first is the chapter on
the culture industry written by Horkheimer and Adorno together in
their *The Dialectic of the Enlightenment*.[26] We shall go back to it in
chapter 6. The second is Leo Lowenthal's collection of essays *Literature, Popular Culture and Society*,[27] which is a model of fieldwork
in this genre. Lowenthal charts a deep change in the imagery of

popular culture when, checking through the mammoth weeklies of American domestic life, the *Saturday Evening Post, Harper's*, and the like, he finds a shift completed by the 1920s from heroes who are captains of industry to heroes who are 'celebrities', a quite new category including sportsmen, star actors in film and theatre, all alike in that their fame is to be looked at, not to do. This is the moment at which capitalism moves from its productive to its consumerist phase. It is the adolescence of the spectacular society with whose weird features we shall end this book.

The last contribution to the Institute's journal, the *Zeitschrift* (or, 'writing for the time') which must be on all media bibliographies is a second essay of Walter Benjamin's, 'The work of art in the era of mechanical reproduction'.[28] Benjamin, as we saw earlier in 'The storyteller', is not an accessible writer. He was taught by and admired the Jewish scholars of hermeneutics (or interpretative principles) who deliberately sought enigmas and polysemic (multi-meaning) interpretation of the sacred Jewish books, the *kabbalah* and *torah*. He is epigrammatic and purposefully inconsistent. In the essay in question, he stresses that the sacred quality of a work of art, its 'aura', is lost by limitless reproduction. Only Giotto's frescoes in Assisi have aura, their reproductions do not. But novels and films are always reproductions. There is no original in any useful sense (the manuscript has a kind of aura because the great man wrote it down, but it isn't *the* work). Thus, although the sacred aura is lost by mechanical reproduction, reproduced art has radically more democratic possibility than aureatic art. The latter, Benjamin claimed, had 'cult value', the former 'exhibition value'.

One isn't perfectly sure on several occasions whether Benjamin is a mourner at the funeral of old traditions and values or herald of the new age of mechanically reproduced, newsy and exhibitionist art. But certainly the type of the new art is for him, writing in the 1930s, the film. He rebuts the elitist charges against the film (made by the Leavises and by Adorno) that film 'is a pastime for helots, a diversion for uneducated, wretched, worn-out creatures ... a spectacle which requires no concentration and presupposes no intelligence' and he writes in repudiation (p. 236):

> Mechanical reproduction of art changes the reaction of the masses toward art. The reactionary attitude toward a Picasso painting changes into the progressive reaction toward a Chaplin movie. The progressive reaction is characterised by the direct, intimate fusion of visual and emotional enjoyment with the orientation of the expert.

Such fusion is of great social significance. The greater the decrease in the social significance of an art form, the sharper the distinction between criticism and enjoyment by the public. The conventional is uncritically enjoyed, and the truly new is criticised with aversion. With regard to the screen, the critical and the receptive attitudes of the public coincide. The decisive reason for this is that individual reactions are predetermined by the mass audience response they are about to produce, and this is nowhere more pronounced than in the film.'

In homely terms, Benjamin tells us that we might miss the point of Picasso, but (by god) we spot every nuance in the Levi commercials. And he anticipates the state of mind of the home viewer and listener a generation later (p. 242):

Distraction as provided by art presents a covert control of the extent to which new tasks have become soluble by apperception. Since, moreover, individuals are tempted to avoid such tasks, art will tackle the most difficult and most important ones where it is able to mobilise the masses. Today it does so in the film. Reception in a state of distraction, which is increasing noticeably in all fields of art and is symptomatic of profound changes in apperception, finds in the film its true means of exercise. The film with its shock effect meets this mode of reception halfway. The film makes the cult value recede into the background not only by putting the public in the position of the critic, but also by the fact that at the movies this position requires no attention. The public is an examiner, but an absent-minded one.

Films, of course, have come a long way since then, and there are now degree courses, National Film Theatres and Institutes, and honoured film critics. But much stands in Benjamin's account of how progressive ideas and responses work in culture, especially in the bleakness of his conclusion. He notes there – with extraordinary prescience – the transformation by Fascism of politics into aesthetic spectacle: the mass military parades of tanks, helmets, motor-cycles, miles of men – 'A million eyes, a million boots in line.' Hitler's Nuremberg rallies, celebrated in Leni Riefenstahl's infamous and seductive movie *Triumph of the Will*, expressed and reinforced the power of Fascism. Benjamin declares that such aesthetics can only be fulfilled by war. In a frightening epigram, he ends (p. 244):

Mankind, which in Homer's time was an object of contemplation for the Olympian gods, now is one for itself. Its self-alienation has reached such a degree that it can experience its own destruction as an aesthetic pleasure of the first order.

One may recoil a bit sceptically until one remembers the compulsion with which we all have watched the terrible beauty of nuclear explosions on a television or cinema screen. Benjamin's response as Marxist to the aestheticization of politics, the making of it into gorgeous or sinister spectacle, is to politicize art. At first glimpse we may feel fed up by this ('I'm bored with politics'), but not if we remember that politics for him and his friends was the envisaging of human happiness in the future.

Notes

1 See Marx's essay, 'A critique of political economy' in *Marx and Engels: Selected Works* (Lawrence & Wishart, 1980).

2 Mark Poster, *Foucault, Marxism and History: from Mode of Production to Mode of Information* (Polity Press, 1985).

3 Anthony Smith, *The Politics of Information* (Macmillan, 1978).

4 Marshall McLuhan in his book *Understanding Media* (Routledge & Kegan Paul, 1964), is author of the famous slogan, 'the medium *is* the message', by which deliberate overstatement he meant to emphasize what I have said here about mediation.

5 In *Television: Technology and Cultural Form* (Fontana Collins, 1974), p. 19.

6 See R. K. Webb, 'The Victorian reading public' in *Penguin Guide to English Literature: Dickens to Hardy*, ed. B. Ford (Penguin, 1958). See also Louis James, *Fiction and the Working Man 1820–1840* (Cambridge University Press, 1965).

7 See Raymond Williams, *The Long Revolution* (Chatto & Windus with Penguin, 1961)

8 See James Curran and Jean Seaton, *Power Without Responsibility* rev. ed. (Sage Publications, 1988).

9 In *Imagined Communities* (Verso, 1983) p. 39.

10 Raymond Williams's phrase, in *The Country and the City* (Chatto & Windus, 1973).

11 See Matthew Arnold's *Culture and Anarchy*, first published by Elder, Smith in 1869.

12 Q. D. Leavis, *Fiction and the Reading Public* (Chatto & Windus, 1932).

13 One of her colleagues traced the effect of these forces on the writing of the plays. See L. C. Knights, *Drama and Society in the Age of Jonson* (Chatto & Windus, 1936).

14 Reprinted in *Education and the University* (Chatto & Windus, 1943). See also his rejection of Marxism in general and the Russian revolutionary leader-in-exile, Trotsky, in particular in an article 'Under

which King, Bezonian?' reprinted in *Selections from 'Scrutiny'* (2 vols, Cambridge University Press, 1970).

15 F. R. Leavis and Denys Thompson, *Culture and Environment* (Chatto & Windus, 1932).

16 George Sturt, *The Wheelwright's Shop* (Duckworth, 1906). H. S. Lynd, *Middletown* (Constable, 1937).

17 There is plenty of evidence. See, recently, Harry Braverman, *Labour and Monopoly Capital* (New York Free Press, 1974).

18 See I. A. Richards, *Practical Criticism* (Routledge & Kegan Paul, 1924).

19 For example in his *Nor Shall My Sword* (Chatto & Windus, 1972), and *'Anna Karenina' and Other Essays* (Chatto & Windus, 1967).

20 Denys Thompson, *Voice of Civilisation* (Muller, 1942), and *Between the Lines* (Hutchinson, 1947); the first about advertising, the second newspapers. My own book, *The Imagery of Power* (Heinemann, 1972), is an attempt to re-write Thompson's first title for the television and colour-photography age.

21 Richard Hoggart, *The Uses of Literacy: Aspects of Working-class Life and Entertainment* (Chatto & Windus with Penguin, 1957).

22 Its history is comprehensively told by Martin Jay, in *The Dialectical Imagination* (Heinemann Educational, 1973).

23 In Herbert Marcuse, *Negations: Essays in Critical Theory* (Allen Lane, 1968), p. 95.

24 In a letter quoted by his collaborator, Theodor Adorno, in his book *Prisms* (Merlin Press, 1968), p. 109.

25 T. W. Adorno, *Minima Moralia: Reflections from a Damaged Life* (New Left Books, 1974), p. 224.

26 T. W. Adorno with Max Horkheimer, *The Dialectic of the Enlightenment* (Allen Lane, The Penguin Press, 1973).

27 Leo Lowenthal, *Literature, Popular Culture and Society* (Doubleday, 1961).

28 In *Illuminations* (Jonathan Cape, 1970).

3

The Books of Numbers

These two traditions of mass cultural theory are no longer separate, and certainly no longer to be set as contraries to one another between which the theorist must choose. The liberal, thinking always of the protection of individuals, still knows that Society-with-a-capital-S is a great Thing which crowds upon the individual, invading him against his will or without his even noticing and making him thereby less his own man. Society as a structure for someone who thinks like that – and most of us do, most of the time – is pictured in ways close to that of the Marxist. The Marxist who has taken to heart the lessons taught from Frankfurt is no longer the vulgar figure who reads Lenin as Holy Writ and believes the mass media to be straightforwardly repressive, holding on the one hand that their ownership is routinely concentrated in the bosses' hands so they simply speak in the bosses' voice, and on the other that the poor, put-upon proletariat is cowed and bullied into believing whatever it is told. The new Marxist theorist has taken to heart the key word 'mediation', and knows that whatever people do with the mass media, as producers or consumers, they do it in particular, local, actual lives. Both theorists, in other words, have to be faithful to the facts and the truth.

But of course the moment we speak the simple words 'facts' and 'truth' both liberals and Marxists turn disdainfully on us to ask, how we know them to be the facts and who can ever say what the truth is? Indeed, in the human sciences at large today, truth is taking a terrible pounding from what is called relativism, a term we need to keep by us in media theory. The relativist believes,[1] put at its simplest, that all judgements or claims as to truth are relative to the circumstances in which they are made. In the (silly) slogan often produced at this point, 'There are no absolute truths'. This contention rests upon the view that we each live within a community of belief which sets the standards of evidence, the authority of tradition, and the criteria of rationality. Relativists further argue that between such communities of belief there is and can be no agreed court of appeal, and therefore that what is true for somebody living on the other side of the world, or was true for somebody living five centuries ago, has in each case irrefutable validity. It is, or was, 'true for them'.

There are certain points where the devout relativist must give very literal ground. The earth is round, whether or not medieval peasants thought it was flat, and the Inquisition came to get people who thought otherwise. The defensive move against this is generally to say that there are differences in kind between the truths of natural science and the relative truths of human experience, especially as these touch upon questions of value. At these points, they say, the most we can hope for is tentative agreement on *interpretation*, which can only be grounded in a community of shared belief.

In terms such as these, relativism must be given a long run for its money. It becomes at times silly, as when its advocates say that nothing can be ever done or said in judgement about how another culture lives, even when we believe that culture to be doing something terrible. This priggishness would prevent, in a Rider Haggard sort of example, our rescuing the Maya child of the sixteenth century from the priests about to sacrifice her according to the peculiarly horrible custom of Mexican Indians at the time, because it was fine by their beliefs and anyway the little girl thought she was going to eternal bliss. The daft relativist denies any common human nature, as rooted in naming and necessity, in the facts of shelter, food, sex, and death. But a scrupulous relativist makes the categories of fact and truth sit below a question mark, and since the very designation 'mass' in 'mass media' betokens factually huge columns of numbers, we shouldn't ignore him.

The earliest proponents of intellectual relativism, Isaiah Berlin tells us,[2] were the Neapolitan, Vico and the German, Herder, writing respectively at the beginning and the end of the eighteenth century. They were part of the wide, mixed current of new ideas which started to flow unevenly through Europe at that time towards the modern age. But where Vico and Herder stressed contextual thought, the variety of human understanding bedded in different languages, the special nature of the study of people as opposed to things, the Enlightenment in general put its faith in the absolute reach of human reason, and its limitless power to explain everything.

I have referred to this process in the first two chapters, and later to the British philosopher, lawyer and politician, the great planner of the new kind of society, Jeremy Bentham. Bentham, writing prodigally for the half-century from 1770 to 1820, saw before anyone else the nature of the new kind of industrial society, and that its most obvious feature was its sheer *mass*, the massive numbers of people who composed it. They not only came together vastly from their scattered places in the countryside, they bred and increased no less vastly in the dark new cities. Bentham realized that a special kind of social arithmetic would have to be invented, capable of organizing these masses and trying to resolve rationally the violent clashes of their wishes and needs which were certain to occur. He started from the famous dictum of what was called utilitarianism that all social decisions be decided in favour of their utility, or 'the greatest good of the greatest number'. The greatest social good was people's common happiness, roundly translated as their material welfare.

In the 1820s and the terrible slums of Manchester or London, material welfare had a clearly quantitative measure: enough food and clothes, fuel and clean water. The Benthamites concluded that as long as they could assemble enough facts about the society, then the social calculus ordered by the rational principle of the greatest good of the greatest number would leave men in no doubt what to do next. We meet Bentham later, in chapter 5, as the first architect of modern prison surveillance and rehabilitation; that also was governed by his numerical principle. It was plainly true to the Benthamites that everyone would be better off if enlightened rulers scrubbed out the skulls of the criminal class. The facts spoke for themselves.

The heritage of Bentham goes deep in all industrial societies, and nowhere more so than in the study of mass media. Bentham followed the philosophical master of Enlightenment empiricism, the great Scotsman David Hume, who showed that *physical* events and objects – Newton's apple falling to the ground, the sun apparently rising in the East every day – could only be explained in terms of *mental* events and objects, what Hume called 'impressions and ideas'. Hume allied this endeavour to a radical scepticism about everything – the apple might fly upwards tomorrow – from which it followed that the only way to discover reasonably reliable regularities in life was to watch carefully what happened, collect great piles of such observed information, and infer the probability of certain outcomes from their comparative frequency of occurrence.

It sounds obvious today, after 200 years of scientific observation and induction. There is a logic to statistical inference, but it takes a lot of working out and making watertight. Hume's method turns less on proof than on probability. It is hard to establish a natural *law* (which is fixed); the best you can usually do is to falsify your hypothesis, so that at least that way you can discover what is not a law.

Hume was followed by the first statisticians of the nineteenth century, Galton and Gauss, intent on showing how to collect reliable facts with Hume in one hand for method, and Bentham in the other for policy. Of course, the facts themselves had to be chosen for their human relevance, but once you knew the ones you were looking for, you practised the utmost scruple in not tainting them, twisting, or distorting them for fear that your scientific inference would not be reliable. As in the scientific laboratory, so in human activity, the social scientist must keep antiseptic his 'sense-data', so-called because those were the facts which presented themselves to the senses of touch, sight, hearing. (Smell and taste don't get much of a chance in social science.)

The grand theorists of the human sciences, Marx and Mill, Durkheim and Weber and William James, who codified procedure as mass inquiry got going, and social policy was worked out to make the filth and cruelty of industrial capitalism more bearable, set a clear breach between collection of the facts and giving them a meaning. Facts are, by this token, the real things out there; values are personally chosen and attached to the facts by human volition. You stand back and decide what facts you want – how many children watch violent after-10 p.m. movies? This is a clear value-decision, taken let us say because you want to estimate the effects of TV violence on ten-year-olds. The facts are then collected in as methodical and sterilized a way as possible, whatever your preferences about the outcome. Then you get to work and see what they mean, always respecting their factuality of course, but placing them in an interpretative context.

This is the classic separation between fact and value made by empiricism. It finds a familiar parallel in the separation made by liberalism when writing history or reporting daily news, between fact and opinion, and it stems at about the same time from the same social arguments and the same class. Of course, one knows what they mean, and part of a proper education is to learn how to detect opinion masquerading as fact, partisanship dressing itself in the judicious robes of impartiality. But empiricism has taken some hard knocks for supposing that the fact : value distinction is watertight, and nowhere with greater force than in media studies. The whole concept of ideology, with which we deal in the next chapter, is intended to get purchase on the necessarily partisan nature of our knowledge, on the truth that knowledge is a practical instrument which we bend to serve our interests.

So, too, the theorists of language, particularly of speech-acts,[3] point out that in speaking we *do* something; we do not only speak truths or falsehoods. To say 'I promise' or 'you ought to help' is not exactly to make factual statements, but to *act*, or to make what J. L. Austin called 'performatives'. As such, an empiricist cannot classify either utterance or the justification which goes with it in one of his two boxes. Similarly, in pointing to a mushroom and saying 'That's poisonous', we not only make a factual statement which can be checked, we affirm a value, in this case the pretty straightforward value of not being poisoned. Here, too, empiricism can't distinguish facts from values.

Either way, these are arguments for deciding upon the very grounds of knowledge, whose technical name is epistemology.

II

The same arguments bear directly upon empirical practice in media studies, which for three decades or so from the mid 1920s to the late 1950s simply *was* media theory in the USA. Of course the dispute between empiricists and others is not only part of the human sciences, but of thinking about human experience in any context whatever. The most ordinary domestic puzzling out of life-difficulties casts us in the first place as empiricists or rationalists: as those who will try to find such probabilities as may help deal with the wild unpredictability of events, or as those who hope to tease out a convincing connection between their thoughts and the world such that the two come together in a reasonable pattern.

The vulgar empiricists fell upon the human phenomenon of the mass media with satisfaction. All over the teeming USA of the period between 1920 and 1950 the social scientists deployed the gleaming apparatus of statistics and, as they believed, compiled (without prejudice) the piles of figures which would enable this unprecedented new society of immigrants to understand itself. They sorted out, in the first instance, the numbers of audiences: for newspapers, for movies, for Presidents. Perhaps the most famous product of the empirical school of media inquiry is *The People's Choice*,[4] the study which analysed the way voters took their decisions at times of Presidential and Congressional elections. The book is so significant because of its attempt to isolate and measure the factors which come to bear upon such a decision from so many quarters: traditional categories such as class, gender, geography for sure; but then the subtler mediations of newspapers, radio, newsreels, rallies, workmates, close friends and so forth are all given tentative place in a hierarchy of differentially loaded factors.

This is the best kind of empiricism, but it introduces, perhaps painfully, another arrival at the social scientific festival, the functionalist. The functionalist, as the story goes, stands unnoticed just behind the empiricist's shoulder. *His* view is that human institutions and practices have the function that they maintain in one way or another (which the theorist must specify) the ordering and powering of society. If they are *dys*-functional, they impair the social machine. Empiricism is held to be functionalist. It piles up the accounts of how many people go to the movies, read pulp thrillers or a given newspaper, in order to show how their freely chosen leisure life functions as an adjunct of the social order and the political economy. It is sharply criticized in its mass media versions by the Marxists, who accuse it, with some accuracy, of simply endorsing the way things are and of betraying the responsibility of intellectual inquiry to criticize. Marxists who want to argue, also with justice, that the mass media systematically protect the ruling class, obstruct radical change, defend capital and deride the Left, dismiss empiricists as the stooges of power, uncritical describers of a changeless world, who choose their research topics to help keep things that way.

The trouble is that Marxists also may have their Functionalist bodyguard just behind them. If they believe, as Marx taught, that the social base of society is its economic forces and all else (Church, Law, Army, Education, Art) is the superstructure built up on the base and given its determinate form by the 'real foundations' below, then the mass media must be merely a function of those economic forces.

It is a circular but still not a pointless quarrel; that is the paradox. To speak of social function makes obvious enough sense, but it only does so if we are unusually faithful to the local history, the facts indeed. And then empiricism turns of necessity into theory, since no one can simply amass facts without some idea of what they might be going to mean. How, after all, could one choose from the inane, unstoppable flow of events? You count people going into cinemas, no doubt, but you have to have some idea of what they are doing. Better to think of those facts as *actions*, people doing something, and then to acknowledge that actions are only intelligible if they are placed in some kind of narrative. Millions of people in cinemas means something different in a society with very high unemployment (the USA in the 1930s) as opposed to one with full employment (the USA in the early 1950s, when cinema numbers hit their peak). To know what the millions mean, we need to know if those audiences were bored or just cold, too poor to do anything else or in love with Rudolf Valentino.

III

Empiricism, in Hume's version, is very compelling. As Hume was at pains to make clear, it was unmistakably theoretic. Mindless number-collecting is impossible, therefore; even train-spotters *mean* something by their numbers. They count and classify. The two basic classifications of empiricism in media studies are producers and consumers. This is the simple complementarity of their analysis. Some people put out the message, others heed it. We study, empirically, one half or the other.

Roughly speaking, the Marxists have taken the producers as their subject and the liberals have taken the consumers. But the division of labour is not quite that simple. If it worked like this at first, it is because the implicit assumptions of each sent them that way. Marxists followed the master into the records of capital. He thought of empiricism as he thought, respectfully, of Darwin; 'One must put up with the mere English way of doing things', he wrote in a letter to Engels. Empiricism pretended to be theory-less, and Marx, as one of the giants of scientific rationalism, was nothing if not theoretic. But he had to have the facts, and taught by example that to find the power of the ruling class at work you must go down into the machinery of the economic base, take it to pieces, measure it, and determine the way it produces for the benefit of its owners. This is not empiricism as Hume saw it – there are no 'sense-data' in such research, but there are plenty of numbers and counting.

Empiricism in a truer sense suited the liberal cast of mind and its unstated assumptions. Liberalism, as we saw, takes its strength from its strong trust in individuals, and although it is itself decidedly a theory, it thinks of itself as a minimal theory, so fundamentally self-evident as not to be a theory at all. 'There's no such thing as society', the liberal says. 'Can't you see that we're all just people?' A yet further assumption about intellectual inquiry flows from this, known in the trade as 'methodological individualism'. By its lights, the researcher refuses to treat any data within grand theoretical frameworks. Data themselves are strictly individual, and will only yield up very local truths by being treated individually. Liberals are often led by their dispositions to connect their view of individual people and their theoretic rejection of theory in this way. Isaiah Berlin puts it with celebrated neatness in a little folk-proverb: 'The fox knows many things, but the hedgehog knows one big thing.' More elaborately, foxes are diverse and multifarious in their thought, and hedgehogs love one Big, all-explanatory Idea.[5] Marxists are hedgehogs, liberals are foxes.

But as I said, the two world-views are no longer so simply counterposed in media studies. Once upon a time, in the 1930s, when to the Frankfurt School such a hedgehog view of Goebbels' propaganda-dominated Third Reich seemed self-evident, the Marxists supposed that the new mass media roundly and successfully told the masses what to think. At the same time, liberal researchers saw commercial culture as deadening and trivial, but were committed to the hope that, given critical self-awareness and a liberal education, individuals could stand up to culture and win their freedom.

Both schools learned to take in the other's washing: the Marxists became more empirical, the liberals more theoretical.[6] The quintet who dominate American empirical research of the sort which still sets the terms and tone of nearly all the work there, Lazarsfeld, Katz, Berelson, Klapper and Schramm,[7] were committed to working in the fine grain of individual experiences, then agglomerating these into large tendencies. Thus they spoke up for the powers of individuals to make their own political decisions for themselves, whatever the massiveness of the mass media pushing at the door of their attitudes. They documented the continuingly solid presence of family and friends in a world where communication systems were so global, swift, and momentous. And they showed how various were the imaginative and fantastic uses people made of the narratives of the mass media, how resourceful individuals were in resisting and transforming the pervasive influence of media.

In spite of themselves, however, they were bound to concede much to Marxism's view of the compelling absoluteness of the forces of production. Their very subject-matter endorsed the idea that mass communication, driven by capital, was steadily becoming the energy-centre of all social networks. They cast their defence of individuals defensively: people *resisted* these forces, but there was and is one hell of a force to resist. After all, the choice to study audiences in the first place put the liberal empiricists firmly at the consumer end of things, and a consumer by definition has to take what's coming from production. The symbolic, heady day-dream of free consumer choices through which the advertisers pretend that we drift all day is a largely demeaning, deeply gratifying fraud, as we all agree. We can only choose from what is produced. Much of what is produced we don't need and hardly want (another perfume, another slimline tracksuit, another unit trust, another nuclear missile). But we buy them anyway.

Seeing things from the consumers' end alone, as chapter 7 emphasizes, may give us strong sympathies for the individuals concerned but it also encourages us to ratify their human weaknesses and fat-headedness. We note the millions who watch the latest dismal soap opera, or turn straight to the page 3 girl, and conclude that *Crossroads* and *Matt Houston*, the *A-Team* and *Bugs Bunny*, the *Sun* and the *New York Daily Post* are what audiences really want. So more such products are made because they guarantee the brute size of audiences.

Such conclusions jump from 'watch' to 'want'. In an excellent premise which is at the heart of liberal, that is to say 'anti-masses' theory, we are all members of many but overlapping minorities. But the demands of production which we turn to in chapter 6 drive always toward the streamlining of products, to the reduction of variety and therefore to ease of reproduction, to holding their customers tight and increasing their rates of consumption. So they must deny the mixed identity and multiple self which we all are and have, living as we do in a variety of minorities.

When it goes uncritically along with slogans about 'consumer sovereignty', media research turns into the hireling of the forces of production. It hands itself over to the colossal industry of market research, and beyond question this has taken the techniques of empiricism to new heights of precision and sophistication. Saying so returns us to our political theme. Media theory and the studies it energizes cannot be impartial. It leads either to criticism or ratification of the way of the world. Thus, market research into patterns of consumption helps to control, predict and manipulate that consumption. That is its purpose, even — perhaps most of all — when it is trying to fasten down and describe the smallest preferences and habits in our consumption of mass media.

It is, on the other hand, worth pointing out that the questionnaire-and-interview duo which empiricism developed and market research refined so carefully is indispensable to media theory and never to be taken lightly. Naturally, blithe or unwary empiricism must be warned just how careful you must be with framing questions, checking memory, detecting lies, and suppressing people's unstoppable garrulity about themselves. Our interest in that subject is generally so overwhelming that we are all too ready to believe the interest of others is just as great, and to pour out an autobiography. That partly explains the eagerness with which we search tables of figures, looking, at one and the same time, for a reflection of our ordinary selves in the identical practices of others, and for the confirmation of our superiority in their visibly inferior tastes.

Either way, the pull of the tables of numbers specifying audience and consumer habits is irresistible. It is one of the great pleasures of media research simply to see what people get up to in such vast numbers. There is more than a little, in this attitude, of Michael Caine's 'Not many people know that', and it is none the worse for it. Lacking such interest, with its prurience (no less human for *that*, either), and with its sheer curiosity and powerful urge to recognize human variety, there could not be human science, let alone liberal research.

The trouble is, most such interest goes the consumer and market research way, and the Marxists have surely much on their side when they say that liberal empiricism, always non-committal about its economic allies, is by now in thrall to consumer research, and a creature of the marketeers. The force of such criticism comes out if we test the free market nostrum that consumer choice determines profitability. James Curran, with Graham Murdock one of the pioneer champions of media research from the production end, quotes[8] the then chairman of *The (London) Times* when the Labour-supporting daily newspaper, the *Daily Herald* folded up, as not-so-innocently saying, 'The *Herald* was beset by the problem which has dogged nearly every newspaper vowed to a political idea: not enough people wanted to read it.' You get the idea? All this idealistic politics, especially from the point of view of *those* politics, puts readers off. Give them rubbish – bums and tits. Then they'll buy it.

But when it closed in the 1960s, the readership of the *Herald* was 4.7 million, well above many of today's tabloids, and far more, as Curran says, than the total of all the posh papers put together: 'The *Daily Herald*, lone consistent voice of social democracy in the national daily press, died because its readers were disproportionately poor working class and consequently did not constitute a valuable advertising market to reach' (p. 225). Market research has since matched the working class audience to advertising revenue in both newspapers and television; perhaps the audience was poorer in those days, and more critically wide-awake.

However it was, the crude free-market-as-run-by-consumer-choice view of the world will not do. If we turn to the stout dossier of inquiries by men and women following the lamps of Curran and Murdock[9] down the hugely vaulted but ill-lit naves and corridors of power, we find such choice truths as the Rockefeller family's grip on American media, expressed not in simple holdings of shares, but in the characteristic formation of British and American ruling class power: they control Chase Manhattan Bank, not only because it commands 'strategic holdings' in the three major American TV networks, RCA, ABC, CBS, but also through the structure of inter-locking directorships which connect television to the rest of American capitalism (seven members of the 18-man board of CBS have other Rockefeller positions).

'What do you expect?', people ask. The rich run things, they link up with each other. They are members of one another's clubs. As Murdock points out, access to information in these matters is hard to come by, except when open scandal breaks out in the City and Wall Street, and insider dealing is briefly in the news, not in the sex-and-money soaps. The ruling class keeps its deals to itself, and even more its quarrels and conspiracies and eliminations. So neo-Marxist research is hard to do: the difficult way forward is indicated in chapter 6. But work such as Curran's and Murdock's is richly empirical from the other side – historically specific and materialist, they might prefer to say. When Murdock shows us[10] that the ceramics, oil and banking conglomerate Pearsons buys up the *Financial Times*, Longmans, Penguins, Madame Tussaud's and the London Planetarium next door, and Warwick Castle, he lights up a cause-way which shows us where capital itself is heading, and how it may move to dominate the entire range of our consuming lives, from the petrol we burn in the car, the newspapers we read in it, the china cups in our picnic basket, to our standing in the queue on Bank Holidays for the waxworks or the castle.

IV

What now follows is a brief case of samples, displaying the figures which provide the essential ground for the study of mass media and public communications. They have their inherent fascination, as I said. It is simply amazing that American schoolchildren spend half as much time again watching television as going to high school. But then it is reassuring that in Britain at least only 2 per cent of the 4–7 age group is still watching by 9 p.m. Out of the figures of production and consumption, we can build as full an account as possible of the practices which constitute the two halves of all this endless, worldwide activity.

Many of the figures go out of date very quickly, and the new sources are quoted in my notes. They are principally here as an object-lesson, and bunched together accordingly for ready reference. The lesson teaches that mass media are just that: masses of people consuming masses of products; masses of capital in very few hands driving the whole mammoth machine. The lesson of all subsequent chapters is just how little and how much use these raw figures are. We always need more figures, no doubt, and have to make them speak. By themselves, they are dumb and dead. Only our recovery of the contexts, practices and purposes of local life and knowledge will make them get up and walk.

First selection: a British consumer medley

Table 1 Hours of TV watched, by age groups

Age group	Hours per week
4–7	21.9
8–11	24.7
12–15	22.5
Adults	29.2
UK population average	28.4

Source: British Audience Research Board, January 1987

but age group 4–15 watches 23 hours per week January–March, 17 hours per week July–September, presumably because the sun comes out.

At 8 a.m. 20 per cent of all households have their TV on; from 4 p.m. to 10 p.m., 50 per cent; at 12 p.m., 7 per cent. By 9 p.m. only 2 per cent of the 4–7 age group are still watching (BARB, as above).

It is also important to note that 23 per cent of all families are

Table 2 Television and radio: average viewing and listening in the United Kingdom, per week, by age

	Television viewing				Radio listening			
	1984	1985	1986	1987	1984	1985	1986	1987
Age groups (h : min per week)								
4–15	16:10	19:59	20:35	19:14	2:46	2:24	2:12	2:07
16–34	18:16	21:36	21:10	20:03	11:42	11:42	11:24	11:18
35–64	23:24	28:04	27:49	27:25	9:59	9:43	9:56	10:16
65+	29:50	36:35	36:55	37:41	8:01	8:04	8:27	8:44
Reach[a] (percentage)								
Daily	74	79	78	76	46	43	43	43
Weekly	90	94	94	93	81	78	75	74

[a] Percentage of UK population aged 4+ who viewed television for at least three consecutive minutes or listened to radio for at least half a programme over a day (averaged over 7 days) or a week.
Source: *Social Trends 19*, © Crown copyright 1989

one-parent families, 46 per cent have no children, and only 31 per cent fit our usual picture of the nuclear family, as having two parents only, and at least one child (HMSO census figures, 1984). 97 per cent of all households have TV; 43 per cent have two TVs; 36 per cent have VCR (*Social Trends*, HMSO, 1988).

These details give rather more meat to the naked histograms which follow.

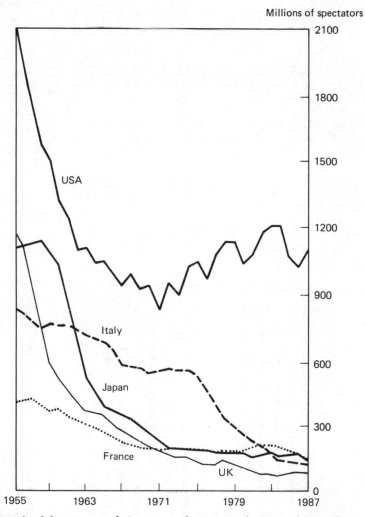

Figure 1 Movement of cinema audiences in the United Kingdom and other countries, 1955–1987. (*Source: Social Trends* 19, © Crown copyright, 1989)

Table 3 Average weekly household expenditure in the United Kingdom on selected leisure items; by household income, 1985 (in £s, with percentages)

Leisure items	Gross normal weekly income of household (£)						All households (%)
	Under 100	100– 150	150– 200	200– 250	250– 300	Over 300	
Alcoholic drink consumed away from home	1.71	3.70	5.42	6.64	7.76	10.90	5.30
Meals consumed out[a]	0.97	2.18	2.52	3.73	4.30	7.66	3.18
Books, newspapers, magazines, etc.	1.41	2.02	2.29	2.84	3.05	4.06	2.42
Television, radio and musical instruments	2.06	2.85	3.93	6.10	6.48	7.85	4.36
Purchase of materials for home repairs, etc.	0.60	1.45	2.06	2.40	3.85	7.53	2.66
Holidays	0.94	3.05	4.42	3.35	6.45	10.88	4.28
Hobbies	0.03	0.02	0.08	0.05	0.08	0.23	0.08
Cinema admissions	0.02	0.07	0.06	0.10	0.14	0.21	0.09
Dance admissions	0.04	0.08	0.09	0.22	0.18	0.30	0.13
Theatre, concert, etc. admissions	0.04	0.10	0.18	0.22	0.29	0.53	0.20
Subscriptions and admission charges to participant sports	0.07	0.20	0.47	0.61	0.78	1.48	0.53
Football match admissions	–	0.03	0.07	0.07	0.06	0.10	0.05
Admissions to other spectator sports	–	0.02	0.03	0.02	0.04	0.08	0.03
Sports goods (excluding clothes)	0.04	0.11	0.26	0.39	0.58	1.72	0.47
Other entertainment	0.10	0.21	0.22	0.37	0.46	0.64	0.30
Total weekly expenditure on above	8.03	16.09	22.10	27.11	34.50	54.17	24.08
Expenditure on above items as a percentage of total household expenditure	11.8	13.5	15.1	15.5	16.8	18.5	15.8

[a] Eaten on the premises, excluding state school meals and workplace meals.
Source: Family Expenditure Survey, Central Statistical Office

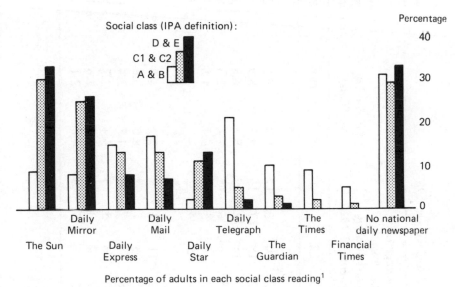

Figure 2 Reading of national daily newspapers in Great Britain: by social class, 1984. (*Source: Social Trends* 16, © Crown copyright, 1986)

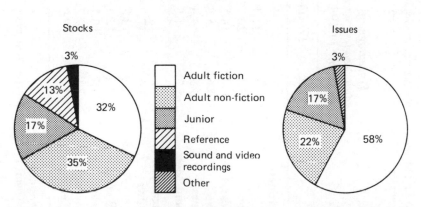

Figure 3 Public libraries in the United Kingdom: percentage of stocks and issues by major type, 1986–1987. The 'other' category for issues includes computer software, sound and video recordings, microforms, manuscripts and printed maps. (*Source: Social Trends* 19, © Crown copyright, 1989)

Table 4 Reading of selected magazines in Great Britain: by sex and social class, 1987

	Percentage of adults reading each magazine in 1987		Percentage of adults in each social class reading each magazine in 1987						Readership (millions)		Readers per copy (numbers)
	Males	Females	A	B	C1	C2	D	E	1971	1987	1987
General magazines											
TV Times	19.5	21.4	21	22	22	20	20	17	9.9	9.2	3.0
Radio Times	19.2	20.7	26	26	23	18	17	16	9.5	8.9	2.9
Reader's Digest	16.0	14.5	20	20	18	15	12	9	9.2	6.8	4.3
Smash Hits	4.6	5.8	5	5	5	6	6	3	–	2.3	4.8
Weekly News	3.5	4.4	–	2	3	4	5	5	4.5	1.8	2.4
Exchange and Mart	5.7	1.9	3	3	4	5	4	2	–	1.7	7.7
Women's magazines[a]											
Woman's Own	3.4	17.7	8	10	12	11	11	9	7.2	4.8	3.8
Woman	1.9	13.7	6	7	9	8	7	7	8.0	3.6	3.1
Woman's Weekly	2.1	12.9	7	7	8	8	7	8	4.7	3.4	2.6
Family Circle	1.7	10.1	8	9	7	6	5	3	4.4	2.7	3.9
Good Housekeeping	2.0	9.2	15	12	7	4	3	2	2.7	2.6	6.4
Woman's Realm	1.2	7.9	4	4	5	5	5	5	4.6	2.1	3.0

[a] Includes male readers

Source: Social Trends 19, © Crown copyright 1989

Second selection: US consumer comparisons

Table 5 Utilization of selected media: 1950–1987

Item	Unit	1950	1960	1970	1975	1980	1982	1983	1984	1985	1986	1987
Households with:												
Telephone service	Per cent	(NA)	78.5	87.0	(NA)	93.0	(NA)	(NA)	91.8	91.8	92.2	92.5
Radio sets	Per cent	92.6	96.3	98.6	98.6	99.0	99.0	99.0	99.0	99.0	99.0	99.0
Average no. of sets	Number	2.1	3.7	5.1	5.6	5.5	5.5	5.5	5.5	5.5	5.4	5.4
Television sets	Millions	3.9	45.8	58.5	68.5	76.3	81.5	83.3	83.8	84.9	85.9	87.4
Television sets	Per cent	9.0	87.0	95.0	97.0	98.0	98.0	98.0	98.0	98.0	98.0	98.0
Colour set h/holds	Millions	—	0.3	20.9	46.9	63.4	71.4	73.9	75.8	77.7	80.1	82.7
Av. viewing p/day	Hours	4.6	5.1	5.9	6.1	6.6	6.8	7.0	7.1	7.1	(NA)	7.2
Av. no. of sets	Number	1.01	1.13	1.39	1.54	1.68	1.75	1.79	1.78	1.83	1.83	1.86
Cable TV	Per cent	(NA)	(NA)	(NA)	(NA)	19.8	29.0	37.2	41.2	44.6	46.8	48.7
VCRs	Per cent	(NA)	(NA)	(NA)	(NA)	1.1	3.1	5.5	10.6	20.8	36.0	48.7
Commercial radio stations												
AM	Number	2232	3539	4323	4463	4589	4668	4733	4754	4718	4863	(NA)
FM	Number	676	815	2196	2767	3282	3380	3527	3716	3875	3944	(NA)
TV stations: total	Number	98	559	862	953	1011	1065	1106	1138	1182	1235	1290
Commercial	Number	(NA)	515	677	706	734	777	813	841	883	919	968
Cable television:												
Systems	Number	70	640	2490	3506	4225	4825	5600	6200	6844	7600	7900
Subscribers served	Millions	0.01	.65	4.5	9.8	15.5	21.0	25.0	30.0	31.3	37.5	39.7
Daily newspaper circulation:												
Number	Millions	53.8	58.9	62.1	60.7	62.2	62.5	62.6	63.1	62.8	62.7	(NA)
Per capita	Number	0.354	0.327	0.305	0.282	0.275	0.269	0.267	0.267	0.263	0.263	(NA)

Source: Statistical Abstract of the United States, 1988, US Department of Commerce, Bureau of the Census, Washington, 1988, p. 523. Referred to as *Abstract* in tables 6–9 below.

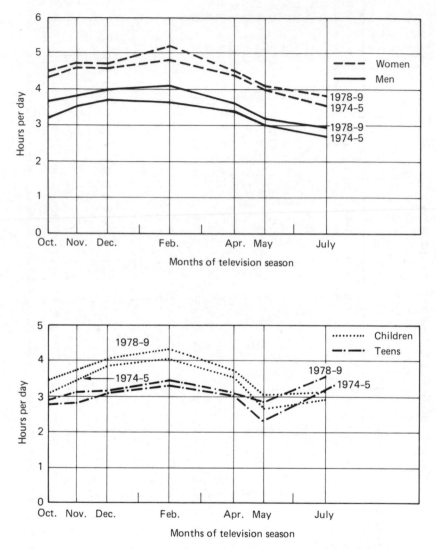

Figure 4 Average hours per day spent viewing television by selected population groups in the US: 1974–1975 and 1978–1979. (*Source: Social Indicators III: Selected Data on Social Conditions and Trends in the US*, US Department of Commerce, Bureau of the Census, 1980)

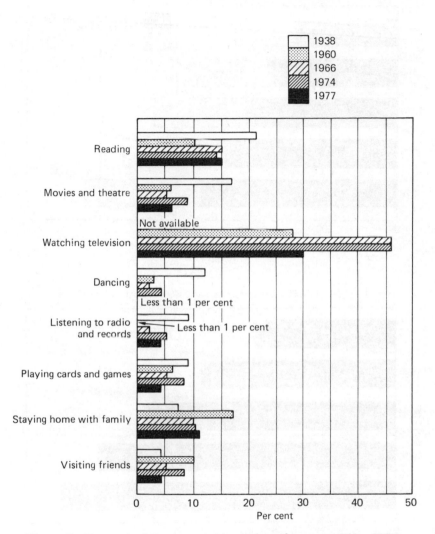

Figure 5 Favourite leisure activities, selected years: 1938–1977. (*Source: Social Indicators III: Selected Data on Social Conditions and Trends in the US*, US Department of Commerce, Bureau of the Census, 1980)

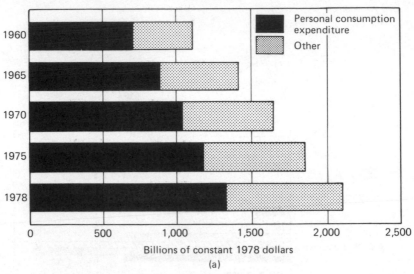

TOTAL GNP

Billions of constant 1978 dollars

(a)

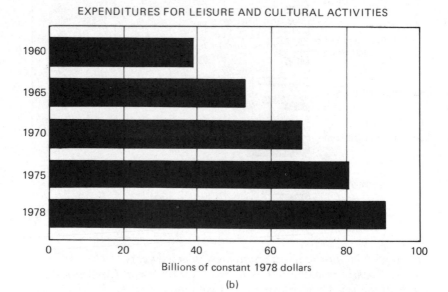

EXPENDITURES FOR LEISURE AND CULTURAL ACTIVITIES

Billions of constant 1978 dollars

(b)

Figure 6 Gross National Product (a) and Personal consumption expenditures for leisure and cultural activities (b) selected years 1960– 1978. (*Source: Social Indicators III: Selected Data on Social Conditions and Trends in the US*, US Department of Commerce, Bureau of the Census, 1980)

As remarked in chapter 6, the proportions in figure 6(a) and growth in Figure 6(b) are constant in relation to a growing economy (i.e. to the fact that more money is in circulation).

Third selection: the forces of production

Table 6 US Public television stations, 1968–1984

Item	1968	1970	1972	1974	1976	1978	1980	1982	1984
Stations broadcasting	153	190	220	238	253	272	281	291	303
Total weekly broadcast hours	8534	12217	15587	18321	22096	26064	27643	30337	32293
General programmes	4671	7697	7904	10868	14329	17929	19508	21418	23154
% of total hours	54.7	63.0	50.7	59.3	64.8	68.8	69.6	70.6	71.7
Instructional programmes[a]	3863	4520	7683	7453	7766	8135	8135	8919	9139
Average weekly broadcast hours									
per station	56.1	65.3	70.9	80.7	90.9	95.8	99.8	104.3	106.6
General programming	30.7	41.1	36.0	47.9	59.0	65.9	69.4	73.6	76.4
Instructional programming	25.4	24.2	34.9	32.8	31.9	29.9	30.4	30.7	30.2

[a] 'Instructional programmes' are for use in the classroom.
Source: Abstract, p. 526.

Table 7 US Public broadcasting systems – income by source: 1975–1985 (in $m, except as indicated)

Number of stations and income source	1975	1979	1980	1981	1982	1983	1984	1985[a]	% distribution 1975	1980	1985[a]
Number of CPB-qualified public stations	169	210	217	238	255	266	275	288	(x)	(x)	(x)
Public television stations	260	281	290	293	299	300	304	316	(x)	(x)	(x)
Federal government	92.3	163.2	192.5	193.7	197.6	163.7	167.0	179.6	25.3	27.3	16.3
State and local government[b]	156.6	245.5	271.6	277.5	301.0	318.3	334.5	363.0	42.9	38.5	33.0
Subscribers and auction/marathon	42.3	86.1	102.3	130.8	162.5	196.4	215.2	246.7	11.6	14.5	22.4
Business and industry	25.1	57.9	72.4	86.8	100.5	119.8	144.7	170.8	6.9	10.3	15.5
Foundation	28.7	20.4	23.5	19.3	22.1	24.9	27.8	43.7	7.9	3.3	4.0
Other	19.8	30.4	42.6	60.8	61.5	76.0	85.0	97.5	5.4	6.0	8.8
Total income	364.8	603.5	704.9	768.9	845.2	899.2	974.2	1101.3	100.0	100.0	100.0

[a] Preliminary figures.
[b] Includes income received from State colleges and universities and, beginning 1979, from other tax supported colleges and universities.
Source: Abstract, p. 526.

Table 8 Number and circulation of US daily and Sunday newspapers, 1960–1986

Type	1960	1965	1970	1975	1978	1979	1980	1981	1982	1983	1984	1985	1986
Number of newspapers:													
Daily: total[a]	1763	1751	1748	1756	1756	1763	1745	1730	1711	1701	1688	1676	1657
Morning	312	320	334	339	355	382	387	408	434	446	458	482	499
Evening	1459	1444	1429	1436	1419	1405	1388	1352	1310	1284	1257	1220	1188
Sunday	563	562	586	639	696	720	736	755	768	772	783	798	802
Circulation (millions):													
Daily: total[a]	58.9	60.4	62.1	60.7	62.0	62.2	62.2	61.4	62.5	62.6	63.1	62.8	62.5
Morning	24.0	24.1	25.9	25.5	27.7	28.6	29.4	30.6	33.2	33.8	35.4	36.4	37.4
Evening	34.9	36.3	36.2	35.2	34.3	33.6	32.8	30.9	29.3	28.8	27.7	26.4	25.1
Sunday	47.7	48.6	49.2	51.1	54.0	54.4	54.7	55.2	56.3	56.7	57.5	58.8	58.9

[a] All-day newspapers are counted in both morning and evening columns but only once in total. Circulation is divided equally between morning and evening.
Source: Abstract, p. 528.

Table 9 US Television – expenditures for network advertising, 1980–1986

Type of product	1980	1984	1985	1986	Type of product	1980	1984	1985	1986
Expenditures	5147	8557	8313	8600	Horticulture	15	29	30	29
Apparel, footwear and accessories	131	237	161	181	Household equipment, supplies and finishings	225	266	275	335
Automotive	529	808	848	927	Insurance	74	109	99	131
Beer and wine	242	448	428	535	Financial planning services	20	66	60	79
Building material, equipment fixtures	59	105	97	88	Jewellery and cameras	119	140	129	139
Computers, office equipment and stationery	57	374	249	222	Laundry soaps, cleansers and polishes	306	367	397	398
Confectionery, soft drinks	281	393	388	359	Movies	103	167	138	143
Consumer services	178	369	303	379	Pet products	144	175	175	157
Department and discount stores	94	215	161	139	Proprietary medicines	430	670	700	761
Food and food products	844	1365	1502	1513	Publicity and media	34	58	50	49
Freight and industrial development	7	53	40	27	Restaurants and drive-ins	132	352	416	439
Gas, lubricants etc.	71	58	49	45	Tobacco products	8	10	6	1
Home electronics equipment	50	79	36	40	Toiletries	765	978	955	874
					Toys and sports goods	93	165	152	138
					Travel, hotels and resorts	72	108	102	113
					All other	64	393	367	359

Source: Abstract, p. 531.

Table 10 Videocassette recorder penetration in selected regions, 1983

	No. of TV sets in use (n)	No. of VCRs imported (n)	VCRs as percentage of TV sets (%)
Western Europe	119,222,000	16,844,000	14.1
United States and Canada	189,280,000	14,426,000	7.6
Middle East	2,470,000	1,938,000	78.5
Australia and New Zealand	6,422,000	1,561,000	24.3

Source: Benjamin Companie, 'Media institutions, technology and policy', in *Mass Communication Review Yearbook*, ed. Michael Gurevitch and Mark Levy (Sage Publications, 1987), p. 563.

Table 11 Proportion of British press revenue derived from advertising in 1979

Category	(%)
National dailies	44
National Sundays	44
Regional daily and Sunday papers	66
Local weeklies	85
Total newspapers	59
Trade, technical and professional journals	64
Other periodicals	47
Total periodicals	54

Source: James Curran, 'The impact of advertising on the British mass media', in *Media, Culture and Society: a Critical Reader*, ed. Richard Collins et al. (Sage Publications, 1986) p. 312. See chapter 6 for further use of this indispensable collection.

Table 12 Costs as a proportion of advertising revenue in the British press

Category	1960 (%)	1973 (%)	1975 (%)
National popular daily	60	85	100
National quality daily	40	55	65
National popular Sunday	65–70	95	115
National quality Sunday	40–45	60	70

Source: James Curran, 'The impact of advertising on the British mass media', in *Media, Culture and Society: a Critical Reader*, ed. Richard Collins et al. (Sage Publications, 1986) p. 316.

This short medley concludes with a fragment of the content-analysis of programmes, where empiricism and criticism come together. It reports on the violence-content of some US children's television in 1960, when everybody was just as worried about the question as they are now. The interested reader could compile her own list from this month's telly, if she can face a hundred hours of it.

... the authors monitored and analysed a week of television in late October 1960, from 4 p.m. to 9 p.m., Monday through Friday. Figure 10.4 summarises their findings. It can be seen that commercial television brought to children fast-moving, exciting fantasy, with broad humour and a considerable amount of romantic interest. The authors considered the content to be 'extremely violent'. Shootings and sluggings were frequent; in fact, more than half the programme hours consisted of programmes in which violence played an important part. The authors, it should be pointed out, did not take all of the violence seriously.

For example, the cartoons and slapstick films they deemed were intended to be funny, rather than exciting, were disregarded in the analysis. Nevertheless, in the hundred hours analysed there appeared:

12 murders
16 major gunfights
21 persons shot (apparently not fatally)
21 other violent incidents with guns (ranging from shooting at but missing persons, to shooting up a town)
37 hand-to-hand fights (15 fist fights, 15 incidents in which one person slugged another, an attempted murder with a pitchfork, 2 stranglings, a fight in the water, a case in which a woman was gagged and tied to a bed, etc.)
1 stabbing in the back with a butcher knife
4 attempted suicides, three successful
4 people falling or pushed over cliffs
2 cars running over cliffs
2 attempts made in automobiles to run over persons on the sidewalk
A psychotic loose and raving in a flying airliner
2 mob scenes, in one of which the mob hangs the wrong man
A horse trampling a man under its hooves
A great deal of miscellaneous violence, including a plane fight, a hired killer stalking his prey, two robberies, a pickpocket at work, a woman killed by falling from a train, a tidal wave, an earthquake, and a guillotining.[11]

These foregoing figures are little more than gestures towards the details called empirics in media research. In several cases they bear directly on what is said hereafter, especially in chapters 6 and 7, but their principal message is to suggest how their implications may be checked, what the discrepancies are between the overall pattern of numbers and the actual conduct of life as it is lived. When statistics are reliable, in a well-known bromide, they only 'give us permission to proceed'.

Notes

1 See, for a fair summary and a rough treatment of relativism, Bernard Williams, *Morality: an Introduction to Ethics*, rev. edn. (Cambridge University Press, 1976).

2 Isaiah Berlin, *Vico and Herder: Two Studies in the History of Ideas* (Hogarth Press, 1975).

3 John Searle, *Speech-Acts: an Essay in The Philosophy of Language* (Cambridge University Press, 1969), also in Chapter 4, n. 5. See the useful exposition of the idea in Michael Stubbs, *Discourse Analysis* (Routledge, 1983). See also J. L. Austin, 'Performative Utterances', *Philosophical Papers*, (Clarendon Press, 1961).

4 Paul Lazarsfeld, B. Berelson and H. Gander, *The People's Choice* (Columbia University Press, 1948). See also Elihu Katz and Paul Lazarsfeld, *Personal Influence: the Part played by People in the Flow of Mass Communications* (Free Press of Glencoe, 1955).

5 Isaiah Berlin, *The Hedgehog and the Fox* (Weidenfeld & Nicolson, 1953).

6 Their gradual reconciliation is well described by the editors themselves, James Curran, Michael Gurevitch and Janet Woollacott, in their introductory essay, 'The study of the media' to their *Culture, Society and the Media* (Methuen, 1982).

7 In addition to the texts in note 4, see Joseph Klapper, *The Effects of the Mass Media* (Free Press of Glencoe, 1960). Schramm is cited below, note 11.

8 James Curran, 'Capitalism and control of the press 1800–1975', in *Mass Communication and Society*, eds James Curran et al. (Edward Arnold, 1977).

9 For strong examples of Graham Murdock's work, see his contribution to *Mass Communication and Society* (1977) (see n. 8, above); 'Capitalism, communication and class relations' (with Peter Golding); and his 'Large corporations and the control of the communications industry', in *Culture, Society and the Media*, eds Michael Gurevitch et al. (Methuen, 1982) (n. 6 above).

10 Murdock (1982), as above, n. 9, pp. 118–20.

11 The content-analysis is quoted from another famous piece of empiricism by Wilbur Schramm, Jack Lyle and Edwin Parker, *Television in
the Lives of our Children* (Stanford University Press, 1961), pp. 11–
12.

4

Theories of Ideology

The first three chapters provide the prehistory and foundations of a theory of media. As I warned in chapter 1, 'theory' is not a magic word and 'theoreticism', which is the hard determination to get everything tidied away and explained in a single system, can lead people into very rigid and ridiculous ways of thought. A theory is, among other things, simply a means of including a wide range of apparently related events and phenomena within the terms of a single set of descriptions. As we also noted, a description may turn into an explanation, but either term denotes our knowing more about what is going on. Theory permits us to describe and perhaps explain what is going on more tidily and comprehensively.

So, at first sight, a theory of media is just the same as a theory of human or animal communication. But although such a thing may be envisageable it would require putting so much all together – a theory of meaning and structure in language, a sociology of the variety of dialects (how class speech varies, for example), a model of mutual comprehension and misunderstanding, all these before one got anywhere near books and television. The likelihood is it would be impossibly top-heavy and elaborate. A theory of media here signifies a theory of *public communication*[1] and as we have made clear, this means a theory allowing us to describe within its framework a threefold structure of interlocking social practices. But putting things in this way is formidably abstract. Let us unpack it a little.

A theory has a *structure* in the sense that the descriptions which it makes possible connect with one another. Such descriptions (or, sometimes, explanations) build up into a larger, more inclusive account of what is happening. The most familiar form of such theory is a *narrative*. When we ask what is happening politically in a given society, we typically answer ourselves by telling a story in which the key concepts are the protagonist (hero) and the antagonist (villain); the general plot or action, which makes individually detailed behaviour explicable; the chronology, or beginning, middle and end of the action (to understand what is happening we need a history). These are the simplest units of that popular theoretic form, the story, and we learn them continuously from our babyhood. Taken together, these conceptual units (or ideas) come together in a narrative framework or structure. In the proposed more technical structure of our media theory, the three interlocking parts or zones are more like systems than like individual ideas or concepts. Nor is their systematic nature always obvious. It is probably better for anyone inquiring into mass media or public communications to think of these three zones as *bundles* of social orders and practices which we may classify in the following three ways.

1 *Orders and practices of signification*; which is to say all those social activities which systematically signify, symbolize, or have *meaning*. The most obvious example is language itself. Language serves as the basic type of meaning system, with its special rules of the lexicon (dictionary), syntax (grammar), and its smallest units (phonemes, morphemes). However, we shall tackle signification through the procedures of semiology in the next chapter, where semiology aims at nothing less than the study of all signs and how they mean what they do.

2 *Orders and practices of powers*; a heading which is the cue for following those many occasions in public communication when power is exerted *over* people, and when power is simply generated of its own accord *in* a person. In the first case we see power exerted over others whenever we open a newspaper or watch television: the language and images direct the audience to think and feel largely as those with the power of production prefer. It is this sense of power we refer to when we speak of 'manipulation' by the mass media. Power may also be inscribed much less visibly in social practice, as when we are subject to the most commonplace routines of everyday life, particularly as these dictate while we hardly notice it the ideas and vocabulary of our common-sense picture of the world. Manipulation in the first sense may be quickly spotted at work in the opinions and persuasions which the powerful seek to instil in us. They transpire in the generally believed narratives of the day. Power in the second sense is contained in the unnoticed limits of our language, those which define and regulate such key moral notions as 'the individual', 'a person', 'identity' or, in another context, those which fix us in our social space, like the vocabulary of the law or

the handbooks of state bureaucracy and social security. We know that power of this kind is everywhere, that indeed it *is* the social order in action, but it is often hard to catch it so. Lastly, power may be created *in* a person by the power of a communication. This is not the association usually called up by the word 'power', but it is a familiar experience. A novel, film, piece of music or a speech may be readily described as powerful and we feel empowered by them even if that feeling may express itself in many different ways (applause, tears, inspiration to be a better person, etc.).

3 *Order and practices of production*: by which I mean not only what economists mean by production – the manufacture of commodities for market – but also what is implied by the theatre, film and television usage, 'producer', where the person so described organizes his colleagues in the act of production of a play, film or TV programme. Again, more largely, production refers to all our creative activities with regard to communication: to our 're-producing' the story we watch in the cinema out of the million stills on plastic circling in the projector. It also refers to our production in our imagination of the story locked in black marks on white paper bound into a book. The practices of production include writing as well as manufacturing, the programme planners and buyers of CBS or the BBC as much as an actor, journalist or cameraman.

Signification:power:production. These are the three zones of media theory commended for our attention here. They have the merits of simplicity and inclusiveness, but another theorist could of course come up with different components for a similar structure. Nevertheless, I contend as modestly as possible that these will serve a student quite well enough to order and focus what is already a bursting and chaotic field of force, as well as an academic subject which is as yet quite unformed.

II

In each case, the *orders* are so-called because they have levels of importance in analysis; their attendant practices start, as emphasized in my first chapter, with history. The student of a medium cannot go wrong if she begins carefully with its history. Hence our history of alphabet and print; hence also, with an eye on the practices of production, our history and elementary exposition of electronic media.

History itself, however, cannot avoid being theoretic, as the brief biographies of Liberalism and Marxism in media studies brought out, and as the subsequent short history of empiricism underlined. A fact is only known to be such by means of our eradication of what is not wanted from round about it. Facts are spotted because we have the concepts as lenses through which we see what we are interested in. Liberals deploy the facts they do because they are interested in the liberty of individuals to move freely through society. Marxists pick out their facts because their preoccupations fasten upon the oppression, not of individuals but of classes, by those with the capital which gives them their power.

Both the traditions which are at the origin of media studies and its forms of cultural expression unite in their ferocious criticism of the giant structures of culture whose drive for commercial profit seems to destroy the humanness of the world they are supposed to serve. Liberals and Marxists alike see the great juggernaut of production crushing out the human potentiality which production is there to express and cherish. Liberals put the blame on industrialization, Marxists on capitalism. But their diagnoses lie close together, however far apart their concepts and their solutions.

This is the reason why media studies and its attendant theorists pounced upon the critique of ideology as the solution of their problems. As long as the discussion of culture was confined to novels then, as Q. D. Leavis demonstrated, analysis could be conducted by the individual critic at work upon the single writer. Once the discussion of culture was broadened to take in the multiple authorships of films, newspapers, television programmes, then criticism had to turn to the study of structures of production and their collectivities, however sensible it might still be to attribute malignancy to these institutions. Lord Beaverbrook didn't actually write each daily issue of the *Express*; Alexander Korda assembled vast production teams and casts of thousands in Egypt to make *The Four Feathers*: a critic can hardly treat it as though Korda were its only parent.

Accordingly, media theory began, some time around the 1950s, to work with the rather loose concept, 'ideology'. Once more, to understand its usefulness and limitations we need to look briefly at its history and the way the word took on the layers of its meanings. It started out with the movement in Germany at the end of the eighteenth century known as 'the Enlightenment' when ideology simply entitled the study of systems of ideas (the suffix '-ology' meaning 'study of'). But Karl Marx and his great collaborator Friedrich Engels in notebooks written together in 1846–7, but published rather later, gave the word a characteristic twist. In a famous formulation, Marx and Engels wrote, 'In any epoch the ruling ideas are those of the ruling class, i.e. the class which is the ruling material force is at the same time its ruling intellectual force'[2] (p. 64). They went on to a rehearsal of their theory of class struggle as being necessarily produced by the contradictions in capitalism between capital and labour, and noted that the ruling class of capitalist systems, the bourgeoisie, naturally created a subordinate fraction of a class which would work out and circulate its preferred ideas. This is the birth of ideology as a theory of partisan interests: that is, the view that the ruling class favours best those ideas which preserve its own property and power by persuading everybody else that things are just fine as they are, and that the ideas, values and frame of mind which suit them so well, suit everybody else at the same time.

This is not necessarily a hypocritical state of affairs, and indeed Marx was hardly interested in whether bourgeois states of mind and feeling were pure or not. In a contemptuous aside he observed, 'The bourgeois always supposes that the conditions which made for his own emancipation will suffice for the freedom of the whole world.' Certainly, we are familiar with the millionaire property owner (or prime minister, or president) who noisily asks why the unemployed don't work their butts off like he did, there being nothing else to stop them making their fortune as well.

The ideology which Marx saw at the heart of capitalism was the form of political and moral valuation summarized earlier as liberalism. The crucial place it gave to the freedom of individual action, and the fulfilment and self-awareness of the personal identity at the heart of the individual, fitted perfectly with the economic facts. Capitalism demanded the prompt circulation of privately owned capital and the unfettered play of market forces in competition for profits, the highest of which would go to the most efficient and successful product.

The trouble in 1847 (which still stands in the rather different version of capitalism now running the world) was that such a system, as Marx and Engels clinchingly demonstrated, creates terrible waste and poverty, and in order to have winners on this scale, makes for millions of losers at the same time. In those days, they were the insurgent urban proletariat in the insurrections of 1848; today, the starving millions and the guerrillas of Africa and Latin

America. Liberal ideology, however, is dreamed up to hide those consequences, or to show that in spite of them, all will be well. It is an ideological theory intended to gain triumphant victory for partisan interests. We see it at work in every classroom of the Western world where schoolteachers urge the values of creative individualism upon children much too poor to do anything except to deride them. For Marx and Engels, the whole process is a fix, and we shall therefore refer to this as the fix theory of ideology. According to the fix theory, 'ideology' can only smell very fishy. It is, as Clifford Geertz puts it,[3] both 'mask and weapon' (p. 201).

In another, more kind-hearted version of the theory of ideology, its system of beliefs and values are seen as a way of taking the strain of everyday life. Fix theory is, so to say, strong on sociology. It grounds its explanations very solidly indeed in the facts of social class advantage and the will-to-power inscribed in every political circumstance. The trouble is that it is so crude. Once you have got hold of the idea that *any* attempt to justify advantage or power may be ideological, then it is easy for *all* intellectual or educational argument to be accused of being a fix. This doesn't mean that much of the message of the mass media is not ideological; it plainly is, as we shall see when we come to consider some deservedly celebrated criticisms of news broadcasting as inherently ideological. But it is far too simple-minded to describe everything baldly as 'ideological' in the sense of being a fix.

For a start and in order to do so, the ideology-critic has to treat all men and women as 'bloody fools'.[4] Marx and Engels dealt blithely with this problem by simply designating all those who credulously believed an ideology which ran bluntly against their own best interests as being in a state of 'false consciousness' which prevented them seeing what was plain to the intellectual vanguard. But we may well object that such a psychology is too brutal, and that people may well accept beliefs and values which don't really speak to their deepest preoccupations (let alone their self-interest) but they either can't see what to do about it, or hope that their children may do all right even if they don't, or simply and rationally think that the alternative would probably be worse.

This is the so-called 'strain' theory of ideology, which has the great merit of acknowledging that the world is a painful, contradictory and muddled place, and that people in having, as people, to believe *something*, have to make do as best they can with the bits and pieces of ideology which they find around the place. These bits and pieces make up a pattern of sorts, and as Geertz says, 'in the

modern world at least most men live lives of patterned desperation'
(p. 204).

Ideology-critique veers between fix and strain theory according to
whichever best suits the subject-matter in hand. The trouble with fix
theory is its cast-iron self-righteousnes; it always knows better than
we do what's going on. The trouble with strain theory is that it turns
profound beliefs into a mixture of pain-killer and safety-valve: without them we'd go potty. This also is unattractively supercilious. It is
with our beliefs and ideologies that we brace ourselves to change the
world. We battle to make them *rational*, not just intoxicating.

A subtler, more intellectually responsive way with both versions
of the theory would be, according to Geertz, to treat ideological
arguments and symbolic actions as *texts* or, in another key phrase,
speech-acts[5]. If we do so, we then have at our disposal the much
more complex and delicate array of literary-critical (or practical–
critical) instruments which we met in chapter 2. If we treat ideologies as texts, we can analyse the variety of their rhetoric and the
expectations of their audiences, whether of the *Washington Post* or
the *Daily Mirror*, the President's press spokesman or any old television ad. If we treat ideologies as utterances which are in turn *spoken
actions,* then, as in any ordinary conversation, in order to understand them we have to give them a context, try to recover the
speaker's intentions in speaking so, and ask what he or she is *doing*
in talking this way.

These admonitions hold for all ideological analysis. But first we
should glance at the way in which such analysis became important
to media theorists, and to an aspect of ideology's grip on the
structures of everyday life which is rather less simple-minded than
the versions of ideology so far considered.

III

Ideologizing, like any other process of thought, is an imaginative
business. We devise symbolic fictions in our heads and try to match
them to the world.[6] But, as the fix theorists insist, this is an unequal
process if other people with more power are tyring to persuade you
to match *their* symbolic fiction or model against the world rather
than yours. And as we saw, the mournful analysis of the new media
theorists in Britain and in Germany in the early 1930s was that
commercial or capitalist fictions were winning this little struggle
hands down.

When mass media theory really began to get going as a wide-spread intellectual activity this easy victory became the most problematic question in the whole inquiry. Casting backwards over the field and thereby finding the Frankfurt Institute, the thinkers who were most convinced of the inherently political nature of their researches rediscovered during the 1960s the work of Antonio Gramsci, the Italian Communist of the early 1920s.[7] Gramsci was an early leader of the party and a representative of the Fiat car-worker unions in Turin. But he was dedicated to the importance of strictly intellectual struggle in the class war, and as such edited and wrote most of the party newspaper *L'Ordine Nuovo (The New Order)* until Italy's Fascist ruler Mussolini gaoled him for being a communist. Although he was released into hospital after eleven years, his health was broken and he died in 1937 in his forties.

The point of this very terse biography is that Gramsci had two theoretical workplaces: the journalist–editor–agitator's tiny office near the factory, and prison. In both, however, he addressed himself, not to the brutally visible features of the Italian state, but to what he called the 'hegemony' (in Italian, *egemonia* or the presence of power). He tried to give hegemony a special, elusive resonance in political analysis. Hegemony for Gramsci was the heavy, saturating omnipresence of the way things are. It refers to the most everyday facts of life as these are lived within the forms and structures we like to think of ourselves as having freely and independently chosen: marriage and family, home and its customs and possessions, our deepest feelings and beliefs, our leisure and ordinary expenditure, our bodily awareness and health, our friends. This is the domain of everyday consciousness, and ideology is obviously too light a word to signify its volume and extent. In identifying hegemony as the revolutionary crux, Gramsci did not always do much more than name the problem. He only had one solution to the pervasiveness and weight of a hegemony always dominated, of course, by the dominant class, but produced by absolutely everybody. His solution was gradual and painstaking education of the masses by an organized Communist intelligentsia.

This was the prominent part of Gramsci's analysis which made such an appeal to teachers trying to work out how to teach about the new media without just saying that they are all terrible. After all, Marxism had originally taught that social revolution was inevitable and the dictatorship of the proletariat historically assured. Liberal educationists, on a more modest scale, had nevertheless been confident that good teaching could, as it were, immunize their students against the worst effects of mass culture. Both on the large political platform and in the small space of classroom effectiveness, what was needed was an explanation of the power of culture in general, and the mass media in particular, to disarm criticism and prevent change. Gramsci provided it. The analysis of hegemony returns us to the deliberate blurring of the distinction between description and explanation mentioned at the beginning of chapter 1. In order to understand how hegemony invades and pervades our common sense, we have to describe as closely (and as unexpectedly) as possible the three 'orders' of communication and media listed at the start of this chapter: signification, power, production. What anthropologists call ethnography is our best method: a highly specific narrative about the form of life in front of us, but a narrative always suspicious of its own common sense.

The great usefulness of the ideas of ideology and of hegemony is that both teach us to be suspicious. Handling them, it is not easy to forget the universality of deception, conscious or otherwise, nor the extent to which people want to dominate others, and to make their arguments win over ours. But beyond face-to-face disputes, ideology and hegemony are terms which permit us to study the strictly structural weight of social institutions upon our thought and living. We all tend naturally to believe that we are free individuals, and cheerfully overlook the circumstance that we have little choice but to think along the lines organized for us, above all, by the massive information institutions – schools, universities, newspapers, television, societies and associations, churches, political parties. These are the agencies of *power*, and therefore of ideology. Any version of the truth, we should remember, is necessarily attached to its power to win a hearing.[8] Truth can't win by its purity as we'd like to think; it must have muscle.

These observations warn us that the study of ideology is necessarily deep. We have in play the twin, complementary theories of fix and strain ideology. We have also the requirement that ideology (and hegemony) should be studied as texts, and that texts of all kinds, like our speech, are *active*. And so to understand speech as action, as we do all the time, is to interpret it according to the very long-standing system of literary and linguistic criticism – what the Elizabethans understood by Rhetoric.

Rhetoric in the Elizabethan grammar school was the study of the many figures of speech, each with its own effects and purposes. It was only in much later times that 'rhetorical' took on its derogatory connotation, as meaning a lot of cheap verbal decoration on top of what someone is really saying. If, however, we try to recover the original sense — always a hard thing to do — we are then asking the student of ideology to be also a student of the multiple dimensions of a text. Our ideological texts, Geertz tells us, are ways in which we match a symbolic, imaginative structure of ideas, images and emotions to the world-out-there. These ideas and images which give form to our feelings and explain them to us resemble, metaphorically, maps we use to guide ourselves towards action in the social world. They are stories we tell ourselves about ourselves,[9] in order to work out what to be and do. Famously, the number of ways in which stories may be interpreted, the different things they can mean to different people, are manifold. They may be true or false, a help or no help at all in what we have to do. We can only penetrate these depths on a sort of tripod, sociological, psychological, and cultural, which is to say interpretative. We situate the texts under inquiry on a social ground (class, nation-state), within a psychological framework (everyday habits of feeling and modes of thought), and then try to follow the cultural figures which the stories mark out on this terrain.

IV

No one can do everything, however. The nature of the intellectual enterprise of practising media theory is given a rousing send-off in the final chapter. Here, in specifying how to study ideology which is such a key term in the media theorist's dictionary, it is enough to say that however we define a text — the front page of a newspaper, a single film, a week or a lifetime of television programmes, even an individual's biography whether lived or written down — we have to put it back in context, give it history and social meaning. We have to ask what it meant to the people who spoke, wrote or lived it, and what they *intended* it to mean; and we have to see how well it matches up to the reality-out-there with which it was to deal.

All these activities include *us* as participants as well as observers.[10] We cannot, in other words, conduct these inquiries without ourselves having a value-position of a deeply entrenched kind, and this position can, in matters to do with public media, hardly avoid being political. There is then the problem, especially given the powerful leverage of the fix (or 'interest') theory of ideology, that our analysis is simply a matter of cheering on the side we want to win. By the same token, quite a lot of media research as well as media performance is, crudely, a matter of facing that part of the audience which will clap the loudest. Probably the most available resolution of this pull between being-on-one-side and wanting-to-tell-the-truth-even-if-it-hurts is the classic one of the intellectual: that he and she conduct all inquiry in the names of liberty, equality and fraternity. This trinity was, of course, the great banner of the French Revolution, and at a time properly conscious of women's rights, we might better translate the last of its terms as solidarity, or perhaps, community. In any case, that leaves us media theorists in ideological study taking the side of the weak or the oppressed or, more broadly, the people: all those who are both subject and object to the holders of power, whose business is profitable manipulation and ideological victory. More ringingly, let us say that the critic of ideology names for what they are lies, bullying, hypocrisy, cruelty, greed.

Put like that, only liars and bullies would not enlist to the colours. The media theorist, settled in his self-righteous conviction of being on the side of virtue, can show by his criticism of ideology who is putting the fix on whom. Or, in a more sympathetic mood, he can turn to the same business and show how this bit of ideology is taking the strains of domestic life in our times.

What are central, then, are the ideas or controlling concepts which each brings to inquiry. In a famous instance, the French Marxist philosopher Louis Althusser[11] designated the great social institutions of information, culture and education, 'Ideological State Apparatuses' (ISAs). It was an attractive label and has had a long run for its money. He argues, as a Marxist may be expected to argue, for the fix theory, but on a very grand scale. All these institutions – schools, colleges, newspapers, broadcasting – are bits of apparatus for the state to use in order to manage the consent of society. For Althusser that is their function, whatever the odd individual may try to do.

As one might expect, a lot of people, especially teachers, expostulated angrily with Althusser, and his is certainly an example of the theory at its most assertive and impersonal. All the same, it is pretty obvious that a stable modern state, characterized by its giant institutions of capital, production, surveillance and weaponry, cannot afford to leave its broadcasting media (and its education) entirely to themselves, to subvert the stability of the state if they choose. The whole point of official education and informal culture is that between them they will allow the parent society to reproduce itself in a sufficiently recognizable form for the next generation. So, yes, the public media (to go no further) can be plausibly described as ISAs in much of what they do.[12]

The truth in Althusser's accusatory phrase is shown in an exemplary series of studies by the University of Glasgow Media Group,[13] which began in 1976 and is still continuing. These happily titled volumes address themselves to the main news programmes of the BBC and commercial television networks in Britain, and offer to show how wholly these programmes present news as the State itself would naturally prefer. They show in careful detail how the list of items on the nine o'clock and ten o'clock news reports accurately follows an implicit hierarchy of relative importance such as a civil servant might draw up. They show how this agenda is presented as the natural, self-explanatory and common-sensible way to see things. And they show how the imagery of presentation, whatever the personal political views of the presenter, interviewer or reporter may be, frames the situation, makes it safe and endorses the way things are as seen from the offices of those in charge. Thus, cabinet ministers are interviewed either in quiet voices in a big room or from behind an imposing battery of loudspeakers. Local political figures – councillors, say, or union spokesmen – are interviewed as they move down the street and in the wet.

In a later, notorious instance,[14] the Glasgow group analysed the reporting of the British all-out miners' strike of 1984–5 on television news. They showed convincingly how fearsome the miners' pelting of police with stones and brickbats was bound to look if the cameramen stood, as they would understandably do, behind the lines of police shields. In an experimental response to this criticism widely made by the miners themselves during the strike, a camera crew worked alongside the pickets, scattering in front of the horse-back charges made by police, with the free use of their heavy clubs on any head or back in their way. When this happened, it is no surprise how different the news looked in terms of the responsibility for violence, the extent of beating, the simple fairness of the conflict.

A clinching instance of what then can only be called gross bias by news institutions whose legal charter requires 'balance' and impartiality as part of their duties to state and civil society is given by a news transcript in which the same events are under discussion. In a magisterial analysis, building (as he says) on the procedures of the Glasgow group, Len Masterman quotes this following exchange between the TV interviewer and a senior union official from South Yorkshire:

Nick Ross: Mr. Taylor, how on earth do you explain what happened at Orgreave today?

Jack Taylor: Well, I think you should be asking that question to the police, not just asking it to me. They were in a position today where we saw scenes that we … well, I thought we'd never see them in Britain. We had people on horses, policemen, riding into crowds of miners with batons swinging. We had policemen with dogs, we had policemen by the thousand there. It's O.K. you saying to me how can I explain it. I'll tell you what, everyone seems to assume that it was equal. What we had was miners in tee shirts and jeans and running pumps. And we had police in shin-guards with riot shields, with long staves, attacking working people.

Nick Ross: Mr. Taylor, can I get this right for people who saw the news footage earlier? Your interpretation of what happened is that 5,000 miners, striking miners, were peacefully picketing. The police then stormed the picketing miners.

Jack Taylor: Today there we had a situation where policemen were really *beating* miners. Now if they believe they can beat us into submission as well as starve us into submission, they don't understand us.

Nick Ross: Well, some people, Mr. Taylor, will certainly agree with what you say. I suspect that the vast majority will be *astonished* at hearing your account, particularly since there are so many reports from independent witnesses. I've got one here, for example, from a garage owner nearby who says that the pickets smashed his doors, took three of his cars and set them alight – so many independent people are saying that it was pickets who were running amok, not the police.

Jack Taylor: I'll tell you what, I was there. I was there, and I can tell you what I saw. I saw policemen … in fact I were chased along a road three hundred yards myself and the problem is if you were the back one you got a beating. I were pulled by the hair to the ground, and if you want witnesses I can bring you witnesses to say that was right. Now if you are telling me that this is the sort of country that you and me are looking forward to for the rest of us lives, I'll tell you what we want to have a re-look.

Nick Ross: … In our Westminster studio is Eldon Griffiths, Tory MP, who is Parliamentary Spokesman for the Police Federation. You heard that Mr. Griffiths – what is your assessment of what happened today?

Eldon Griffiths: I think you used the right word and you said it was

> astonishing that Mr. Taylor should paint a picture
> of the police attacking the pickets ...
>   (*Sixty Minutes*, 18.6.1984)

The ideological framing of these incidents makes it clear where the
state apparatus is standing, all right.

In another admirable study of British television news, Philip
Schlesinger[15] speaks of its social function as being the construction
of reality for all those of us who, like Nick Ross and Eldon Griffiths
in the quoted extract, weren't there. It is a phrase – the construction
of reality – which draws attention to its own contradiction; what is
real to our eyes is what somebody else constructs, makes up. Of
course it lends itself usefully to the fix theorists of ideology, whose
theory is most at hme with the increasingly visible pressures of the
State to get the official news broadcasts told the way it wants them
told.

It is at such moments that conventional ideology-critique has most
to reveal. Even setting aside, however, many people's instinctive
incredulity at what they are told by the news (however much they
would miss it if it were taken off), news itself is only a very small
proportion of newspapers, and even less of broadcasting. And in
spite of novel meaning 'new', novels are not news in any conventional sense. When we turn, therefore, to all these other, innumerable narratives of a society, standard ideology-critique is too simple-
minded to be much help, and the required connection with the study
of literary texts, the practical criticism of stories, needs to be set out
more firmly.

V

I shall do so by starting from my last, but for my purposes most
valuable primer on 'how to study ideology'. Krishan Kumar's remarkable essay[16] 'Holding the middle ground' purports, innocently
enough, to explain the form, content and personnel of BBC news
and political magazine programmes. I shall want to extend its grasp
a very long way further.

Kumar starts from the central place of the BBC in British cultural
life noting – as we see in chapter 6 – how unlike all other broadcasting corporations it is in this. He shows how its historical formation
and its good luck enabled it to occupy, first and comprehensively,
the huge new tracts of leisure time which have opened up and

expanded since it got its charter in 1926. Now that charter enjoined
upon the BBC duties as to its balanced coverage of national events
and its strict impartiality as between social groups in conflict, even
where one of any such pair of opponents might be the government.
An early test of this impartiality was Britain's first General Strike in
1926, and the Director General steered round the problems at that
time by doing as he was told while not allowing the BBC to become
simply the Prime Minister's microphone.

Gradually, with assorted bumps on the way, the BBC assumed its
unique authority. The Second World War did much for this, and
further confirmed as significant, reassuring, known and even loved
figures, its globally celebrated newsreaders: Alvar Lidell, Stuart
Hibberd, Howard Marshall, John Snagge, and others. When these
men announced themselves as reading the news to people in Britain
crouched in air-raid shelters and to partisans in Nazi-occupied
Europe who could get to a radio, they were not only believed, they
were trusted.

Kumar follows the institutional history which put such men, and,
gradually their women colleagues, in such a venerable public position. He then notes that as the social climate in Britain changed
post-war, as regional, class and colour differences became more
strained and visible, the nationally honoured newsreader transmuted
gradually into the institutionally monumental programme presenter.
The changing history of Britain, the breaking up of a settled class
authority, the struggle of regions against London – Scotland, the
North, above all, the six counties of Northern Ireland – meant that
the settled social agreement of wartime was gone. Yet, as Kumar
explains, the BBC was enjoined by statute and duty to look for 'the
middle ground' where it is believed that citizens of goodwill can
always find common cause, can settle quarrels, and can understand
and reconcile the 'extremists' who by definition were off that middle
ground, away on the edge of things. In so far as the BBC was, in the
genuinely Roman sense, a forum for national debate it was driven to
the dangerous issues precisely in order to see how to balance the
account. Dedicated from its foundation to liberalism and the value
of individual freedoms, the BBC was bound to define balance as its
central value, and to believe that reasonable action, and even truth
itself, lay always *between* two points of view, in the middle, away
from extremes, moderately and sensibly available to someone who
weighed up the opposing cases.

The emblem of the politics of balance became the presenter. The
great corporation developed a special breed of men and women

amongst whom by 1990 the best-known names in the tradition include Robin Day, Richard Dimbleby and his no less famous sons, David and Jonathan, Richard Baker, Brian Redhead, John Timpson, John Humphries, Sue Lawley, Anna Ford and many others. These names indicate what Kumar calls the 'style of presentation, compounded equally of aggressiveness, scepticism, irony, and detachment in which we can most easily observe the role played by the professional broadcaster in the BBC's strategy of survival' (p. 248).

Such presenters speak for *us* against the interest groups they interview or hear from. They talk to Cabinet ministers, protesters, strikers, and even on past occasions, terrorists, and turn to tell us what these people are saying, having stood up for what they and, on the whole, we believe to be the middle ground we are always looking for. In Kumar's sketch, still in my view vividly accurate nearly twenty years after it was written, we see a model of broadcasting responsibility towards its own best constituency.

For, as I said, to see the importance of the presenter in this way is to enlarge the model to take in broadcasting itself. As the presenter, so too the programme editor, the channel head. The presenter holds his position a little way out in front of us but representing us. He organizes and makes coherent the many voices and points of view and items of news in his programme. He becomes present to us as a moral style, recognizably that of his broadcasting channel (commercial, local or pop channels work in just the same way – disc jockeys are to pop shows exactly what the solid political figures are to the news magazines). So, too, the pattern of programmes itself balances the many voices which speak through them, balances also what is guessed at as the range of tastes and preferences, possible uses and gratifications of us, the audience and the people. Thus, a typical evening's viewing will include the children's programmes, the news, the soap opera, the quiz show, the chat show, the situation comedy, the news again, the documentary, the tough thriller (it's getting late), the news magazine, the fringe variety show (later still) and the bought-in American cop serial (off-the-peg, after midnight stuff). Such a front page represents another kind of balancing act, between the innumerable minorities who make up the mass audience.

The balancing continues within categories of programme. The comedies make comic the situation of as many different social groups as they can get in: say, unemployed itinerant workers (*Auf Wiedersehen, Pet*), senior citizens still with life in the old dog (*Last of the Summer Wine*), single career women with bitter-sweet but fundamentally comic love-affairs (*Thirty Something, The Mistress*), deadbeat or dedicated students (*The Young Ones, Fame*), or complete cross-sections of a social world (*East Enders, Coronation Street, Crossroads*). Like the model or cognitive net of the novel as I described it earlier, this range of programmes is a net or membrane stretched round society, holding it together, trying always to get everyone in. As new groups rise to public consciousness and are in danger of exclusion, then corresponding television programmes emerge to bind them into the texture of narratives which holds the middle ground and keeps it as widely available as possible.

We can use this expanded version of Kumar's model to understand the relative balance of any broadcast text: the news pages of the *Guardian* or the *New York Times*, the list of new books put out by a publishing house, the range of displayed magazines in the newsagents. In each case, an editor or proprietor has chosen as balanced a texture of narratives as he or she believes will match the constituency for which the company in question plans its production.

Seeing things this way takes, of course, a bit of practice (it is apparent, for example, in examination papers). But it brings together the theory of ideology and the disciplined practice of literary criticism in a unity which should make it possible to hold together the vast flow of stories from mass communications in a single current. It is the first stage of our own specific and simple method.

Notes

1 Raymond Williams points out that 'public communication' is entirely preferable to 'mass media' as a term with which to describe our subject matter (in his *Communications*, rev. edn. Penguin, 1979). It reminds us that these matters are ours, the public's, and escapes the inaccurate superciliousness of 'mass'. The trouble is that the term 'mass media' is very thoroughly dug into everyday usage.

2 Karl Marx and Friedrich Engels, *The German Ideology* (1846–7), ed C. J. Arthur (Lawrence and Wishart, 1970).

3 Clifford Geertz, 'Ideology as a cultural system', in his *The Interpretation of Cultures* (Basic Books, 1973; Hutchinson, 1975).

4 A criticism made in so many words by E. P. Thompson in his attack upon the ideology-critique of Louis Althusser, title-essay in Thompson's *The Poverty of Theory* (Merlin Press, 1978).

5 See, in this connection, Paul Ricoeur's difficult essay 'Social action considered as a text' in his *Hermeneutics and the Human Sciences*

(Cambridge University Press, 1971), and John Searle's also difficult short book, *Speech-Acts: an Essay in the Philosophy of Language* (Cambridge University Press, 1969).

6   Richard Gregory proposes a model of all psychological processes on these lines in his brief essay, 'Sketch of a psychology of fiction', reprinted in *The Cool Web: Patterns of Children's Reading*, eds. M. Meek, A. Warton and G. Barton (Bodley Head, 1976).

7   Antonio Gramsci, *Selections from the Prison Notebooks*, tr. and ed. Q. Hoare and G. Nowell-Smith (Lawrence and Wishart, 1971).

8   Such a way of putting it anticipates the work of Michel Foucault, whom we shall meet properly in the next chapter.

9   Geertz, (1973), p. 448 (see n. 3 above).

10   'Participant-observation' is a term coined by anthropologists to describe their position half-in and half-out of the (generally alien) peoples and societies they study. For a very good short essay on the subject, see David Hargreaves, *Social Relations in the Secondary School* (Routledge & Kegan Paul, 1967).

11   See Louis Althusser, 'Ideology and ideological state apparatuses' in his *Lenin and Philosophy* (New Left Books, 1971).

12   Read the excellent essay from which I summarize this argument by Stuart Hall, 'The rediscovery of "ideology": return of the repressed in media studies', in *Culture, Society and the Media*, eds. Michael Gurevitch, James Curran et al. (Methuen, 1982).

13   Glasgow University Media Group, *Bad News* (1976), *More Bad News* (1980), *Really Bad News* (1982), all published by Routledge & Kegan Paul. Their best-known spokesman is Greg Philo.

14   Also very well treated by Len Masterman, in his seminal book *Teaching About the Media* (Comedia, 1985). The quotation below comes from pp. 119–20.

15   Philip Schlesinger, *Putting 'Reality' Together: The BBC and its News*, rev. edn. (Sage Books, 1988).

16   Krishan Kumar, 'Holding the middle ground', *Sociology*, 9 (1975), reprinted in *Mass Communication and Society*, ed. James Curran, Michael Gurevitch et al. (Edward Arnold and the Open University Press, 1977).

5

From Semiotics to Discourse

I

We have the beginnings of a method in the study of ideology. But in
the last chapter I spoke blithely about what this or that *meant*, as
though meaning itself were not a decidedly tricky quantity. In our
everyday, common-sensible dealings with the world, we have to
proceed with business-as-usual as though all we said were plain as
day. We have to live within the belief that the language we use has a
straightforward relation to the world, and that when I use the word
'table' to refer to the thing 'table' – this assembly of bits of wood in
front of me – then the relation between the two tables is perfectly
clear. What linguists call the 'signifier' is just that: the black marks
on white paper 't-a-b-l-e'. It signifies in speech and writing the
'signified', the thing itself on which we put down our book and cup
of coffee. Of course, the 'signified' – the thing itself – is already
conceptualized in virtue of being a table with a table's uses and
purposes. 'Signifier', therefore, refers to a *humanly identifiable* object. 'Signifier' plus 'signified' together constitute the '*sign*' (often
represented as 's/S').

The world, however, is not an amenable place. The upheaval and
expansion in media technology which we saw accelerating so rapidly
through the nineteenth century brought about widespread and thor-
oughgoing revisions in the common pictures held of communication.
Books had, after all, been around a long time, even if not always in
print. The picture they implied of the relation of word to thing was a
simple one: that language was at once a mirror and a lens. It could
be made, if you were disciplined enough, to *reflect* the real world
faithfully so that it could be seen clearly. Alternatively, if the lens of
language were ground well enough, you could look through the
words and see things as though nothing were in the way.

Telephones, radio, photography, impressionist painting, moving
pictures, Strindberg's plays, symbolist poetry, Henry James's novels,

[handwritten marginalia: to form a concept or concepts out of observations / experience data etc]

2. denoting
any perceptible
distinction
between
one speech-
sound &
another.

Einstein's equations, were all tokens in the 1880s that the workings of representation could no longer be taken for granted. Soon after the German philosopher Gottlob Frege began his work on sense and meaning in language (*Sinn und Bedeutung*), the American philosopher C. S. Peirce began his efforts to devise a theory of how *all* signs, whether derived from a phonetic alphabet or from an ideogrammatic system, came to mean something to the human mind. Peirce was as intent upon the signification of, say, paintings as upon words: alphabets, photographs, speech and canvases are all equivalently signs which stand for something completely different. Yet children learn quickly and easily to see them as that other, different thing. How does it happen?

It should be emphasized at this point that Peirce's and Frege's inquiries were not into psychology. The question they put was not, what goes on in our heads to make sense of these squiggles on the page? It was, what is the system *in the sign* which does the signifying for us? The name given to such inquiry was 'semiotics', which means the study of signs and meanings themselves. The two names of Frege and Peirce distinguish two parallel approaches to the study of language-as-sign-and-meaning which has become the dominant field of all the human sciences for the past half-century. Peirce commands the grand theory of semiotics. His work is committed to finding a large, structural description of all signifying systems. He wants, like all scientists, both to identify the elementary particles of signs and to reintegrate all the components in a single structure. Frege, we may say, bent himself to the study in detail of what language actually does, if we study it unimpeded by the view that it is a mirror of nature.[1]

Frege and Peirce were the pioneers. The two names perhaps better known to media students in the same genres are Ludwig Wittgenstein and Fernand de Saussure. Wittgenstein's great book *Philosophical Investigations*[2] was only published in English in 1953, although his ideas had been circulating in typescript for several years. He is gestured at throughout as contributor to this book's modest manifesto for media theorists and practical citizens. For now his powerful name serves to advertise his drastic development of Frege's ideas into a view of language and thought which has re-shaped the human sciences and permeates this book.

Wittgenstein began on a quite different track. Following his own version of the philosophic doctrine known as Logical Atomism, he was determined that in his first, no less famous book, the *Tractatus Logico-Philosophicus* (1921) he would establish the basic linguistic units within which one could tell the truth. But he then jettisoned his own argument. Having spoken of language as a picture of the world, over the next two decades he worked out a much more three-dimensional view for the *Investigations*:

> Our language can be seen as an old city: a maze of little streets and squares, of old and new houses, and of houses with additions from various periods; and this surrounded by a multitude of modern sections with straight regular streets and uniform houses. (p. 8)

The image of a city didn't satisfy him. He produced the now celebrated metaphor of language as a 'family of games', and gaily contended that there could be no general theory of games. Some features are common, some drop out, new ones appear, as one moves from cards to solitary ball games to team games and so forth; all, however, are *games*. So too with language, and understanding how language works is, he said, a matter of *looking* and *seeing* (Wittgenstein's italics). When we do look and see we find, Wittgenstein tells us, that we use these many games according to their rulebook in order to match the language which gives form to our thought against the world-out-there.

It is this matching motion of the mind with its linguistic or visual models of the world which is one key to a theory of media. Wittgenstein's way, like F. R. Leavis's, was to work from the practical examples to hand, from what people actually said. Semiotics, on the other hand, starting from a very different tradition, wanted to dismantle the whole of language as physicists dismantle matter, and then provide a theoretic model to show how it all comes together in a structure.

Semiotics and linguistics are of a piece in this project, and Fernand de Saussure is the man who, in his *Course on General Linguisitics* of 1916,[3] devised the technical model followed by semioticians thereafter until Umberto Eco's magisterial *A Theory of Semiotics*[4] in 1976, which we turn to shortly. Saussure is the second architect of the subject after Peirce, and much more accessible than Peirce. He it was who defined the sign as signifier and signified *together* (for which his algebra was s/S). But his radical move was to argue that language can only be analysed in terms of itself: all reference to what is out there is quite arbitrary. 'D-o-g' could just as well have referred to the quadruped which goes 'miaow'. Language, in his formula, is a closed self-referential system. We can only know what it means according to its 'principles of difference', such that 'table' has nothing in its meaning to do with 'able' or 'babble'. We tell them apart by simply learning the differences which give the sounds their conventional meanings. This principle of difference is inscribed in the nature of language and right across its vocabulary. It is *basic*, and it was this basic form which Saussure called *la langue* (literally, the tongue) which semiotics and linguistics possessed as their true subject. *Parole* (literally, the word) was the actual daily speech of innumerable individuals, and not his business.

II

The French semiotician who most boldly took up Saussure's ideas was Roland Barthes, and his *Mythologies*[5] is another of the short list of absolutely essential texts for media theorists. It is also a brilliantly mischievous book, and begins with 30 or so very short essays which exemplify the method. Many of them were written as separate magazine pieces but each takes a commonplace or an exotic cultural text, like soap powder advertising, toys, the latest Citroen car model, Einstein's brain, striptease, and decodes the signs which encode the text. Thereafter in an extended essay, he explains the semiotic method and situates it in the general study of what he calls mythology but which for our purposes might as well be called ideology.

This move is made in spite of Barthes's saying:

> The writer's language is not expected to *represent* reality, but to signify it. This should impose on critics the duty of using two rigorously distinct methods: one must deal with the writer's realism either as an ideological substance (Marxist themes in Brecht's work, for instance) or as a semiological value (the props, the actors, the music, the colours in Brechtian dramaturgy). The ideal of course would be to combine these two types of criticism; the mistake which is constantly made is to confuse them: ideology has its methods, and so has semiology. (p. 137)

It is puzzling that he does not consider himself to have effected this combination of both types of criticism, especially since he, a genial and gregarious man in everyday life, regrets that

> the mythologist cuts himself off from all myth-consumers, and this is no small matter ... the mythologist is condemned to live in a theoretical sociality; for him to be in society is, at best, to be truthful: his

utmost sociality dwells in his utmost morality. His connection with
the world is of the order of sarcasm. (pp. 156–7)

Well, sarcasm is not the most endearing of manners for sure, and the
mythologist here sounds like someone whose truth-telling takes the
unpopular form of puncturing other people's falsehood. In other
words, Barthes's mythologist blows the whistle on ideologues trying
to work the fix.

However, Barthes's myth is a good deal larger text or 'type of
speech' (as he calls it himself) than the kinds of ideology encountered in the previous chapter. He says roundly that almost any
cultural object may be treated textually. All have their mythic properties, and all are proper objects in 'the province of a general science,
co-extensive with linguistics, which is semiology' (p. 111). He continues with an axiom, 'Semiology is a science of forms, since it studies
significations *apart from their content*' (my italics). This is the doctrine of the pure formalist, whose analysis is only of formal relations, in this case not only the signifier and signified (objects which
are in the wholly different categories of word and thing), but also
the 'correlation which unites them ... the sign, which is the associative total' (p. 113). He gives the example of a bunch of roses sent to
a sweetheart. The flowers are a *sign* of devotion. Their meaning is
the duo: flowers-and-feeling. In a useful illustration, Barthes points
out that for Freud a dream is 'the functional union' of its narrative
and its interpretation. A sign is similarly the functional union of
word and object.

Barthes's mention of Freud is no accident, of course. Freud is as
strong a presence in the thinking of all semioticians as Saussure and
Marx, for all three were, in very different fields, grand initiating
theorists of structuralism. Structuralism, in a nutshell definition, is
the theory that all human organization is determined by large, social
or psychological structures which have their own irresistible logic
independent of human intention, will or purpose. For Freud the
structure of the psyche, for Marx the structure of economics, and
for Saussure the structure of language all precede the individual
human subject or (as it is often put) human agent, and pretty well
determine what he or she can do in all circumstances. Even if we do
not turn structuralism into a theory which inherently denies individual free will, its practitioners certainly have clear in their sights
the project to get the individual off the middle of the stage of the
human sciences. Barthes follows the lessons of his great predecessors, Freud, Marx, Saussure, in seeking to 'de-centre the subject', to

prevent all those studying human society from doing all their thinking in terms of single people, generally men, trying to sort out the world round about them in rational, principled, consistent ways. Barthes in particular and semiotics in general start from the premise that language 'speaks' the individual, rather than the other way round. In short, his view is that the forms of language are so pervasive and so strong that they form the essence of self and society. He repeats Saussure's dictum that language can only be analysed in terms of itself (the principle of difference in *langue*), not in terms of what people are doing with it in ordinary utterances (*parole*).

In action, Barthes performs his analysis of signs and myths very jauntily and engagingly, all by means of a neat little device. He picks up the distinction between signifier (word) and signified (object). He translates them into 'meaning' and 'form'. The meaning of a sign, or myth, is most simply illustrated if we think of a photograph. Barthes's device, as he said, is an economic and extremely useful one for understanding visual images on a screen as well as verbal ones on a page. Indeed it may be criticized for being rather *static*; excellent for a photograph or a cinema still, it is not really elaborate enough for a novel or a whole movie. But we need not concern ourselves too much with its limitations. The meaning–form analysis is extremely useful as a way into more searchingly practical criticism of the narratives of media. Here is how it works.

Take a photograph, let us say, of an extremely pretty girl. Such a picture is replete with meaning: with the girl's own vitality and charm and the biography it suggests, her character, working life, class, family. She is looking straight at you, as photographs may, as though you were the only person in the world she could be interested in. She has soft, candid eyes. Part of the meaning of the photograph is the corresponding fantasy it releases in the person looking at it. 'Suppose I met her. Would she like me?'

Now give the photograph a form. The picture I have described would be easily found in an advertisement. The advertisement might be for perfume, say, or soap; it might be for clothes or something less obviously connected with a pretty girl like an insurance company or an investment house. Whichever it is, these commodities are not the form. The form in this case is the mythical concept of master-symbol, feminine sexuality. We see that at a glance, and what happens is that the rich jugful of meaning which we have in a snapshot of a pretty girl is poured into the mythical form or concept marked 'feminine sexuality'. As it is poured out, so the meaning becomes thin and all but disappears. No longer *this* girl with all her life, but the vague, ubiquitous myth of sex. This is so conventionally true, that we don't need the whole picture to work with, as advertising agencies well know. A mouth, a curl, a patch of brown skin, together suggest all that is needed, and by *withholding* all the plenitude of meaning provided by the real girl, the mythic symbol is made even more potent.

There is a reciprocal motion from meaning to form and back again. We can learn the trick of signs and images by pouring one into the other. Barthes writes:

> ... *quantitatively*, the concept is much poorer than the signifier, it often does nothing but re-present itself. Poverty and richness are in reverse proportion in the form and the concept: to the qualitative poverty of the form, which is the repository of a rarefied meaning, there corresponds the richness of the concept which is open to the whole of History; and to the quantitative abundance of the forms there corresponds a small number of concepts.' (p. 120)

This is characteristically compressed. Here concept and what I called mythical symbol are synonymous: in our example, female sexuality. (It is worth observing in passing that in our culture at least most such symbols, and there aren't many as Barthes says, have to do with power, whether sexual, military, economic or political.)

Barthes contends that *concept* or mythical symbol, and *form* are reciprocally rich and poor. In our imaginations, feminine sexuality is a very general, transparent concept (or myth). Its physical embodiment, or present, literal form (the girl) is rich with quantitative possibility. There are millions of such girls, each of them filled with her own vivid actuality and biography. When we look at her for herself we are drawn back from the symbol and the myth to *the* (her) form. When we look at the myth, her uniqueness thins out and becomes transparent. Through a detail (a curl, a slender wrist, above all, a smile) we see the rich historical myth of sex itself fill up once more with its vast power, bigger than a million individuals.

It is important *not* to see this as a fight between the mythical concept or symbol (boo) and the real life of the form or body (hooray). Take a different example, which will call out differently stock responses (and none the worse for that) from the decent spectator. We are looking at an Oxfam poster depicting in black and white some of the innumerable starving and wretched of the earth. Because all such starving millions are black in Africa or brown in

Asia and Indian America, so are the people in the photograph. Furthermore, since three-quarters of those starving millions are children under twelve, so are these. The picture is in black and white because it would cost Oxfam much more to circulate it in colour.

But there are, as we would all agree, semiological decisions involved in keeping the picture black and white. Colour photography somehow, but fatally, suffuses all its subjects with glamour, particularly on television. A colour photograph, especially of a foreign country, appears intrinsically exotic. It is something to do with dazzle, which is why the inevitable shimmer of the dots-and-lines composing a TV image look glamorous (a point to return to in chapter 8). Not only that. The anthropologists and economists who originally did so much of the bloody, political work of bringing these desperate circumstances to the notice of the world brought back black-and-white photographs. Such photographs seem to us to bear witness to their own integrity. The great tradition of news photographers is rooted in black-and-white. Such men were weaned on *Picture Post*, the great British photographic magazine which followed Tom Harrisson and the empiricists of *Mass-Observation* straight into the Second World War. From Bill Brand then to Don McCullin today, reporters of their kidney built a tradition of bleak, accurate and immediate photography and reporting. Its people were always *there*, where Asian children were being bombed and starved, whether in Korea, Indonesia, Vietnam, or elsewhere. The politically conscientious class of the rich western societies learned a way of seeing from them. The familiar technology of the black-and-white film gathered a special semiotic richness. We know that such pictures are *true*.

Their truth, politically speaking, is more mythical than formal. Their signified has greater resonance than their signifier. That is why the meaning–form relation is not solved critically by cheering on the living individual against the general myth (the mistake an unreflective liberal makes). This, however, is what Barthes implies. He reminds us that 'what the concept distorts is of course what is full, the meaning' and continues 'I do not wish to prejudge the moral implications of such a mechanism' (p. 123), but all the same his analysis constantly rings with the sarcasm of the man who is blowing the whistle on somebody else's use of mythology as a fix.

If things *are* fixed as between meaning and form, myth and actuality, there's no saying who should win. 'In general myth prefers to work with poor, incomplete images, where the meaning is already relieved of its fat, and ready for a signification' (p. 127). This need

not be so. The starving children are, if we force ourselves to look at
the probability, already cared for sufficiently not to starve (they were
picked out by the photographer) or else, in a grimmer realism, those
particular children are already dead. *Their* living form, poor things,
is all at the service of the myth. The mythic symbol – compassion for
the wretched of the earth – has great power, however. It might even
one day cause more of the rich to do something about the wretched
of the earth. In the meantime, the form of these skeletal infants
pours into the mythic symbol enough energy to make a few
thousand liberal-minded people send cheques to Oxfam.

III

The point is this: the meaning–form distinction (or, if you'd rather,
the particular image–mythic symbol distinction) is simply a useful
device for our practical analyses. In saying so, I am pulling away
from the semiotician's formalism towards a main preference for
heuristics in this book and its method. Heuristic inquiry, I suppose,
may be defined as inquiry into lived experience. The formalist,
however, is concerned less for the content of life and more for its
forms and structures. In school, algebra and geometry are formalist
disciplines. Physical geography or history are heuristic ones. The
literary criticism in which we have seen the origins of media studies
goes both ways. The formalists tell their students to study form and
structure: in literature (as in film), imagery, rhythm and metre,
figures of speech, pattern in the balancing of character, the framework of plotting, everything in the work which we can see diagram-
matically. The 'lived experience' teachers ask students for personal
responses, for accounts of the *effect* of the work on their own
'sincere and vital emotion' in D. H. Lawrence's phrase. They teach
full human recognition of the diversity of life rendered in the work.
They look for pondered interpretation of what the work means in
terms of its author's intentions in relation to what the students
themselves understand of life.

It is banal to say so, but of course media theory must be formal
and experiential together. (A theory *is* a bit of algebra.) Semiotics
gives us some of the formal apparatus. It is then up to us to turn it
to practical application.

Barthes's meaning–form device is a useful place to start. It is easy
to see how to use it, for instance, in the case of heavily mythicized
genres (or types of narrative) in the cinema. The readiest example is

the Western. Anybody familiar with the genre only needs tiny cues from the form in order to fill up the myth container. What the classifications of rhetoric call metonymy is its standard figure of speech, for metonymy works by using a part to suggest the whole. A metaphor works by substituting the attributes of one object for attributes from another, the more *un*alike the better. Visual images, particularly in film which needs to compress linear effects into simultaneous ones, are largely metonymous. Thus, when we see in *High Noon* the clock, the railway line, the waiting desperado play-ing his harmonica on a tilted chair, the pale, ageing, anxious face of Gary Cooper and the open, innocent one of his beautiful new bride Grace Kelly, the metonymies deftly recharge the ancient myth with the electricity of suspense. In *High Noon* the balance of meaning and form is kept equivalent. Myth and experience are at poise, and when this is so we have the structure of a great movie.[6]

The same is true of paintings, from the study of which, for their iconographic meanings, semiotics is a more formal derivative. Icono-graphy is, literally, the study of images, generally sacred ones, but is relevantly unlike semiotics. For iconography insists upon the practi-cal meaning and *usefulness* of the icons to the people who made and adored them. Such inquiry is largely historical, as an illuminating study like R. W. Scribner's semiotics of medieval church-teaching *For the Sake of Simple Folk*[7] brings out so fully. The iconography of medieval woodcuts was a way of teaching a congregation which could not read to be devout, and to be schooled in the sacred mysteries. But it is a necessarily practical inquiry to find out what those icons meant. The traditional split between theoretical and practical reasoning forces its way between iconography and semio-tics. Iconography can tell us *what* the great *Last Judgement* of Michelangelo in the Sistine Chapel meant to its author and his patron. Semiotics can tell us *how* those and all other forms signify. The difficult thing is to do both.

In his *A Theory of Semiotics*,[8] Umberto Eco offers the most comprehensively formalist statement of the subject since Peirce and Saussure. It is a daunting book and noticeably missing from most of the literature of media theory for that reason. It is, however, one of the classic texts of the subject and quite apart from a proper piety towards it, we need it for our basic theory and method in two important ways: the first as grounding Barthes's device in a larger frame of reference; the second as marking the conceptual limits of semiotics and moving us on to try out discourse for our purposes.

Eco borrows his biggest idea from particle physics. The physicists, as we saw in our short history of early electronics, work either on the basis that the world is made up of elementary particles whose necessary presence they theorize, or on the basis that it is made up of waves whose motions they predict and seek to verify. Eco takes so-called field theory in order to posit 'the format of semiotic space'. He breaks with the traditional triple axis of linguistics, phonetics–lexicon–syntax, in an effort to show that the *codes* (a key concept) by which we turn the sound of words into intelligible discourse are more like elementary particles in their operation than the mechanical-sounding principles of the dictionary and the grammar book. He writes, 'A code is commonly supposed to render the elements of two systems equivalent, term by term (or strings of units by strings of units)' (p. 125). That is, the code by some conceptual change which matches or triggers a kind of transformer in the brain 'renders the two systems equivalent'. Reading is an instance. It is a deep puzzle to explain how runes on the page become sounds in the ears. Eco is trying to describe how the code can be capable of effecting this transformation in all signifying circumstances. To do so, he needs the freedom and pliability of a none the less systematic view of meanings as bombarding one another in semantic space, just as electrons bombard one another in nuclear-physical space. Any such view will go far beyond the fixed categories of grammar to- wards a 'hypercode' which gathers together subcodes, some of them 'strong and stable, others weak and transient such as a lot of peripheral connotative couplings' (p. 125). Thus phonology un- changed for centuries and semantic fields (which we could para- phrase as zones of meaning around a concept) which can change quite quickly must be interdependent within the hypercode. Eco adds arrestingly, 'The code is not a natural condition of the Global Semantic Universe nor a stable structure underlying the complex of links and branches of every semiotic process' (p. 126).

This last assertion runs against the grain of our habitual thinking about language. We take for granted the basic changelessness of language. Eco offers as an illustration of his theme a box of magne- tized marbles, after shaking which we could establish its 'system of attraction and repulsion by which some are drawn to one another and others are not' (p. 124). (We can see the likeness in this simple image to the electronic tube in which 'bombardment' – a chaotic- sounding idea – produces finely controlled electric current.)

> ... If the marbles, when free, represent a model of an informational
> source with high entropy, a system is a rule which magnetises the

marbles according to a combination of mutual attractions and repulsions on the same plane. The code which, on the other hand, couples different systems is a *biplanar rule* establishing new attractions and repulsions between items from different planes. In other words, every item in the code maintains a double set of relations, a *systematic* one with all the items of its own plane (content or expression) and a *signifying* one with one or more items from the correlated plane. (p. 126)

Entropy is the physical law which causes waste, loss or decline. Information charge wastes away; meanings fade. Eco is hunting for a way of representing the conservative and radical forces of meaning. Semantics at once conserves old meanings and introduces radically new ones with every new sentence or image. Eco is averse to the 'tree' diagrams of linguistic textbooks which take meanings down many separated paths. 'A denotative marker [i.e. primary meaning] may be very short-lived, while a connotative marker [i.e. associative meaning] can be stably rooted in a social convention' (p. 85). The problem for him is to discover a theory and so render intelligible the *system* which is holding meanings in this busy semantic space, and which will tell us why and how the semiotic code works.

Eco ultimately rejects Chomsky's view that such a code is built into the innate structure of the human brain. He is resolute that the magnetization of the marbles of meaning is a strictly cultural, transitory and therefore historical process. In stressing the historicality of meaning, he sorts well with the tenor of this book. You find out how history impregnates our actions with meanings by looking and seeing. But Eco takes semiotics off in a redoubtably formalist direction. We need his guide to codes, certainly,[9] his strong sense of mobility *and* system in semantic space, but the gap between his formalism and the good media theorist's attention to practice is very wide. It is what we mean when we say, 'Eco is very abstract'. We cannot readily enough turn his theoretic system into the currents of actual, historical experience.

IV

In an effort to close the gap between theory and experience, a number of writers about media have followed the French *maîtres à penser*, Jacques Lacan and Michel Foucault, in speaking of 'discursive practices'. The idea of a discourse is looser and baggier than a code, and in its recent technical sense 'discourse' has designated the variously formal fields of official conversation in the culture. It takes something from the field theory which Eco uses, in suggesting a flexibly defined but systematic range of intellectual and cultural reference, with its own local rules and conventions about how language organizes meaning within semantic space. Examples of discourse, following Foucault's magisterial studies,[10] include law, and the systems of punishment; medicine, and the institutions of hospital, clinic, the doctor's surgery and the routines which go with it; rationality and its cognates, particularly irrationality and madness. Foucault then extended the notion of discourse vastly to take in the systems of self-reference, self-fulfilment and self-awareness which constitute the moral heart of contemporary life. In the four-decker series which begins with *A History of Sexuality* and its terse essay in the history of language, he proposes that, commanding all the other formal discourses of modern institutional life which he has charted, the discourse of sexuality in relation to the self is the most pervasive and penetrative of all, locking us in the innermost prison of the society which he sees us as having made for our own perpetual incarceration.

Foucault's bleak, compelling and fluent documentary of discourse is exemplary for the media theorist. The trouble has been that discourse and its sibling 'textuality' have been horribly and pretentiously overworked in both media and historical studies. For a while, *anything* could be counted a discourse, the more wildly so as psychoanalytic aid was called in from Jacques Lacan[11] to identify the subconscious excesses which led people to ignore and indeed to repress their own subjugation by the power of old discourse. This procedure was most enthusiastically enlisted by film criticism as it began to assimilate the great surge of upsetting energy released in so timely a way by the new cultural feminism of the past 25 years.

Lacan's most famous dictum is doubtless 'the unconscious is structured like a language', and he follows that by turning our natural dreaming life into a *signifying*. He analyses dreams as Saussure analyses syntax. First, this analysis moves along a horizontal axis, the syntagm. The syntagmatic structure organizes all the units of a sentence which move laterally: for instance, the agreements of subject-noun, verb, object. Second, analysis may move vertically *down* the paradigm. Paradigmatic structure organizes those units of a sentence which, although fixed laterally by the syntagm, may vary 'downwards' until organized by the paradigm. Syntagmatic rules are not affected by changing the subject from 'I' to 'she'; paradigmatic ones are. So too with the verb: 'I make' changes to 'she spoke' on the paradigmatic chain.

Lacan's daring idea was to apply this axis of analysis to the dream. Syntagm was then the linear or horizontal narrative of the dream. The paradigm was its symbolism. The two together constituted the interpretation (there are obvious parallels with Barthes's meaning–form device). Lacan then attached this model to a revision of Freud's protocols in which the infant psyche, fixated by birth upon the mother, is torn violently away from this primal reciprocity by the jealous discovery of the precedence of the father. Unconscious desire to recover that impossibly perfect communion with the mother mobilizes the psyche for the rest of its life, for better or worse. Sublimation of that desire, or transcending its neurotic distortions, gives rise to culture.

I cannot compress Lacan's version of Freud into a few paragraphs, and in any case the job has been unbeatably well done by Terry Eagleton.[12] What is important for understanding discourse is how Lacan aligns semiotics and psychoanalysis in order to release new interpretative theory. In his celebrated hypothesis of the infant's 'mirror phase', Lacan generalizes a variety of mirroring experiences. These include the commonplace and delicious game of the baby's throwing things out of the pram in order to have them given back ('Where's it gone?' 'There.'). The baby finds in this exchange a signified to match its own signifier. This hitching together of the self and the world, thereby conferring a sign on the infant, has clinching force when the small child works out that the image in the mirror is its own reflection (not an easy thing to do). Gradually, however, the child loses its happy grasp on that reflection; the reflection is no longer filled up by the child to its satisfaction. It sees the ambiguities of the reflection, the absences, the displacements (left to right, right to left; the reflected face is half the width of the real one). These ambiguities are metonymies for the drastic displacements which take place in the psyche and are driven deep into the forgetfulness of the unconscious. The child is weaned, loses the mother, yields to the father. Freud and Lacan agree that life thereafter is an endless search for that perfect 'oceanic' happiness in which child and mother could unite. As in metaphor, the radically 'other' had the same identity as oneself. From puberty on, all thought is a metonymy, an inherently tragic failure to hold on to more than the bits and pieces which have to stand in for the perfect unity of infant happiness. As Eagleton has him say, 'This potentially endless movement from one signifier to another is what Lacan means by desire' (p. 167).

It is theory of this sort, whether political or psychoanalytic but in any case semiotic, which describes itself as post-modernist. The post-modernists see human experience as irretrievably fragmented, and individuals as necessarily exiled in the modern city of strangers. We, on the other hand, may feel briskly unsympathetic even while we concede the force and terror in Lacan's vision. For all the term 'post-modernism' does, by definition, is stop history. It implies that after the experience of modern politics and war, the modern psyche, modern art and media, all we will find is the endless acreage of the waste land. After the natural, settled ease of the language spoken at home, in public we can only hear the unnatural, self-conscious drawing-attention-to-its-own-process of modern international speech. Nevertheless, we rejoin to the Lacanians that settlement remains a usual human experience, even if all film critics leave home restlessly and soon. And even in adult life, men and women can find, if they're lucky, the unity of signifier and signified in art or in life which gives them back the sign of their own happiness.

It should be apparent, even in this summary, just how attractively versatile Lacan's ideas looked to students of visual media. The jumps, foreshortenings, close-ups and panning shots of a capable movie all lend themselves to a theory whose first premise is the brokenness of experience. Much creative and intelligent work has been done on these lines, especially in *Screen*, the house magazine of the British Film Institute. Feminism found in Lacan a way of iden-tifying the cruelty and arrogance of unconscious patriarchy in the male-dominated cinema. Unhappily but also comically, the height of what Garnham roundly calls (as we see in the next chapter) 'the Lacanian madness' brought interpretations of such extreme dottiness and jargon-clotted circularity as to discredit the venture altogether. The zest of the master for paradox, punning, deliberate obscurity, oracular sentertiousness and other Parisian gestures led many of his disciples at *Screen* into a macabre dance up cemetery road.

Foucault is only a way out of this dead end if we take him for his method, not his message. His message, to say it again, is that modern 'carceral' society has devised unprecedentedly penetrative and invisible modes of oppression and imprisonment. Indeed we are most dominated, according to Foucault, when we are least aware of it. The fatuous slogans of bodily awareness and sexual-technical freedom celebrated amongst the miles of charred flesh along the

August beaches of the Mediterranean and Malibu hold in thrall their victims as securely as manacles. The language of selfhood, self-discovery and self-enrichment is for Foucault yet another deadly prison. The value terms inscribe servility and 'the discourse of power' in the body itself.

The phrase, 'the discourse of power' is perhaps Foucault's best-known contribution to method in media theory. His claim is that *all* arguments as to truth are driven by the will to power. To make a truth-claim is to make a power-claim in the same breath. Knowledge is therefore never 'disinterested' (in both the strict sense and the everyday one: it is never impartial and it is never bored). To possess, reveal or create knowledge is to do the same for a form of power.

Foucault documents this claim on his part by following in the first place the creation of modern (i.e. from the late eighteenth century onwards) forms of intellectual inquiry.[13] He sees the advent of medicine, psychology, pedagogy, criminology, law, all of them the great intellectual products of the Enlightenment's determination to light progress on its road by human reason, as being mere instruments of state repression. Each discipline marks out an area of body and mind for its control. First the mad and the sick, then the children and the criminals, then domestic life and its great untamable, sex. Each is brought under the terrible domination of language, the discourse of power. Thereafter, we may say if persuaded by his bleak picture (and it has great persuasive power), such modern 'policy sciences' as management theory, time-and-motion study and industrial relations, are all discourses of power written out and given their charter in order to control, without its even noticing, an increasingly passive, docile society.

Such a theory has obvious grip for anyone swayed by the fix theory of ideology (and no rational person could fail to be). Foucault gives historical depth and procedure to the method outlined as a first stage at the end of chapter 4. Kumar's 'Holding the middle ground', I suggested, gave us a diagrammatic form for the whole territory of social narratives. Foucault's classic study of the prison, *Discipline and Punish*, shows us how to mark the dominant landmarks of the discourse and their historical contours upon such a map.

The vital word in that last sentence is 'dominant'. Someone could reasonably object that 'discourse' bounds no clear area of inquiry, and 'discursive practices', Foucault's pet phrase, even less. There are any number of discourses within the official curriculum alone and new ones keep turning up. As for 'discursive practice', well, all that presumably indicates is the dozens of activities that go on under the heading of, say, legal discourse: courts, solicitors' offices, traffic wardenship, house conveyancing, conditions of sale on the back of shop goods, school rules, and so on.

Foucault, however, saw the field of a discourse like the physicists see the electromagnetic field. It is defined, not by its will to truth, but by its will to *power*. A discourse seeks power, and that is what marks out its range. Furthermore, its quest is always historical – it is at work in specific times and places, its field of force accumulates. So to find it out, we need to do history. Hence his study of the birth of the prison. The modern prison came out of the Enlightenment and coincided with the other 'carceral' institutions of industrial society codified by Foucault: the clinic, the lunatic asylum, the school, mental and manual work itself. The menace was the new, reforming version of the prison which was first conceived in the early 1800s.

At that time Jeremy Bentham, earliest designer of the mass society numbers books, thought up a prison which would be utterly unlike all preceding prisons as they had existed for thousands of years. His *Panopticon* would be built in a vast circle surveyed from a central watchtower. All the cells would be barred like a cage, without solid walls. The watchtower would permit endless surveillance of every prisoner, alone in his cell. Foucault plots the rapid development of surveillance in all modern societies from the *Panopticon* onwards. He sees them as endlessly watchful of consciousness itself. A prison is no longer somewhere for prisoners to rot, but a place where their very character is penetrated, changed; in the jargon, 'rehabilitated'. He saw this as the type of modern governmental control. Its language, as is always the case, is the key to its form and meaning.

Discipline and Punish shows us how to study a discourse. The media theorist builds it into his account of ideology, its drive to dominate *and* its help in taking the strain of life. In so far as he breaks clear in his criticism of the surveillant, cold oppression of ideological discourse, he refuses Foucault's grim determinism. In another compelling example of discourse analysis, Edward Said[14] studies the form and content of what he calls 'orientalism', the subjugating discourse by which Western imperial nations built up a picture of the Oriental, whether Arab or Asian, his wiles, inscrutability, cruelty and little erotic festivals. Said shows us these brutal and ignorant stereotypes in order to liberate us from them. By the same token, media students might study the various discourses of novels, television, movies, or just gossip as they handle, say, domesticity, childhood, warfare (one should, of course, say 'defence'), landscape. Thereby they will grasp how these modes of speech, thought and imagining make for freedom or for imprisonment, for human virtue or for the dark.

Notes

1 Frege and Peirce are unnecessarily difficult texts for our purposes. However, Richard Rorty in his seminal book, *Philosophy and the Mirror of Nature*, (Basil Blackwell, 1981), makes the case against seeing language as a simple mirror of reality. Non-philosophers will find the last part of the book the most accessible.
2 Ludwig Wittgenstein, *Philosophical Investigations*, tr. G. E. M. Anscombe (Basil Blackwell, 1953).
3 Fernard de Saussure, *Course on General Linguistics* (1916) (McGraw-Hill, 1965).
4 Umberto Eco, *A Theory of Semiotics* (Indiana University Press, 1976).
5 Roland Barthes, *Mythologies* (1957), tr. Annette Lavers (Jonathan Cape, 1972; Paladin, 1973).
6 Peter Wollen, in *Sign and Meaning in the Cinema* (Secker and Warburg, 1969), gives a very sensible guided tour round these procedures.
7 R. W. Scribner, *For the Sake of Simple Folk* (Cambridge University Press, 1981).
8 Eco, see n. 4 above.
9 Eco shows us how to use his ideas practically in a new collection, *Essays in Hyperreality* (Picador Books, 1987).
10 Michel Foucault, *The Order of Things* (Tavistock Press, 1966); *Madness and Civilisation* (Random House, 1967); *The Birth of the Clinic* (Tavistock Press, 1973); *Discipline and Punish* (Penguin, 1977). This is only a selection from a life's work. As this chapter says, *Discipline and Punish* is the most important work for media theory. See also, however, vol. I of *A History of Sexuality* (Penguin, 1979).
11 Jacques Lacan, *Ecrits: a Selection* (Tavistock Press, 1977).
12 See Terry Eagleton, *Literary Theory* (Basil Blackwell, 1983), chapter 5.
13 For the relevant works, see n. 10 above.
14 Edward Said, *Orientalism* (Vintage Books, 1979; Penguin, 1987).

6

Institutions: the Political Economy of Media

I

Politics is not only to do with power, and spotting the extent to which our culture makes us free or oppressed is not the only goal of media theory. One of the things that make people fed up with politics is the endless quarrelling about whether things are going right or wrong, and who could do better. Politics, as I put it earlier, is the study of how the world is and how it ought to be. If we can agree roughly that the point of living is to lead a good and happy life and to act morally, then we have to have the *chance* to do these admirable things (it would be very hard indeed to be a good man in hell[1]). Politics in real life is the business of arranging those chances, and it is perfectly obvious that the power to arrange anything so far-reaching *and* the power to live a decent enough life on behalf of yourself and the people you love are alike political matters. Most sensible people do not want to be in charge of other people's lives; wanting power a great deal is rightly thought of as a fishy business. But unless they take some power over their own lives, they won't be able to act freely – and therefore well – at all. To be a genuinely free man or woman is to be on the way to being a virtuous one. Put like that, freedom is not just an individual circumstance in which you can do well or badly, it is a virtue in itself.

This short preamble in moral politics is intended to encourage those who blench at the phrase 'political economy'. On the argument of this book, political economy is both heart and hinge to its progress. It is the heart because unless we know how the colossal resources of the media and information industry are allocated and who controls this busy movement, we cannot understand why its forms and contents are as they are. Even as one-to-one a communication as a novel, in which the meeting between writer and reader looks as direct as possible, is itself produced by the relevant corner of the vast publishing industry, with its editors, booksellers, reviewers, advertisers, printers, binders, distributors and warehousemen. Political economy is the hinge of this book because its intellectual framework shifts us with a jerk from the analysis of consumption to that of production. Ideology-critique and semiotics have to work with what they can get: the books, films, television programmes, newspapers and the rest available on the open market. They then show how the internal machinery of their contents works.

Political economy, every bit as historical a study as all we have learned to do so far, carries us into the mode of·production itself. It therefore puts questions, as a matter of practical analysis, about what it is right for anyone to own, about what is done with such power and how the structures of productive power themselves generate a momentum far beyond individual control. Necessarily, also, it poses questions with no particular consolation for the political Left or Right about how things might be differently ordered, and whether it would be better if they were. The answers to such questions are not predictable. Few people, for example, in the large and on the whole self-satisfied elite which pronounces on culture in Britain, expected that the second commercial channel from the IBA, Channel Four, would become the triumph it has. Only a handful inside the industry who saw the possibilities for small production companies commissioned by programme had strong hopes that this would be a better way to produce television than through 'the vast, insane bureaucracy' (the words are those of a producer) of the BBC.

But Channel Four is a happy exception, and political economy cannot be confined to the analysis of British media. Indeed, its disciplinary premise must be that world media have, as Enzensberger predicted twenty years ago,[2] come together in a vast, universal system of:

> news satellites, colour television, cable relay television, cassettes, videotape, videotape recorders, video-phones, stereophony, laser techniques, electrostatic reproduction processes, electronic high-speed printing, composing and learning machines, microfiches with electronic access, printing by radio, time-sharing computers, data banks. All these new forms of media are constantly forming new connections both with each other and with older media like printing, radio, film, television, telephone, teletype, radar and so on. (pp. 13–14)

II

For all the play made in earlier chapters with the idea of a universal system, it still sits uneasily with the analysis of culture. The Leavises and the Frankfurters alike saw commercial culture as a productive monolith, certainly, and also as a lethal menace. The way round its frightfulness was to find genuine works of art which were immune to the poison, and build from those an image of a redeemed future, whether for a few individuals (the Leavises) or for a revolutionary socialism (Walter Benjamin, if not Theodor Adorno). Political economy, however, exempts nothing, not even the work of art. But since until recently the preponderance of teachers of media were formed in study of the traditional humanities, and since, moreover, culture with a big C retains a socially high prestige position in English-speaking communities, there is deep resistance to treating the production of culture as part of commodity exchange.

This is particularly noticeable in the making of official cultural policy. Its institutions such as Arts Councils, educational curriculum writers, Federal or State funding committees for arts centres, television channels with obligations to high culture and the like, all these worthy bodies express the view that their wares are above market considerations. They are heirs to the deep split effected in nineteenth-century thought between feeling and reason, a split which was canonized in the forms of most national curricula. Science was presented as the rational, powerful and public mode of thought. The arts were taught as being emotional, subjective and private in their relevance. By this token the arts were not trivial; they cared for the realm of values, but values were personal, indisputable and private. There was (and is) no disputing them, only agreement between individuals to differ.[3]

This version of the arts is still effective. It is at the bottom of the subsidy system. It holds that good art communicates straight to the individual's heart, unimpeded by class, colour, gender or any other accident. And in spite of all that is said and done about the sponsorship of the arts by commerce, such sponsorship is supposed to be proof that commercial interests are capable of transcending themselves and giving charitably to that superior level of being which exalts feeling and pays no profit. Sponsorship is the token paid by capital to show that it isn't so bad after all. Certainly, they say, if you want art, you must pay for it. But art really has only a transcendental value. Subsidy and sponsorship acknowledge the need for this value on everyone's part, because the market can never satisfy it.

A political economy of culture has to reckon with this decidedly ideological version of artistic value, but only as a function of the distribution of cultural commodities and the nature of cultural institutions. These institutions define cultural policy as the business of finding audiences for the work of art, not works of art for the audiences.[4] This direction is compounded by the view of the creative artist, the popular version of whom is as somebody driven by a vision and therefore living in spiritually beneficial poverty. This vision impels the artist to create works which will probably be rejected by the market because they are, in some mysterious way, ahead of their time. It is the gratifying public duty of policy-makers to provide audiences by subsidizing the gap between creative vision and philistinism.

But my contentions about the looseness of the idea of 'mass' in the phrases 'mass media' and 'mass audience' hold strongly in this predicament. There are no masses, only varying sizes of overlapping minorities.[5] The creative artist in his or her singleness of purpose can only create within the structures and processes of the market. This is the given fact, and however it may have been voiced first by Marx, it is now the commonplace of any senator whose mouth is hired to speak for business in his country's parliamentary forum. The capitalist mode of production attracts *every thing* to its equivalence in exchange value. That is what capitalism *is*, and the best reason why it is morally imperative to detest it. Social relations within it are dominated and shaped right through by the relations of exchange – buying and selling in the market. The creative artist simply cannot create anywhere else. And the obvious fact obtrudes into the pious view of cultural policy-makers and teachers that the market, first, is where most people *do* satisfy their cultural needs (if that's the right word) and preferences.

This doesn't at all conclude: so much the worse for high culture. It only concludes that high culture is bound into the entire system. It will find its audiences according to the chances it gets and takes: new novels sell respectably at 15 pounds or 25 dollars; new paintings are displayed in Bond Street and the Rue Lafayette for umpteen thousands in any currency; new movies are made for the long or short road from the local cinema to the home video-recorder. In each case, these commodities take their luck in a peculiar, hectic and far from free or open market economy. The media theorist must put her faculty for critical discrimination, her training in semiotics and her model of ideological analysis down amongst the abstractions of political economy. Doing so, she renounces nothing of her moral sense; indeed it should be sharpened. For political economy deals in the relations of production, and these determine, or let us say, set limits to the terms of every transaction between men and women in society.

Practising political economy is the same as learning any new discipline. It alters our conceptual framework. We incorporate the new concepts as best we can into our existing frame of mind. It is not, however, like learning a foreign language from scratch, nor are its practitioners required, at least for the purposes of this book, to be highly numerate.

Adorno and Horkheimer[6] long ago pointed out that capitalism in the modern era moved to appropriate and industrialize all those domestic, leisure and cultural areas of life which earlier capitalist production left alone. Capitalism is impelled by its logic to seek and then to saturate new markets.[7] In its early phase, capitalism was intent upon profits from extraction and heavy manufacturing: its form of communication was the train. By now, having moved through the car and the aircraft as its subsequent modes of transport and communication, its new form is electronic communication and its typical commodity consumer goods. Trains, cars and aircraft are still built in millions, of course; but the leading edge of capitalism and the source of the most burgeoning profits is information technology and all it includes.

Hence the big barons turned to the industrialization of culture, defined by Garnham as 'the production and circulation of symbolic meaning', a definition which fits easily with semiotics in the previous chapter. In the cultural industries we find the four standard features of the capitalist mode of production:

1 mass production and distribution of commodities;
2 capital-intensive technology;
3 managerial organization of highly specialized divisions of labour;
4 cost-effectivity as the criterion of success, i.e. the maximization of profit or, in the production of State culture, competitive victory over rivals.

(It should be noted that the first three features occur in the cultural industries of the socialist bloc,[8] but this isn't a point we can pursue here.)

In his great work, Marx defined capital:[9]

In itself the sum of money may only be defined as capital if it is employed, spent, with the aim of increasing it, if it is spent expressly in order to increase it. In the case of the sum of value or money this phenomenon is its destiny, its inner law, its tendency, while to the capitalist, i.e. the owner of the sum of money, in whose hands it shall acquire its function, it appears as intention, purpose.

But as both Marxists and the non-Marxist followers of Keynes have agreed since Keynes published *his* classic in 1936, *The General Theory of Employment, Money, and Interest*, capital doesn't have things all its own way. It is fraught with structural, ineradicable contradictions. These twist its workings into peculiar shapes and always prevent the perfection of what its ideologues dream of as 'the free market economy'. The contradictions occur at once between capital and labour. The labour force resists exploitation as best it may, and struggles to win back for wages as much of the surplus-value (profit) taken by capital as it can. In addition, capitalism is harried by a statistical law of its own mechanism by which the rate of profit is always falling in the long run.

These contradictions are endemic to capitalism in all its forms; the cultural industries generate more contradictions of their own. These result from the nature of competition within the cultural industries for a quadrilateral of always finite resources and no less finite prizes.

Producers are competing in the first place for a share of finite consumer income. Within the general tendency of the past 40 years for prosperity to rise for at least two-thirds of the population in the rich nations, households approach a set limit for the purchase and consumption of essentials like food and clothing. Obviously both food and clothing industries try frantically to persuade people to buy more clothes and eat more food, but there is a limit even in our overweight, overdressed society. As a proportion of household expenditure, the budget for cultural goods and services (new videos, compact discs, theatre or cinema tickets, even holidays) has not been rising in line with increased income.[10] This puzzling slowness in cultural expenditure may be connected with the second finite in our frame: time.

There are limits set to the amount of time we devote to our cultural life. For those in work or in official education, these limits are obviously set by the hours of the working week and the time taken to travel to work and college. After that, there are more or less conventionally set times for sleep and meals, at the end of which, as they say, the time is *free*; it is your own, to do with as you like. Now the competing companies do all they can to take more time off you. They open access to their products by, for instance, removing the box office and the journey to the cinema or the concert hall. They bring ever less realistic, because humanly uninterrupted, celestially perfect musical performances into your home. They sell you the video-recorder, and although its signal is much murkier than a good television and its film image downright awful, it's all easier and cheaper than turning out on a cold night to the moviehouse. The cable and satellite broadcasters edge into your sleeping time with films after midnight, the early morning shows break into breakfast in the hope of persuading their advertising sponsors that they have audiences to sell at half-past seven in the morning. These inroads are real but marginal.

There is, however, for those on the side of anti-commercialism a gratifying resistance involved. For, as I said, the time set aside for cultural pursuits is *ours*. Leisure time is free time. It is to some large extent what people work *for*, and it is therefore powerfully averse to manipulation, unpredictable and excellently wilful in its choices, and deeply attached to its value as unregulatable. As Garnham drily puts it,

> Cultural consumption is particularly time-consuming in the sense that the most common and popular forms of culture, namely narrative and its musical equivalent, are based upon manipulation of time itself and thus they offer deep resistances to attempts to raise the productivity of consumption time. (1983, p. 6)

The finite quantity of time makes it the object of fierce competition. That quantity continues to increase slightly, as cultural life draws back to the home, the cassette, the video, and the book. But even then, the cultural industries are beset by recalcitrance.

Capitalist production depends on the successful mass production and distribution of its commodity. The more sold, the lower the price can be dropped, the higher the marginal rate of profit and the more efficient the economies of scale. To regulate this process, capitalist production typically builds in the deliberate tendency of the commodity to become obsolete. This cycle of purchase–obsolescence–replacement is standardly smoothed along by advertisements persuading consumers to replace what is still new. The cycle is the dynamo of capitalism. However, it is also important to that production that innovation is kept as cheap as possible. This year's car should be as like as possible to last year's car. New technology costs a lot. The research towards and development of a prototype is the most expensive stage of the productive sequence.

These necessities run solidly up against the demand of cultural activity that its material be freely chosen and, preferably, new. Of course a gradual selection of old favourites is chosen by the culture at different class levels and canonized as classics. The film, music and book industries are each immensely relieved when any work moves out of the dating process in this way and onto the timeless shelf of classics, since regular sales can then be assured for a long, safe time (especially if the classic becomes officially examinable, and appears in the syllabuses).

But, by and large, the first value of a cultural product is its novelty. If you watch people in a video-hire shop, they will put back the videotape they know they have seen, unless it's an old friend. The queue is longest for the latest thing. Cultural consumption resists in this way the drive of production towards stereotyping products. Each product – film, novel, music – resembles the development of a prototype. Of course when the industry finds a success, it tries to replicate it as quickly and easily as possible, as Q. D. Leavis saw in her analysis of bestsellers. After *Jaws*, then *Jaws II, III, IV*. But sequels rarely work, and even the Catherine Cookson or Barbara Taylor Bradford novel has to provide *some* novelty.

The costs of production are huge compared to the costs of reproduction, as one would expect. And the success of novelty is a matter of luck or accident. It can't be planned for, as witness the fact that in the record industry only one in 9 singles and one in 16 LP discs makes a profit.[11] The difficulty is to smooth and stabilize this erratic curve by creating a broad, settled repertory which supports risk. The neatest example is the creation of news as a commodity everyone wants, which gets old and goes bad *immediately*, The news holds all men at least to TV, radio and newspaper. But no one buys yesterday's news.

Not only have the cultural industries to manage the contradictions between mass-production and innovation, they have to control as best they may the relative durability of cultural goods and people's deplorable refusal to treat them as private property. Books, movies, cassettes don't wear out easily and people lend them readily. Worse, they lend their cassettes and the crucial pages of their expensive books for pirate copying. The cultural good becomes a public good, however much the industry tries to stop the traffic by copyright laws.

In an effort to control these surging contradictions, the cultural-industrial companies have begun in a selective way to ignore profits on their films, videos and cassettes and to push the profit-making responsibility onto the hardware. The drive to change consumers over to compact disc equipment and domestic video cameras is one example of this process, and the sharp increase in mergers and takeovers within the communications industry is part of the big companies' efforts to control 'vertically' whole domestic systems of hardware and software reproduction, ensuring that once you hire their video and audio plant, you have to use their compatible software as well, because other people's don't fit.

III

Cultural industry still does not escape from the twistpoint of its own contradictions. I stress them since it is precisely from such details that theory of our historical kind must start. There remain two other points on the quadrilateral of resources and rewards which defines the competitive field: advertising revenue and skilled labour.

Broadcasting houses are selling audiences to advertisers; software houses must buy skilled labour. Commercial broadcasters literally sell audiences to advertisers whose investment varies according to the predicted audience size. State broadcasters (Britain, France, Australia, Channel 13 in the USA) are obliged to compete with the commercial stations in order to sustain a comparable level of state funding. Selling audiences is also up against unexpected and fairly rigid limits. In Britain over the quarter-century from 1960 to 1985, total advertising expenditure scarcely shifted as a proportion of the Gross National Product (GNP); it was 1.43 per cent in 1960, and 1.34 per cent in 1985. Twelve commercial stations are competing for a fairly fixed sum each year, and at a time when all other costs are likely to be rising. The figures run clean contrary to the folklore about endless advertising money being poured into cultural organs of all sorts. Of course broadcasting stations can raise extra revenue by extending broadcasting hours, thereby selling new audiences, just as newspapers publish new advertising space. After midnight and before breakfast broadcasting helps, if only in a small way. (In Britain, the BBC can only match these new times out of its existing licence fee. It still has to shut down at midnight; its breakfast broadcasts make do pretty well with studio chat and old news footage.)

Finally, all the cultural industries are competing for a limited pool of skilled labour. Writers, musicians, engineers, actors, cameramen, work in more than one section of the industry. What is then slightly comic is that their deeply entrenched view of the creative artist as an honest, independent journeyman demands that such individuals take to themselves unemployment and the arduous, risky, expensive research and development projects then to be bought up by the big companies. The writer who has not a well-known name bashes out her play and hopes for the best. The wildlife cameraman, a rare, favourite breed, disappears into the delta of the Danube with his camera for two months and comes back without salary, hoping to stick the movie into the *Wildscreen* competitions and make his fortune. So, too, notoriously, the young band in its old dormobile banging away at dowdy gigs is dreaming of a golden disc and the profits it will bring to other people. On the other hand, in all these instances, capitalism has its own problems distinguishing the product from the process of production. 'How shall we tell the dancer from the dance?' the poet asks, and the accountant has the same difficulty.

Understanding the cultural commodity, therefore, is necessarily a matter of understanding our old friend the mode-and-relations-of-production, even though this turns out to be a very jumbled activity. We can set out a few crisp injunctions, however. First, the conditions of production in the media and cultural industries must be seen simply as an extension of conditions in *all* capitalist production. Secondly, study of those conditions should focus on their innate contradictions by way of grasping (and theorizing) their peculiar structure and momentum. These contradictions are in the first place the classic duo of capitalism: the contradiction between capital and labour registered in the wage bargain, and the contradiction statistically innate in the principle of accumulation by which the marginal rate of profit always tends to fall as capital itself hungrily seeks ever wider markets.

The subsequent contradictions of the cultural industries are peculiar to its typical commodity form which is, initially, its *audiences*. (Commodity form looks like a technical term, but means exactly what it says: the shape of the product.) But the industry also makes art objects: films, paintings, plays, concerts, performances, and it is often hard, even contradictory, to divide the object from the process of production. Moreover, the audiences are disobedient and fickle: their time is finite so the market can't expand for ever. They insist on novelty. Their cultural goods they treat as public, not private, property. The goods themselves only wear out slowly. The cultural market is a highly unstable place to trade. It is trading in taste and judgement, the choices people make about how to use their own time in ways which ratify their sense of themselves as individual and distinctive. They watch their own choice of movie, pick their own choice of pictures for the wall, cassettes for the music centre, fiction for the bath and the bed.

This being so, the key figure of the contemporary cultural industries is the figure whose decisions control distribution rather than production. This is an axiom of our political economy. The production of cultural goods is very expensive. Reproduction is cheap. The decisions vital to the industry are those which lead to the most widespread distribution possible. The really powerful and creative figure is, therefore, the person who guesses right about size of audiences, and holds them across a wide repertory. Our axiom, taken from Garnham, is therefore that 'it is not cultural distribution nor cultural production that is the key locus of power and profit' (1983, p. 8). In our study of the political economy of media, we need to look for the editor who matches product to audience, who adjusts the cost of making the movie, the book, the music or the programme, to the spending power of the audience he has in mind. This figure, whether newspaper editor, commissioning editor in a publishing house, programme head or series editor for a television channel, performs the most importantly creative function of the cultural industries. We can set him on her alongside the broadcasting presenter as one who shapes the temper of the times.

IV

Political economy is an uneasy phrase. It designates the point at which two disciplines overlap. Economists have reliable techniques of measurement for historical inquiry; it is their powers of prediction which are shaky, and prediction is what politics asks of them. Ever since Keynes, economics has been a policy science, which is to say a human science obliged to suggest how life might be lived now as well as saying how it was lived then. Keynes changed politics and economics by placing the activities of the state at the centre of the economy. Until Keynes, what is now thought of as neo-classical economics set out to theorize markets as untouchable and as seeking by their own logic an equilibrium between growth and stable prices, employment and low wages. After Keynes's famous formulation of the key concept ('the multiplier') which would permit government finance ministers broadly to control demand and investment, all the equations changed. Capitalism learned to look to the state to solve its market contradictions. The state, indeed, becomes the edge at which politics and economics meet.

There is nothing sanctimonious to say about this development. Some Marxist theorists talk as though the state is simply the central committee of the ruling class, and that when capitalist economies got badly stuck in the late 1920s, this new notion of the state was set up to bail them out. Similarly, the brutal account of the setting up of the national broadcasting houses with the BBC in Britain first, and most European countries, Canada, Australia and ex-imperial dominions following, was that these were ideological loudspeakers for the ruling class. In the Fascist countries no doubt they were. But culture as we have seen (and as we live it, day by day) is a queer, unregulated thing. Part of the reason for having a cultural life is that there we absolutely refuse to do as we're told. It has an inherent subversiveness, which is why teaching it in schools is such a bloody business. Entertainment is always liable to get out of hand. All festivals worry the police. So one cannot look for a neat, peaceful fit between the needs of capital and the uses of culture.

On occasions, indeed, they split apart completely. The high prestige of certain parts of the cultural industry will encourage some capitalists to flout profit in order to support losses. Posh books and posh newspapers have, at times, lost millions while their owners bore the costs for the sake of the prestige shed by association with the particular publication. Ideology and the accumulation of profit do not always coincide.

Where there are splits and conflicts in the structures of modern industrial society, the responsible state generally tries to solve them by setting up some new kind of more or less conciliatory institution. As the deep drive of capitalist accumulation after the First World War took in the new communication technology and the advances war had made possible, it seemed to the many queasy-looking nation-states of the 1920s that the way to reconcile, resolve and heal the wounds of their societies was to set up, in the new, accurate verb, broadcasting institutions.

Of course capital was pouring into the technology, and that also created political as well as economic pressures. A clash between politics and economics impended. In Britain, Australia, even parts of the USA, the spectre of revolution loomed from Russia, Germany and Italy. The British police had even staged a short strike, and general strike waited round the corner. The pointless slaughter of the war was unappeased, and unemployment with pitiful dole money was all there was to greet many of the soldiers returning to 'a land fit for heroes to live in'. At the same time, first radio telegraphy and then full-blown radio had reached the point of take-off into mass production, without anyone having much idea what they would broadcast. There was ample capital looking for a home in radio, and there were social discontinuities amounting to crisis. The British Government brought economics and politics together by setting up the BBC.[13]

This was a historical precedent which has proved repetitious, particularly in Britain but also in many European countries and the once colonial nations. Communications technology was actively developed without having a specific content or context. The state provided both. Raymond Williams points out[14] that home radio gave some of its thrust to the rise of consumer goods in the home, and arrived with the car, motor-bike, camera, electric iron, home telephone, for those whose wages would stand it. The way of life he calls (in what he admits is an ugly phrase) 'mobile privatization' starts from the 1920s, and the radio is its first emblem. The stout, walnut-veneered box with the crocheted twine aperture brought the great mobile world down into millions of private living-rooms.

The BBC shaped and consolidated that process,[15] and in so doing effected more of the reconciliation and restoration of national identity than anyone could have foreseen when the Royal Charter was granted to it in 1924. This extraordinary achievement was effectively the work of one man, John Reith, its first director-general. The BBC has since become in certain ways an exemplary institution: it provided the model, as I said, for a number of state broadcasting houses, notably Canada's and Australia's, but it also gives us a detailed history within which the play of autonomy and obedience, of subversion and conformism, of criticality and nationalism may be seen at work in the industry of the cultural services. It supports the strain and the fix theories of ideology; it created (as it had to) its own semiotics; it is a working model of cultural production in a particular era, and as such offers indispensable evidence against which the media theorist can test his ideas. Since the era of the working of comfortably national cultural economies is now ending decisively, the crumbling old age of this vast but unkillable mastodon contains vivid object-lessons about success and failure in public service broadcasting.

Public service was what Reith devoted himself to. The Royal Charter conferred upon the BBC singular status: in Britain, such charters are enjoyed by a very small number of institutions of which the Universities are the best known. To be chartered is to be independent of any individual party in government, and to have specified duties and conditions of work.[16] In the case of the BBC these included duties of impartiality and balance, as well as larger responsibilities enshrined in the motto cast on the BBC's grand escutcheon in Broadcasting House, Portland Place. It there announces (in Latin) that it will educate and entertain the public, and Reith, an upright, severe, highly cultivated Scot, took his education hard.

He played politics, on the other hand, pretty softly. In a notable exchange at the time of the general strike, he avoided a row by accepting that the government's voice was the voice of the national interest. European and North American broadcasting, even at its most cowardly moment in 1990, would hardly be so obliging. However, Reith not only had a baby institution to nurse, he did not see the BBC at that stage as a source of political information. It had no news department as such, but took its news routinely from the big agencies of the day, like Reuters. Reith saw the subject-matter of the BBC as cultural, and at that date only the Frankfurt school had noticed how fully political culture is.

Much fun is made of Reith these days, for his Scottish dominie's severity, his alleged elitism, his certainty that high culture was good for you and that the BBC ought to educate people up to like it. No doubt a joke or two is deserved. The weird convention of the thirties that newsreaders wear dinner jackets to read radio news is only one of the more potty absurdities about a BBC not without its pseuds, snobberies, and hateful English condescensions. None the less and from the start, the BBC conceived a remarkable mixture of high and popular culture. They had gardening programmes alongside books (classics) at bedtime; they had avant-garde plays beside Shakespeare and Dorothy L. Sayers' detective stories; they had roaming microphones picking up British life on the road and in the street, and they had the great popular ceremonies of national sport: the Derby, the Cup Final, the Test matches.

The divisions in taste were plainly signalled, it is true. The BBC gradually established its own orchestras – itself a remarkable move to make – and one of these was for light music and played on the radio waveband then called the Light Programme, and one was called the BBC Symphony Orchestra, which played on the carefully titled 'Home Service' and was presumably heavier. The Third

Programme, while it gave nothing away in its name, was avowedly the channel for the intelligentsia and high culturalists. But all three were there on the air for a whole nation to listen to, and Reith's vision of a gradually self-educating people was by no means a vacuous one. Once the Schools and Education broadcasting unit was established, the BBC could reasonably claim that its cultural representativeness was complete. It was no doubt abominably genteel – there are all kinds of comic tales about what couldn't be said on the air that was said every day in the street – but then so was British culture at large. But as a picture of the best, most accessible combination of popular and elite culture at that stage of broadcasting history, it would have been hard to beat.

It is also well known that the Corporation gave its standing the aura of final authority by its handling of news and political opinion in the Second World War. While there were bound to be concessions to propaganda from the Allied side, these were very few, as Briggs's admirable history tells us. In its formal, slightly plummy, truth-telling and dignified way, the BBC news became a world touchstone for reporting a war going either well or badly in a prose which did justice and gave dignity to either outcome. German citizens, who had long ago given up expecting Goebbels' radio to tell them any-thing but lies, listened secretly to the BBC world services and were imprisoned for doing so.

From 1945 its position as a social institution in British life seemed as grand and secure as the Established Church and the Universities of Oxford and Cambridge. Forty-five years later, of course, *all* those respectable bodies are looking much more rickety than they did even in 1979, the year of the dragon, when Mrs. Thatcher came to power. But it is exactly the purpose of political economy to explain how such vast changes come about.

V

The BBC effected its deep roots in the lives of ordinary people by its always being so reassuringly *there*[17]. Its readiness and ubiquity gra-dually assumed a taken-for-granted place in home life, in travelling (as the car radio spread) and at work (*Music While you Work* and *Workers Playtime* were wartime innovations of lasting significance). That is, in spite of Reith's lofty and remote ideals, in spite of its often stilted manner and its distance from the many close, local communities which made up the complex national coalition of the

1930s and 1940s, its continuous, companionable presence in the home made its voice the always audible ground-bass of national culture. Plenty of other activities might call out stronger commitments – sport, cinema, dancing, pubs – but none were as mildly continuous and settled as the BBC.

This political base turned out to shape the reception and development of television. Both BBC channels assumed the same responsible gravity towards the world as had the radio, even while their much cultivated 'middle ground' was breaking up (as Kumar told us it was in chapter 4). When in 1954 commercial television was given Parliamentary permission to proceed in the face of virulent resistance in the House of Lords from Reith, then the Charter and composition of the Independent (i.e. commercial) Broadcasting Authority was on lines very similar to the BBC. The IBA also had its duties towards balance and impartiality as well as education services to be provided by the companies it licensed.

The differences between this conception of public service broadcasting which held in Britain and her one-time dominions such as Australia and Canada, those countries such as France and of course the Soviet bloc where broadcasting was formally delivered by the State, and the USA which had (in 1987) 1290 TV stations,[18] all make life very difficult for the dutiful political economist.

From the start of national broadcasting in the USA, the makers of the equipment easily repelled Federal control in a political climate always hostile to any such pressure. The source of money for programme production came from advertising and the electronic equipment industry. The Federal Communications Commission set up in 1937 regulated market competition and struggled in an always open and embattled situation to issue regulations about impartiality, balance and the rest. A separation arose which compounded these difficulties, between *stations* who make what they can afford and broadcast what they can get of their own and other people's, and *networks* (of which CBS and NBC are the best known) who are far richer and more powerful and who distribute nationally whatever it suits them to take from the stations or overseas purchases. It's fairly easy to buy a station or to set up new ones, as witness various of the evangelical TV churches of the Bible belt. But the real giants are the networks, immune to Federal influence. Public service broadcasting in the USA is, so Williams puts it, 'poor relation of the commercial networks'.[19]

American TV broadcasting remains opaque and appalling to most visitors. Unlike the BBC and its sisters in Australia and Canada, the

American stations have little attraction either to the traditional or avant-garde elites. Serious writers or producers or members of the intelligentsia are unlikely to turn to TV as their prime source of income. Writers will still go to Hollywood first, and political intellectuals to the daily newspapers and the weeklies. But the formation of American broadcasting has an importance going far beyond the quality of programmes in the USA, dismal as so many of these are and interrupted by commercials at least every ten minutes of the 24-hour broadcasting day. For it is the US communications industry which set the pattern for the world industry which it dominated until the Japanese rudely disturbed it in the hardware sector during the 1970s.

The dominance was effected in the first place by the close links of what President Eisenhower (improbably) named 'the military-industrial complex' with the communications industry. After the Second World War, the allocation of frequencies was, remarkably enough, in military hands. RCA, the giant Radio Corporation of America, was not only premier competitor in domestic electronics and owner of NBC the second biggest network, but was also very heavily funded for military research.[20] The Defense Department itself has a worldwide network of over 40 television stations and an uncertain number of radio stations (Schiller says 200, Milman 320). The box-office movie *Good Morning Vietnam* of 1987 gives a bitterly hilarious version of what such stations were for at the height of the war in Vietnam. Beyond this vast military system, however, the broadcasting corporations also have stations of their own and subsidiaries all over the Far East and their own southern subcontinent. And notoriously they dump over the globe the used-up movies and soap operas of three decades at cut prices, so that you can see *Dallas* in Bali, *Kojak* in Finland, and *Sergeant Bilko* in Chile any week of the year.

What is at stake is not just a matter of junked programmes. It is what the marketing agencies call vertical selling, meaning the delivery of a broadcasting kit, especially to new or poor nations setting up their first state systems, comprising delivery systems (broadcasting stations and their network), content (old TV programmes and movies), and reception systems (TV sets). This outfit comes along with its powerful commercial aura, protesting its independence from state or political affiliation and armed with a battery of advertising materials all ready for adjustment to local languages and conditions. Williams writes of this as a planned operation from the USA:

The 'commercial' character of television has then to be seen at several levels: as the making of programmes for profit in a known market; as a channel for advertising; and as a cultural and political form directly shaped by and dependent on the norms of a capitalist society, selling both consumer goods and a 'way of life' based on them, in an ethos that is at once locally generated, by domestic capitalist interests and authorities, and internationally organised, as a political project, by the dominant capitalist power. (p. 41)

Public service ideals have little chance in the face of these smiling forces. But in any case, the political economy of world mass communications is now undergoing further convulsions which will alter it out of recognition and beyond our present powers of prediction. All we can do is map the changes with the intellectual instruments to hand and keep our nerve.

VI

The convulsions of our political economy and the historical ecology in which it lives are presently leading to acute hysteria. These hysterics are not those of terror but of delirious over-optimism, especially on the part of the relevant governments. They speak wildly of 'the knowledge explosion' and the information society. The makers of the relevant technology and plant encourage them to envision a future of endless consumer choice whose type is Manhattan TV for domestic life, and the computerized world stock exchanges for the business end of things. A mixture of cable TV, direct broadcasting by satellite, and indigenous public and commercial services, all vigorously but happily co-existing on behalf of freely choosing consumers fills the fantasy screen of the network corporations.

At the same time, the unexpected revival of the book industry, a generation after Marshall McLuhan announced its demise with such premature confidence, has sent the communication corporations off to buy publishing houses in the rush of such takeovers of 1985–8. (Consumer expenditure on books in Britain has gone up fourfold since 1974.)[21] The Pearson Longman conglomerate which owns Penguin and Longmans group also owns the *Financial Times* and put big financial backing into the short-lived success story of British film-making, Goldcrest Films. That is only one handy instance of a firm trying to spread its productive base as widely as possible across its cultural repertory. It is a process visible in the many big marketing enterprises which tie together the book, the TV series, the serialization in the Sundays or weeklies, the prizes and launches, the translations and the T-shirts.

All such activities lead naturally to the centralization of capital and increase in monopolies. The caliphs of power at the centre of the gigantic international corporations have some of the ugliest faces in capitalism,[22] and as our model of a political economy requires, they are in active partnership with their resident governments. They want to win the day for the technological horse that they are backing in a murderously uncertain race. Most governments believe that the global victors of the mass communication race will bring vast booty home and make their host nations rich like El Dorado. They may be horribly wrong, and whatever happens the cultural consequences will be horrible.

If we return to Britain as our example of broadcasting development in a political economy still acutely nervous about its prospects in competition with Germany, Japan, the USA, we find that over the period 1945–87 the country found by accident a happy fit between its production capacity and its audiences.[23] It could not pick up too much broadcasting space in the electromagnetic spectrum because other European countries were so close, and given this limit there had to be state regulation of the channels. A happy match was made between the money for making programmes and the size of the national audience. Four channels turned out to be just fine. Even if by 1987 Channel 4 rarely pulled in more than 10% of its big brother's audience, it none the less filled its schedules against the odds and with remarkable stuff. Similarly, France and West Germany had the populations and the resources to match distribution to programme. The smaller European countries like Denmark or Holland had much more trouble, since licence fees did not bring in enough money from a small population, and they had to plug into such neighbouring broadcasts as they could afford and were in a language their people understood.

The new distribution technologies upset the relative peacefulness of the rich old European and, come to that, Antipodean countries. Cable TV works by simply passing a signal down a cable in the ground from a transmitter to a receiver. The coaxial cable made it possible to send a larger number of messages along a bundle of cables. The optic fibre system is even more capacious. This system is known as part of the terrestrial or earth-based service, to distinguish it from international satellite delivery or direct broadcasting by satellite (DBS) by which a signal is beamed to a satellite, and bounced off the heavens to be picked up by individual receptor dishes in people's back gardens, presently and vaguely priced between £400 and £700 sterling and $2,000 in the USA. Lastly and more familiarly, new distribution technology includes the portable video readily available for rent; though a bit slower in increase than predicted after the first rush of 1982–3, *Social Trends* reported in 1988 that just over 37 per cent of all British households have a video.

The demand of these new systems for programmes to show cannot be met in any one country. In Britain until now an active protection has worked against imported television: 86 per cent of broadcasting space is reserved for home-made products on both BBC and IBA channels. But of course it will be much cheaper for companies after the new deregulation of the airwaves to buy old programmes from abroad. An hour of old US programme costs a mere 2,000 quid; an hour of newly produced drama is ten times as much.[24]

There are always the contradictions, both structural and historical. Cable and DBS are in violent but unresolved competition. They can't both win. Cable is very expensive to install in cities: you have to dig up the pavements, so manufacturers are still trying to persuade the government to pay for this part, after which householders will buy the channels they want (as in Pay-TV in the US). Obviously the cable companies will only provide programmes where populations are densest, and this will leave at least half of most countries unsupplied. So far in Britain, people haven't bothered much to use Pay-TV where it is available. Of 300,000 homes that could do so less than 20,000 do. In the USA, unreliable figures suggest that only 17 per cent of all households subscribe to cable Pay-TV, and that the homes accepting twenty channels or more only use eight of them in any case. As for buying satellite dishes for the garage roof, that looks even chancier.

Trying to do the sums for the distribution companies is a dangerous pastime. The company sells audiences in units of 1,000 to the advertisers. The bigger the audience, the larger the fee paid for the space. They have to calculate where the costs of pushing out to an extra 1,000 people exceed what they can charge to the advertiser. Digging up the pavements is far too much. The logic of accumulation is centripetal: capital is driven inwards into fewer and fewer hands. To meet the competition of the distributing media, the mutually carnivorous corporations gobble each other up in an effort to dominate as wide an arc of the production and distribution circle as possible.

This tendency, as I said, is fully established in the USA, where (for a passing example) the CBS network is entirely owned by one man, NBC is owned by General Electric (with their vast nuclear and electronic holdings as well as their defence contracts), and ABC by the media conglomerate, Capital Cities. In Europe and the Antipodes, only four dread horsemen are running at the start of the 1990s in this apocalypse. The joyful loosening of Government controls (recommended in Britain by the *Hunt Report* of 1983) in Britain, France, Italy, West Germany, the countries big in communication systems which will dominate the small, has allowed four men – Rupert Murdoch, Robert Maxwell, Leo Kirch and Silvio Berlusconi – to buy up and buy out huge segments of the cultural industries in an effort to commend 'verticality' in production and distribution.

This domination is, in detail, too transitory to document here. We may note that Maxwell's total turnover in 1989 was 5 billion dollars, but Murdoch's empire is much more fully integrated and potentially dominant. He owns 90 per cent of the new continental satellite station, Sky Channel, which dumps a raw staple diet of rock, chat and cheap American serial across Europe, plans a 24-hour news programme compiled by the journalists of his own London *Times* and *Sunday Times* (newspapers whose staffs have both shown ostentatious awareness of their owner's political opinions), and has already bought up 20th Century-Fox's huge film stock for recycling through Sky Movies. Berlusconi rode roughshod over Italian television regulations to crush public sector opposition by the simple technical expedient of starting dozens of wholly local TV stations but making them effectually a national network by simply synchronizing their (identical) output. His choicest move, in a savoury mixture of soap, sexy game shows, mail order shopping by television, and dreadful Latin American gaucho movies, has been to allow local station managers to hire very cheaply Italian housewives short of spare cash as impromptu strippers on local nightclub shows.

These giant ventures are, as always in capitalism, gratifyingly risky. Sky Channel lost millions in Germany (and pulled out of the country in 1988) and Fox Five Channel in the USA had lost $130 million in the two years of its life up to the end of 1988. At times, these four princes are tearing at each other's throats; at other times, as in the new (1989) European Production Consortium, they grandly collaborate. Happily, they are none of them immune to mortality, either in the terms of the market, or in a grimly reassuring reality. But the general point stands: world broadcasting is more than ever before passing out of the hands of peoples and their governments, and into the hands of a quite new kind of tyrant, the Satanic Majesty of media, and alongside the star which he creates, the most potent character in this whole narrative.

In all this babel, governments are largely committed to the view with which we began this chapter, that the system will expand limitlessly, and that the new technology will accelerate, in the jargon, from the first through to the fifth generation, each new wave of equipment making obsolete the old, bringing in new resources and bringing down its own units costs in the classic pattern of capitalism followed by all consumer goods. Governments, caught up in the hysteria, want to press forward with these developments in ways which will benefit *them*.

They are unlikely to succeed. These huge tendencies are *multinational* in significance. Economic benefit, if it comes, will bypass national economies. The delirious commitment of official policy to unregulated competition destroys, in the first place, the ethos of public service broadcasting which many nations have admired, and requires for its success drastic increases in TV watching. Existing cable systems in the USA require 10 to 15 viewer hours per day if the subscription is to match the cost-benefit of broadcast television.[25] Not only is the increase of television watching which the new systems demand a disgusting idea in itself, the good old contradiction we noted that cultural leisure time is *ours* and allocated to suit ourselves is likely to obstruct the creation of an even more assiduous society of viewers than we have already.

If the expansion goes ahead and if it is successful, the result will be to disperse audiences and take resources away from broadcast television, to remove its protection and reduce its revenue, to break up its institutions, and to damage beyond repair the British, French, German, Canadian and Australian production systems – not to go geographically any further at the moment. That is to say, the consequences will be dire both economically and culturally. A thriving industry would go steeply downhill. An area of culture capable of fine work would founder. The conclusions of political economy lead, as they ought, to judgements about the polity which would allow such a thing to happen. The lessons are political as well. Public service broadcasting belongs to the public:[26] the public is the historical agent which should do all it can to retrieve its own best property for itself.

Notes

1   As Edwin Muir points out in a noble poem, 'The Good Man in Hell', *Collected Poems* (Faber and Faber, 1955).
2   Hans Magnus Enzensberger, 'The consciousness industry: constitutents of a theory of media', *New Left Review* 64 (November-December, 1970).
3   I develop the history of these divisions of labour in my *The Management of Ignorance: a Political Theory of the Curriculum* (Basil Blackwell, 1985).
4   I take much in what follows from two indispensable papers by Nicholas Garnham, doyen of this whole field. I begin initially with his 'Concepts of culture, public policy and the cultural industries', a discussion paper written for one of the GLC open forums, held at Riverside Studios, Hammersmith in December 1983. The second is his 'Contribution to a political economy of mass communication', published in the opening number of the journal edited by him and his colleagues in the media studies department of the Polytechnic of Central London, *Media, Culture and Society*. This journal is seminal to the political economy of media and all students of the subject should use it regularly. In 1986, the journal published a selection of contributions, *Media, Culture and Society: a Critical Reader*, edited by Richard Collins, James Curran, Nicholas Garnham and others for Sage Publications. Garnham's 'Contribution' appears there also.
5   See Raymond Williams, *Communications*, rev. edn (Penguin, 1979), for this argument.
6   Theodor Adorno and Max Horkheimer, *The Dialectic of the Enlightenment* (New Left Books, 1973). The chapter on the culture industry is abridged and reprinted in *Mass Communication and Society*, ed, James Curran et al. (Edward Arnold and the Open University Press, 1977).
7   I have tried to show how this happens to sport and leisure in my *Popular Culture and Political Power* (Harvester Wheatsheaf, 1988).
8   As Garnham (1983) points out, p. 2 (see n. 4 above).
9   Karl Marx, *Capital*, vol. I (Penguin, Marx library edition, 1976), p. 976.
10 See *National Income and Expenditure in Great Britain* (annually) (HMSO, 1985).
11 Garnham (1983), p. 8, (see n. 4 above).
12 *National Income and Expenditure in Great Britain* (annually) (HMSO, 1985); table, 'Total advertising expenditure as % of GNP'.
13 All histories of the BBC start from Asa Briggs's 4-volume classic, *The History of Broadcasting in the United Kingdom* (Oxford University Press, 1961–79). See especially vol. II, *The Golden Age of Wireless* (1965).

14 Raymond Williams, *Television: Technology and Cultural Form* (Fontana Collins, 1974), p. 26.

15 See Briggs, vols I and II (n. 13 above).

16 Details and wording together with a list of the Governors are given in *Whitaker's Almanack* (annually).

17 I owe much in what follows to Krishan Kumar's paper, 'Public service broadcasting and its public', in *The Future of Public Service Broadcasting* ed. Colin McCabe and Olivia Stewart (Manchester University Press, 1986).

18 See Table 5, chapter 3.

19 Raymond Williams, *Television: Technology and Cultural Form*, (Fontana Collins, 1974) p. 37. See also Herbert Schiller, *Mass Communications and American Empire* (Kelley, 1970) especially for military detail.

20 See Seymour Milman, *Pentagon Capitalism* (McGraw-Hill, 1970).

21 Figure given in *Publishers Association Newsheet* (January 1987).

22 See James Curran, 'Capitalism and control of the press 1800–1975', in *Mass Communication and Society*, ed. James Curran et al., (Edward Arnold and the Open University Press, 1977).

23 In this last section I rely heavily on Richard Collins's paper, 'Broadband black death cuts queues', first in *Media, Culture and Society,* reprinted in its *Critical Reader,* (Sage Publications, 1986).

24 Figures quoted from UK Government White Paper, *The Development of Cable Systems and Services* (HMSO Command 8866, 1983).

25 Collins in *Media, Culture and Society* (1986), p. 301 (see n. 23 above).

26 See Kumar (1986) in n. 17 above.

7

The Problem of Audience

The public is defined by conventional media theory as audience, and an audience only listens. In the condition of 'mobile privatization' by which Raymond Williams characterized the lives of most of us, listening and watching alone or at home is the sum of our political liberty. We can shout at the television, no doubt, or throw the newspaper across the room, but audience or spectator, solitary members of a huge crowd, are our principal public roles. By and large, media theory studies us like this. In the terms of chapter 3, we consume what we read, watch or hear.

The metaphor has deadly power. It not only carries the categoric weight of the discipline of economics, it is also one of the diminishing number of categories in which an always reductionist public policy works. For the sake of its managerial criteria of bureaucratic forms of organization, cost-effectiveness, efficiency and the rest, public policy must treat its units in as limited and distinct a set of roles as possible. To policy-makers we are consumers, voters, producers or unemployed, taxpayers, clients, crowds, and not much else. We are very rarely citizens, users, actors, participants, democrats. To cast a society as consumers is to see its members as creatures to be fed, housed and kept quiet. It is to set up the politics of bribery, whereby the consumer-as-voter is bribed with extra-fat helpings of consumer goods often enough to ensure the docile stability of his and her vote. It is to make contempt and arrogance the natural feelings of the powerful.

These feelings transpire strongly when a society expresses its anxieties in public about what its consumers are consuming. We saw both liberal and Marxist camps in the 1930s as being equally ready to condemn from their different positions the gullible consumer public, so stupefied by urban life, dreary work, or the reduction by capitalism of everything to an object for buying or selling, that it lived 'at the novelist's expense' a sentimental and brutal fantasy miles away from serious and responsible living. The case was made in the same terms against movies and pulp fiction. It has been made since, and in very strong language, about television.

Of course, the world has been going to the dogs for donkeys' years. In the running battle of the books between Ancients and Moderns – running now for at least 2,000 years – it has always been claimed by those fighting for the Ancients that all this Modern stuff is bad for you (though not for *me*, whose general cultivation and power of intelligent discrimination render me immune to any corrupting influence). It is particularly bad for one's subordinates, womenfolk, servants, children, those sorts of people. The Modernists, on the other hand, have not only protested (as according to Freud's classical protocol they must) against the stifling oppression of the fathers; they have also declared that the new truths of the new books ensured unthought-of liberation for the soul of humanity. The young generation stood at the gateway of a growing emancipation brought about by the form and content of the forbidden books now in their hands, and the forbidden thoughts their brave young fellows had dared to think.

The story is satirized by the classical Roman playwrights. It came to life when the stiff and sanctimonious Puritans of Britain's seventeenth-century Commonwealth closed the London theatres, because plays were bad for people. They were fictions in the first place, and therefore lies, and they displayed corrupt and lascivious goings-on for everyone to admire.

In the middle of the eighteenth century, Jonathan Swift told *The Tale of a Tub* in a way to disconcert both sides of the Ancient versus Modern fight. At the same time the rise of the novel was causing the pursy new bourgeoisie of the eighteenth-century Tory settlement to wag their heads over what their womenfolk were now reading. In *The School for Scandal*, Sheridan's play, Lady Teazle has to conceal that scandalous novel *Peregrine Pickle* which her preposterous husband has given her the gossipy leisure, the large, bright, well-lit rooms, as well as the plentiful housekeeping money to peruse and to hide behind the cushions.

Even before his sympathies for the French Revolution had petered out, and when, indeed, he was making the boldest declaration ever written on behalf of a plain, accessible, commonly human and invigorating literature, Wordsworth pitted his manifesto against the temper of the times, in which

> ... a multitude of causes unknown to former times are now acting with a combined force to blunt the discriminating powers of the

mind, and unfitting it for all voluntary exertion to reduce it to a state
of almost savage torpor ... to this tendency of life and manners the
literature and theatrical exhibitions of the country have conformed
themselves.[1]

And in a long jump to a more recent past, the notorious prosecuting
counsel in the *Chatterley* case of 1960, when Penguin Books were
prosecuted by the Crown for publishing D. H. Lawrence's novel,
made himself spontaneously into a folk-villain by asking defendants
in court whether they would leave the offending novel lying about
for the servants to read.[2]

By 1960, however, novels had long since come to respectability,
particularly in academic and educational circles. The novel had, that
is, been absorbed into the cultural discourse which forms itself
inevitably around all intellectual innovation. Presumably when really
new forms of thought and expression appear in a society there is
a general jolt among its audience, and then the audience variously
responds, with a strong generational bias, by rejection or acceptance. As it does so, it alters the reach and the vocabulary of the
conversation of culture. That conversation either accepts the newcomer, changing it to suit itself, or sees it off at the door, in which
case subsequent generations rarely hear of it. If the culture accepts
it, it seeks also to tame it. The new form or the new thought is put
through the educational mixer-and-processor until it fits the received
educational discourse.

In class society, the sequences of acceptance are strongly competitive. Different groups come forward loudly claiming to know what
is good for others to consume. Where status goes with educational
qualification, as it so visibly does in the industrial nations and their
mass societies, the struggle is one for cultural authority and power.
The argument about who shall consume what, about the imaginative
menu which is good or bad for people, is contested between different sections of the cultural bureaucracy: teachers, critics, editors,
programme makers and planners, respected columnists, librarians,
heads of cultural foundations, professors, film-makers, performers
and assortedly nondescript experts.

At a time when there is so much nervousness about our moral
vocabulary, the argument about the content of culture, especially
with regard to moral change and content, focuses on *effects*. It is
hard to fix this broad tendency in its properly historical context, or
indeed to be sure of what is meant by the word 'effects'. Perhaps we
can say, a bit loosely, that as the liberal politics of the nineteenth
century gradually got established, it put at the centre of its world-

picture its distinctive version of the individual. I set this belief out in chapter 2. The ideal individual constructed by liberalism is a very specific person: rational (but with deep feelings), self-aware, morally autonomous, non-dogmatic, hard-working, sincere, honest. Such a figure is hero and heroine of all the great nineteenth-century novels. He and she are also inscribed in other key discourses of the century, especially those invented, according to Foucault, to consolidate the 'carceral' or imprisoning State. The law is one such discourse, and the legal system also puts at its centre this ideal individual.

Alongside the official discourse of the law go its subordinate and regulatory discourses: criminology, psychiatry, social psychology. For our law is organized around the absolute value of individual moral responsibility. If criminals perform crimes for which they are proved fully responsible, they are guilty. But the doctrines of individualism make such responsibility very demanding. Plenty of people are clearly *not* responsible according to such stringent demands. To explain such falling away from high standards of responsibility, and to devise ways of rehabilitating criminals so that they would assume fuller individual responsibility, the assorted disciplines of psychic management arose and described what it was that made people lapse from their duties.

Such are the beginnings of theories of effects. Naturally they cannot be strictly confined to the requirements of the newly codified legal doctrines of the State. But this is a neat and useful way of understanding how the theory of effects came to figure so prominently in political argument. The legal system, as one would expect, created a new version of criminality and therefore a new kind of criminal. This figure came to be called deviant or delinquent, terms which do no more than put a circle round the offender and label it, 'not like us', abnormal.

The regulation of normality may be seen developing right across the dominant institutions of industrial society, and we are all heirs to it today. The techniques of so-called time-and-motion study by which workers were studied at work in mass production were directed towards controlling and economizing every move so that no time was wasted and more commodities were produced. The people who broke that rhythm were penalized, until enough of them came together in unions and refused to do as they were told. Then a compromise was reached – new pay levels, or a 10-hour day – and production went on. At every point, the system measured itself for the effects of what it was doing and in order to make itself more efficient.

Similarly, in schools a system of knowledge distribution was instigated in which, as Charles Dickens once said, the children were arranged in rows like little pitchers waiting to have their dose of facts poured into their heads. Then once again, supervisors checked on the effects of the dose by examining them. Out of the Victorian list of 'standards' which all children had to reach, year by year, came the giant international examinations industry of today, grading, qualifying and rejecting every child in the first, second and, mostly, third worlds.

The measurement of effects transpires from our old friend the Enlightenment, but on its darker side. The great German thinker, Max Weber, predicted that all modern societies would become locked in the 'iron cage' of their own rationality, of which one typical and remorseless feature would be this self-examination and self-quantification.

It was natural, therefore, once the mass media became officially recognized as somehow problematic to society, that they too would become not only a topic of critical and scientific inquiry, but an institution whose effects must be measured and monitored to see what they were doing to the social order.

II

So far, I have told the story of the measurement and explanation of effects from one end only. I have spoken as though its exercise were invariably an instrument of oppression, as though the self-examination of our society must of its nature be directed towards more discipline, greater productivity, severer routines. This is Foucault's grim tale, and Marx before him had characterized the separation of a man from his work and a person from full citizenship as alienation, in German *Verfremdung* or 'estrangement'.

But liberalism has proved itself, in its good times, capable of taking its best values seriously. Its democratic gains have been real. So when its advocates have fought for a more open school curriculum and a less repressive legal and prison system, their efforts have often led to great gains in freedom. By the same token, the measurement of effects is not always to see how better to control people; it may be to discover inaccuracy and reject it or to identify nodes of resistance in people in order to cheer them on and up. The link in meaning between liberal and libertarian is very important. It lights up the main line of my argument in this chapter. In other words, effects and audiences appear in the version of media theory offered here as the occasion for variety, unpredictability and the dissolution of masses into many minorities. Above all, audiences and the effects they register are not formal units in a formal theory, but practical subjects making active use of the cultural expressions they find to hand.

This affirmation of activity or, in technical language, agency on the part of audiences is not always well received and, of course, not always justified. The cartoon picture of the teenage TV-addict slumped in front of the set, which is much put about by corpulent Joe the couch potato with a six-pack of beer slumped in front of *his* set, has got real truth in it. The picture many parents carry with them of their once adorable small children becoming grunting, inarticulate 16-year-olds plugged into the Walkman every waking hour and at the same time hopping the TV-channels with an attention-span of a few seconds has its dreadful reality also. 'Addiction', as we shall see, is not an unhelpful metaphor with which to understand sons or fathers slumped on the sofa with a pile of video movies and a take-out curry.

Effects are not easy to find. It is not surprising that the best summary of their elusiveness is made in the British Government's *Report of the Committee on Obscenity and Film Censorship*,[3] because on a subject of so much heated opinionation and frenzied arm-waving, it could only be a government committee with its recognized impartiality that could stop the fight. As I remarked early in this chapter, the senior generation is always trying to sit on the junior one and to say what's best for it. One section of the bourgeoisie is always trying to push in front of another one and decide what's best for the world. And all such people believe themselves to be both right and righteous, as I do. Any teacher with guts wants to tell the students what it is good to study. Any parent who is not a monster will want his and her children to be safe, and good, and happy. So there must be political argument and public debate about who is right and what is good. Government hearings and reports provide some of the best examples of such occasions, and good ones, like the Williams committee in hand, pass down good judgements.

The committee begins by distinguishing between the classically liberal view that 'no conduct should be suppressed by law unless it can be shown to harm someone' (para. 5.1), which it names 'the harm-condition', and a wider definition of the law's moral function expressed by some judges, as being to express and affirm common morality whether or not the 'harm condition' is at stake. In

Britain certain Law Lords, and in the USA some members of the Supreme Court, have expressed the view that the Courts should enforce due morality irrespective of the freedoms involved.

The committee observes, not without irony:

> Of course, there are many people who would prefer, or believe that they would prefer, a society less pluralistic than modern capitalist societies, and embodying a stronger moral consensus and a higher level of moral conviction. This yearning for a morally more homogeneous society takes many different forms, belonging, in political terms, both to the Right and to the Left. Some seek the recovery of a consensus which they believe once existed, others look to a new society yet to emerge. (para 5.10)

There are innumerable such voices raised (from Left and Right) about the present effects of mass media. The Report goes on, with redoubtable wisdom, to weigh the claims of freedom of speech as the freedom to say absolutely anything in a babel of ideas good and bad, against the unmistakable nastiness and brutality of some ideas and, indeed, some mass media expressions. Its conclusions are subtle and convincing, and speak up for a scrupulous pluralism. The scruples turn centrally on the question of harms.

The Williams committee is strongly aware of the high prestige of academic social science, and we have glimpsed already the historical career of social psychology as the expert discipline for the measurement and control of behaviour in industrial society. The social psychologists are to be expected as first expert witnesses on the question of whether dirty books and movies are bad for you.

One thing at least social psychology will be stern about is fidelity to the facts. The bravura chairwoman of the National Viewers' and Listeners' Association (UK) attacked Stanley Kubrick's undoubtedly very violent film *A Clockwork Orange* principally because a 16-year-old who had been fascinated by the story had brutally killed a vagrant. The boy had not, it turned out, seen the film. (In any case, he should have been legally excluded from it as under age.)

There are many such tales of alleged causes bringing about direct effects. These may surface in *Clockwork Orange* anecdotes, or they may even have some experimental basis. In a now comically notorious series of psychological experiments in the USA a group of small children were shown violent extracts from a film, and then studied in the company of the Bobo doll, a lifesize inflatable toy with a semi-circular, loaded base to bring it upright whenever it was knocked about. Some kids beat up the doll. More kids beat it up if they watched an adult do so first. Conclusion: children are apt to imitate aggression when encouraged. Incredible.

The obvious difficulty for experimentalists is that they can't replicate real violence in the laboratory. The psychologist has little recourse but to observe actual behaviour or to question the participants. If his observation is in terms of statistics, he has to show in this argument that, say, sexual violence or obscene behaviour has significantly increased given a simultaneous increase of some sort in sexual licence. Some researchers claimed to the Williams committee that pornographic opportunity in Denmark and in Britain correlated with increases in rape. (A statistical correlation is a coefficient measuring agreement in form between two sets of figures, notionally testable for its 'significance', or non-accidental connection.) But there turned out to be no usable measure with which to identify increase in pornographic materials, and no rise in rapes which was not paralleled by a rise in non-sexual crime (indeed sexual crimes remained a low and dropping proportion of all crime). So, no provable effects there.

In sum, although no doubt there *are* effects of the mass media, it is almost impossible to isolate them, and say that direct media exposure of a given type (violence) is the prime cause, to the exclusion of others, of this effect (comparable violence). This is the so-called stimulus-response (or S–R) model, and it is useless. Nor is direct questioning of individuals much help (so beware of the interview schedule, however structured). Confessionality is only one hazard. (Who would want to listen to that Great Bore of the Day, the sex-maniac?) Simple-minded answers are another. For not only does it seem so improbable that seeing *Rambo* 17 times would be what made the wretched Houston or Hungerford killers run amok with their gun collection, the relations of fantasy to action are far too various for such causes ever to be determinate. Some psychiatrists even speculate that narrative-aided fantasy, whether sexually violent or anything else, may discharge the tensions which might otherwise have gone into action.

The Williams committee's business was strictly with the legislation of censorship. In pinning down this aspect of effects-claims, its interest was only in seeing whether such claims were valid enough for legislation to be even relevant, let alone whether it would be just. In trying to sort them out, however, it made the unexceptionable point that different media have different impacts, and that in the often intemperate discussion about such urgent matters as sex-and-violence, the duo which is nearly always at the heart of the censorship argument, this obvious truth gets overlooked. I propose in chapter 8 an account of what happens when we do our imagining from words on the page as opposed to imagining from images on the screen. The Williams committee was indeed affected, as well it might have been, by a screening of the uncut version of the Italian director Pasolini's film, *The 120 Days of Sodom*.

Pasolini was no doubt one of the great geniuses of cinema. He was an indomitable Italian Communist, and assassinated by underground Christian right-wingers. The film takes title and plot from an infamous novel by the Marquis de Sade expounding the creed of vicious, pleasurable cruelty to which he gave his name. Pasolini transports the novel to one of the last corners of the Fascist State in Italy which survived surrender in 1943. In vivid and appalling detail, he recreates the story as the inevitable outcome of Fascism's innate logic. The scenes are pitilessly dreadful. What effect do they have? Any normal person, we say, would be horrified (but gripped). There is undoubted fascination in the film, even though one shuts one's eyes. Some people might certainly be excited by it.

In a sane and dignified paragraph, the Williams committee made the essential points, both about different effects from different media, and about the exceptional place film must take in this discussion.

> ... we should make the point that the violence we have seen on film (from films refused a certificate, or cut before the film could be certified) far exceeds in nastiness anything likely to be seen on television. It is not simply the extremity of the violence which concerns us: we found it extremely disturbing that highly explicit depictions of mutilation, savagery, menace and humiliation should be presented for the entertainment of an audience in a way that appeared to emphasize the pleasures of sadism. Indeed, some of the film sequences we saw seemed to have no purpose or justification other than to reinforce or sell the idea that it can be highly pleasurable to inflict injury, pain or humiliation (often in a sexual context) on others. Film, in our view, is a uniquely powerful instrument: the close-up, fast cutting, the sophistication of modern make-up and special effects techniques, the heightening effect of sound effects and music, all combine on the large screen to produce an impact which no other medium can create. It *may* be that this very graphically presented sadistic material serves only as a vivid object of fantasy, and does no harm at all. There is certainly no conclusive evidence to the contrary. But there is no conclusive evidence in favour of that belief, either, and in this connection it seems entirely sensible to be cautious. (para. 12.10)

Pasolini's film, of course, is not of the kind 'having no purpose other than to reinforce or sell the idea that it can be highly pleasurable to inflict injury, pain or humiliation (often in a sexual context) on others'. It certainly shows that this is true, and it *intends* to show that a certain sort of Fascist has such pleasures, and that they *are* pleasures. Whether all the audience would see the film as intended is very doubtful. Film is just too powerful.

III

Faced with the incalculability of direct media effects, the social psychologists and their effects assistants withdrew with a few commonplace but no doubt useful generalizations. As with so much media theory, the *what* of what is going on is pretty obvious; it is the *how* it is going on which is so unpredictable, and a source of such reassurance to those who fear the effects of the mass media as being bad for everyone else except themselves. The hard but also thrilling part of inquiry into effects lies in uncovering the details and trying to see the common patterns in them. Pattern-seeing must be a consequence of knowing what you're looking for.

Usually this simple point is put by copying the laboratory language of the scientist. The scientist puts on a white coat and posits a hypothesis 'What if . . . ?' He then works out an experiment to test it, not so much to make it work as to try to falsify it. Falsification is the only route to certainty, the philosophers of science tell us.[4] The best you get apart from the clinching certainty of falsification, is probability, and in a statistical form.

Hypothesis-making, though generally used in fundamentalist social psychology, is too slow and one-track a procedure to use in following the quicksilver line of media effects into the crowd. Better to think of inquiry as literally that: inquiry means putting questions, and the right form of thought for dismantling what Stuart Hall calls[5] the encoding and decoding of media messages is 'question-and-answer logic'.[6] Unlike the laboratory scientist, the effects research can't treat people as things, and turn subjects into objects. People keep on moving and thinking for themselves. Worse still for the idea of human inquiry by laboratory rules, they pick up the ideas and theorems of the scientist, and use them for themselves. The so-called hypothesis can't then be kept clean and sterilized for the inquiry, because it has changed the behaviour under inspection (for example, in people's awareness of television cameras. They turn the presence of the cameras to their own purposes).

What the human scientist has then to do in following question-and-answer logic, is to try to think the thoughts of those she is studying. In history this is very difficult but, so the historians claim who do so, feasible. In contemporary research it is easier, although not simply a matter of asking other people (we are too apt to ask stupid questions instead of intelligent ones). The point is to try to recover the purposes and intentions of others, including, if we can, those of which they were not themselves conscious. As I have regularly underlined in these pages, the big *structures* of society play through our beings all the time, and our only chance of freeing ourselves from them is to catch them at work. Recovering the reasons and purposes of others is only possible in so far as the questions we ask about what they were up to are sharp and searching enough. Only then can we get beyond the vast, blank totals of the numbers in social surveys, such as the few provided at the end of chapter 3.

The correct response to those rather boring-looking generalities which are the best that effects research can do by way of their findings is to see what questions to put which would turn them back into explanations of everyday life. A generation ago, a grandee of the topic, Joseph Klapper, listed three kinds of change mass media may bring about as 'conversion', 'minor change' and 'reinforcement'.[7] This is not much help, going hardly beyond a little three-colour spectrum from blinding light (conversion) to familiar shade (reinforcement). But research at that time was – still is – much preoccupied by attitude formation and change. The list takes no account of unintended, often invisible changes, or of the obstruction of change (change often being an uncomfortable nuisance, anyway), of making ready for change (opening people's minds up a bit), or perhaps best of all, of simply *educating* people. New knowledge certainly changes us. Being better educated is a change. But it's hard to say *how* such a change takes place, and what exactly it looks like.

The sequence of communication is set out by Harold Lasswell in a five-part question.[8]

Who? says what? through what medium? to whom? with what effect?

The last part of the question is still pretty bald, but it is true that we can only answer it if we have taken some trouble with the first four stages. If we take enough trouble, we will already have a large part of the answer about effects.

In the empiricist classic we met in chapter 3, *The People's Choice*,[9] Lazarsfeld and his team tried to complicate the idiotically simple idea that people believe all the media tell them, by plotting the motions and emotions of opinion along the channels and mediations of personal influence. They say, not very profoundly, that 'ideas often flow from radio and print to the opinion leaders and from them to the less active sections of the population' (p. 151). This was nicknamed the 'two-step flow of information', and as a model it had the merit of pushing inquiry into the density and clamour of domestic and street life. Once this is done, it isn't hard (but it is illuminating) to devise diagrams of the lines of communication which will show what a very large number of different receivers, mechanical and human, messages go through. Along those lines, the most interesting and complicated changes and exchanges take place in our so-called 'primary groups' – family, close friends, equals and allies at work. And working groups matter more in the field of force set up by personal influence in jobs whose occupants depend very heavily on one another for safety or support: miners, heavy construction workers, oil rig personnel, soldiers in combat, foundrymen.

It's a relief to learn that, after all, human presence counts for more than the screen or the tabloid, especially in relation to the political choices and opinions pursued by the researchers. But the world has moved on hugely since *Personal Influence*,[10] the sequel to *The People's Choice*, was written, and small group research has moved with it. Opinion leaders still count for much, no doubt, whether in a neighbourhood, an institution or at work. But there have been transformations at the root of the relations of production, and where the roots have been loosened, the media influences swirl in.

An easy way to get a grip on the idea of relations of production is to use small group analysis to track the assimilation and rejection of media influence. Where a group is brought closely together by affection, mutual dependence, danger, poverty, tradition, its members' attitudes and values are shaped much more by one another than by the generalizing, abstract fantasies of newspaper, novel or soap opera. Typical examples include the closely knit neighbourhoods of immigrant America – Sicilians, Jews, Slavs – or the powerful solidarity of English working-class streets of the kind given mythic expression in the nearly 30-year-old series, *Coronation Street*. We might call its imaginary location, Hoggartsborough, after the great book mentioned in chapter 2 which so richly described the real history of such lives.

The real history and what Marx called its real foundations are shifting, however. It is a cliché of the tabloid press and the chat show that people's sense of community is waning, and that class solidarity is not what it was, neighbours nothing like as neighbourly as they used to be. Even though the tabloids say it's true, it seems to *be* true none the less. Class formation is nowadays much looser. The move from heavy manufacturing and extraction (steel, coal) to consumer and service capitalism means that men work much less in those close, sweated, dangerous and fraternal conditions. As automation, unemployment, increased mobility and the steep rise in women's service labour all become common experience, solidarity at work, familiarity, and long settlement in one home become less binding. 'Mobile privatization', in the phrase, gives much more space and time to mass media. We may say that the mass media fill up unoccupied space and time in each social identity. They therefore exert their strongest direct influence on the lonely, the ill, the elderly, the very young, the workless, the bored, the itinerant.

This makes them sound like predators upon the unprotected, which won't do. Those groups are wider open to television in particular because they don't have a lot of other company. And as all of us live more of our lives in the small rectangle of the nuclear family, the one-parent apartment, the retirement home, and less of our lives among troops of friends, in public places or crowded rooms or comradely labour, so we turn to and need the many narratives of public communication to keep us, as they say, in touch.

Thinking along these lines makes the relation between mass media and audience almost impossible to think about accurately in terms of effects. We should attend instead to modes of interpretation, which is to say, attending to the cognitive fit between messages and audiences. Cognition denotes the effort of mind whereby we connect what we see to what we already know and, however unsatisfactorily, understand it. The philosopher Kant coined the slogan, 'No percepts without concepts', by which he meant that we cannot know what we see until we have the beginnings of a conceptual scheme to tell us how to sort out the shapes. The tiny baby starts by recognizing the loved face of its mother or its protector, and everything follows from that. Cognition is, originally, the connecting current between percept and concept. As the baby becomes the child, it learns to think abstractly and without percepts, to move from concept to concept, to symbolize them, to think of new ones. This is cognition. It is active thought.

Life teaches each of us our cognitive style. This is the apparatus with which we do our thinking: in a more homely phrase, it is our way of seeing, which includes our frames of mind and beliefs, our scheme of rationality, our deep values and commitments. One major problem of researchers is to classify the many individual ways of seeing into a manageable number of entities. Cognitive styles are shaped by age and gender, class and education, tradition and culture, as well as by the obviously hard facts of life as they knock into different people. These commonplace truths return us to my earlier research ruling: we have to recover the thoughts of others and think them for ourselves if we are to understand audiences or, come to that, producers.

IV

Media researchers into audiences made an initially creditable effort to follow this rule when they started up the unhappily named 'uses and gratifications' studies. As Jay Blumler, one of its leading practitioners[11] says, 'this places the emphasis on members of the audience actively processing media materials in accordance with their own needs.' The trouble is that this designation contains a suppressed sneer: media, particularly television, are used by audiences to 'gratify needs'. 'Gratification' has an infantile ring to it, and 'needs' an over-urgent one. The line from gratify to need is as crudely straight as the line from stimulus to response. Behind these terms we can see the discredited models of psychological behaviourism, the view that all actions are built out of conditioned reflexes, reinforced by success and reward.

In spite of its genesis, however, such work can tell us plenty, so long as the list of possible uses and kinds of gratification is subtle and extensive enough. Denis McQuail[12] suggests a list of four headings, each with several subheadings (p. 174): information; personal identity; integration and social interaction; entertainment. Even if we set aside the pious jargon (personal identity, social interaction and all that), these are only beginnings and still stuck in the vocabulary of genteel therapy and social condescension. McQuail's subheadings variously and vaguely include 'finding out about the world' and 'gaining a sense of security through knowledge' (some knowledge makes me feel decidedly insecure), and such ineffable uses of media as 'identifying with valued others (in the media)' where what it would be like to 'identify with', say, the latest star to play James Bond or his shining, muscle-bound girlfriend is unclear to anybody not in a psychotic ward. So, too, with 'social empathy' and 'gaining a sense of belonging'. These no doubt desirable feelings may be brought about by watching *East Enders* or its competitor prog- rammes of a neighbourhood sort, but if so, such uses are hardly dis- tinguishable from seeking 'information' or 'entertainment', and in any case, better understood in the terms I suggested in chapter 2, as ways of situating oneself in a knowable community of countless others whom one cannot know directly.

It is not quite fair to kick to death quite so improvised as well as impoverished a list as transpires from much uses and gratifications research. What is needed is a speculative grid of frames of mind (or, in another phrase, cognitive sets) whose direct encounter with media messages is the focus of attention. Stuart Hall's paper,[13] considered more carefully in the next chapter, will give us a starting point. He suggests that 'decoding' media messages is, as I say, a function of the frame of mind or cognitive set the audience brings with it. Hall's interest is in encounters between programme and audience of a political kind, and he suggests (for audiences) three 'codes' (what I have called cognitive sets). These are: first, the 'dominant-hege- monic', which is to say the conventional wisdom of the day; the 'negotiated', which is to say much the same as the first but with a few local qualifications thrown in; and the 'opositional', which means what it says but at least allows for such vivid gratifications as shouting at the set.

Audience research has concentrated for a long time on the effects of mass media (supremely, television) on political beliefs and actions in a very down-the-line view of politics. Perhaps this is so because its practitioners are themselves of a class on the fringes of politics-with- a-capital-P (Parliament, Congress, and all that), and they tend to overestimate its importance in the lives of others. Certainly, Jay Blumler's work, amongst the best-known in the field, has been stingingly and comprehensively criticized for its limitations by Nicholas Garnham.[14]

The argument dramatizes the classic opposition between the empiricist and the theoretician. In my judgement, Garnham, cast as theoretician, wins hands down. Blumler contends[15] that many theo- retical, specifically Marxist versions of audience, simple-mindedly claim that political television just reinforces the status quo and further legitimates (or vindicates) the ruling ideology. To Blumler this is crass. His view of the viewer is, in Garnham's phrase, 'anti- party, pro-broadcaster', with a strongly positive valuation of the voter as someone rationally determined to sort out the political issues one by one, and make up his or her mind independently.

Blumler, commissioned to do exactly that, comes up with this bald policy recommendation: 'Broadcasters should act as trustees of the voters' campaign information needs' (p. 68).

For Garnham this decidedly theoretical view of things is just as simple-minded as the parody Blumler offers of the Marxists. It ignores the solidarity of class, the importance of working relationships, the strength of a commitment to a *party* and its values instead of discussing all election material issue by issue. Calling on Colin Seymour-Ure's[16] admirable study for help, Garnham shows that Blumler's model viewer is trapped at home, bamboozled by the purported but fraudulent impartiality of the broadcaster, and pushed without noticing it to be darkly suspicious of socialism and more and more likely to settle in the vote for a selfish life.

Blumler's preferential treatment of the broadcaster is as ideological as any other audience theory. By contrast, Garnham wants a vigorously partisan presentation *of itself* by each political party, and very much more chance for the party of the poorer classes to meet its enemy on equal terms and with enough money. Only with a policy of this explicitly combative nature, will television politics shake the viewer out of 'mobile privatization' into citizenship.

Garnham implies severe shortcomings in most audience research. Perhaps we shall do better, thinking again of Hall's two-sided analysis 'encoding–decoding', to remind ourselves of what is loosely referred to as the 'agenda-setting' propensity of media, but try to give this term a bit more substance. All it means is that the mass media set the cultural-political agenda for one another, and that this only changes within their terms of reference and cognitive set. If we think of this simply as a matter of daily news, on radio, TV, or newspaper, it's easy to follow. Certain events and topics are what *count* as news. If other things happen which don't fit the news-processor's categories, they are either transcribed until they do fit it, or they are ignored. Graham Murdock[17] reckons that news must be framed as *event*. The news-collecting and reporting agencies cannot report process, sequence, the uneven development of history which is life-in-earnest. They have to be able to frame all news as a succession of 'news-as-events', and have the images and commentary to match the events.

These habits – the cognitive nets we throw over life – are thick and heavy. Murdock also points out a less inquired-into tendency of mass media to set not so much an agenda for our public consideration, a phrase which at least implies rational debate, but rather the definition of a world. To say so is to hand back manipulative and dominating mastery to television and print with a vengeance. It is also to insist again on the power of the imagery of advertising, its publicity and glamour, to fix our ways of seeing.[18]

Of course this power and its imagery are not just the malevolent magic of a few advertising agencies; they are the deep drive of the entire political economy of capitalism to keep people consuming, buying, throwing away. The imagery creates a world in which the glamour of consumption shines from magic objects, whose possession will cause you and me to shine in the same way. But when we *do* possess those objects – they include people of course, chunky beefcake, succulent cheesecake – glamour has already removed itself to the next object out-of-reach. So we are kept envying, and envy causes us to buy.

This is the magic circle of an international psychosis. We may not be gripped by it all the time, but its pleasures are real and few people wholly escape it. The ubiquity of its images, their beauty and command, make it hard even to want to do so. Its effects are to fill the social imagination with the fantasies of perfect bodies, perfect health, deodorized experience, headache-less drinking, ageless automobiles, tireless tourism. The most pressing as well as the most absorbing kind of media research that I, for one, can think of would be a documentary venture into the long history Murdock[19] summarizes here:

> Another interesting example of advertising-induced withdrawal from class and controversy is provide by the history of American television drama. In the years immediately after the war, drama slots were dominated by anthologies of single plays, many of which dealt with working-class life. While these were popular with audiences and regularly attracted high ratings, they increasingly worried advertisers who saw plays with lower-class settings as damaging to the images of mobility and affluence they wanted to build up around their products. Accordingly, in 1955 they began to switch their sponsorship to the action-adventure series that were beginning to emerge from the old Hollywood studios. The business advantages were obvious. Drama moved outdoors into active, glamorous settings. Handsome heroes and heroines set the tone – and some proved willing to do commercials, and even appear at sales meetings and become company spokesmen. The series also had distinct advantage for the production companies. The fact that they contained the minimum of dialogue and the maximum of action made them ideal export material. They were intelligible anywhere that audiences were familiar with Hollywood westerns and thrillers. Where the American studios lead, everyone else has followed in varying degrees, and the international market is now central to the economies of commercial television. (p. 146)

These large tendencies hit us with effects in our deepest feelings and the ways of seeing which go with them. Indeed, they frame those feelings and give them structure. This, however, is a process surely invisible to empirical research. The best way to follow it is perhaps to introspect as carefully as we can, and then to listen to what people say about what they do.

It is obvious that introspection may be incisive and theoretic, or it may be just mushy. We must, to say it again, have good questions to put to our own experience. Let us begin by asking why we are frustrated when, as we often say, there's nothing to watch on television. When the evening looks blank, why has it become our natural recourse to get a video-film to watch? Why do the films we find have the forms they do? What, for instance, is so thrilling about thrillers? Asking these things, our first principle should be to discard the obvious answers, which in these realms of experience are generally a way of stopping further questions (hence the uselessness of so many questionnaires). If we answer that we watch a video because otherwise we'd be bored, we might remember what Walter Benjamin says in 'The storyteller' about the cognitive benefits of being bored. When we're bored in a certain spirit, our minds and feelings are just contentedly blank, perhaps recharging themselves, often open to new, even precious thoughts. The boredom of ambling along kicking leaves and stargazing is a restorative boredom.

But deadly boredom is another matter. Deadly boredom is presumably the condition in which a longing for action, mental or physical, is wholly thwarted by circumstances. There is nothing to do. The self, vibrant for action, has no social space in which to move. Such vacancy is more and more blankly available in our time. The ugly wastelands surround every inner city. At the same time, the culture of the rich nations teaches all its members that the good life is fulfilled by effective action. Its heroes and heroines are vigorous, physical, and successful doers. The tension between the ideal and the actual is too great. In point of fact, effective physical action and its excitements are very hard to find. Deadly boredom follows.

In the standardly modern condition, what do the active individuals do? He and she dissolve their identities into fantasy. Selfhood, desperate for action, is dissolved into the intensity of fantastic experience in order to make the impossible momentarily real. Presumably some comparable experience comes about with drug-taking: the hard-edged, specific self and its body dissolve into a realm where the body is left behind and fantasy is the real action. Such a description makes sense of the casual reference to some lad or other as 'addicted' to horror videos, or even addicted to Tolkien's *Lord of the Rings.* The addict dissolves into the fantasy, in such a way that a kind of oblivion ensues from which return to real life is groping, painful and reluctant.

We should not mistake this (highly speculative) argument. Everyone needs fantasy. With fantasies they test their lives against imaginative versions of how things might have gone differently. Psychotic fantasy, however, is circular; there is no way out of the story back into real life. The compulsive video-watcher is caught on this roundabout. A harmless version of the same process can occur, at least temporarily, with soap opera. Take the truly awful *Dallas–Dynasty* family of programmes, where the use to which they are put is much more than half the matter, since what the stories start with is so thin.

Not that it gets us far to say so. Partly they are thin to keep them cheap: a few rich interiors, a couple of vast automobiles with obsidian windows, a panning shot up a skyscraper, a swimming pool. But mostly their thinness – perhaps it may be better put by saying their spaciousness – provides the occasion for personal fantasy, rather than its substance. They are etherealized characters whose simple binary oppositions – family/non-family, men/women, sex-power/money-power – may be the vehicles for any fantastic perambulation. And their circle is closed: each opposition complements the other and resists the other. There is no synthesis, and therefore no exit (and therefore, as we've found, no end to the series).

This repetition is the form of the programme's psychosis; it is regular, but not regulable. In this, it expresses something very generally human, which may begin to explain the success of *Dallas* as export. The roots of psychosis are in all human beings; to play in the imagination with a literally endless circuit of quarrel and reconciliation, threat of power-loss (whether of sex or money) and of relief from the threat, all in the dress and with the beautiful bodies and faces of the advertisement-rich, is to return to the mechanical rhythms of the libido, with no help from the alter ego.

Psychosis designates a rhythm of compulsion and gratification of a regular but unregulable kind in which the play of fantasy upon experience is such as to preclude rational reflection or the direction of action towards diverse ends. In countless narratives on American film and television, the circuit of action is closed to reflection in this way. The obvious, box-office instances are the efficient, precise films of Clint Eastwood. Whether as *hombre* in a poncho or fixed-featured cop, the Eastwood hero is impressively the complement of his psychotic enemy. Mad dogs must be destroyed. Vengeance, one way of naming the circle of psychosis, is as satisfying and as pointless as the violation which started it. The lust to violate the violator goes repulsively deep. This is clear on most American, and indeed British television, as well as in the wider society. Vengeance is blameless. Ethics is returned to ritual. There is no difficulty about moral decision. A man has to do what a man has to do.

V

This is the dark side of the audience. Good old interview-and-questionnaire empirics come up with a much cheerier one. David Morley[20] in particular speaks up for and documents the social and sociable uses of television and his warmly entertaining transcripts remind us that, by and large, families do not just slump round the set: they argue about what's on, fight for the zapper, do the ironing, talk to visitors, shout at the Prime Minister and laugh helplessly at the most tear-jerking stuff on the set or come to that, on the page. Even those who admit to non-stop watching have an agreeable line in self-knowledge:

> The basis of the husband's preference for 'staying in' is clarified later in the interview, when it becomes clear that the key factor is that in going out to a public place this man experiences a loss of the total power which he has established within the walls of his own home. Even if his examples (stretching his legs out, smoking, drinking tea) seem trivial, the point is that it is only in his own home that he can do precisely what he likes: 'Plus you're in your own home. In the cinema you sit in your own little seat with no leg room and no smoking. Three hours with no smoking and I smoke heavy. I'd have to get up in the interval and go out, and you smoke about five in that five minutes and make yourself sick. Plus you can have a cup of tea and do what you like.'
> This man plans his viewing (and videotaping) with extreme care. At points he sounds almost like a classical utilitarian discussing the maximisation of his pleasure quotient, as he discusses the fine detail of his calculations as to what to watch, and what to tape, in what sequence: 'And like evening times, I look through the paper and I've got all my programmes sorted out. I've got it on tonight on BBC because it's *Dallas* tonight and I do like *Dallas*, so ... I don't like *Wogan*, but ... We started to watch *East Enders*, didn't we? And then they put *Emmerdale Farm* on, so we've gone for *Emmerdale Farm* 'cause I like that and we record *East Enders* – so we don't have to miss out. I normally see it on a Sunday anyway. I got it all worked out to tape. I don't mark it [in the paper], but I register what's in there; like tonight, it's *Dallas*, then at 9 p.m. it's *Widows* and then we've got *Brubaker* on until the news. So the tape's ready to go

straight through. What's on at half seven? Oh, *This Is Your Life* and *Coronation Street*. *This Is Your Life* we have to record to watch *Dallas*. I think BBC is better to record, because it doesn't have the adverts. *This Is Your Life* we record because it's only on for half an hour, whereas *Dallas* is on for an hour, so you only use half an hour of tape.

'Yeah, Tuesday. If you're watching the other programme it means you're going to have to cut it off halfway through, and I don't bother, so I watch the news at nine o'clock ... Yes, 'cause there's a film on at 9 p.m. on Tuesday, so what I do, I record the film so I can watch *Miami Vice* and then watch the film later.'

The bottomless pit of this man's desire for programmes to watch cannot be entirely fulfilled by broadcast television, and before he became unemployed they were renting a video film practically every night as well as watching broadcast television. 'If I could afford it, I'd have a film tonight, and every night.' (Morley, pp. 70–1)

He is, in his way, a fascinating folk-figure. His unstoppable soliloquy must do here to suggest just how various are the needs and purposes working themselves out in audiences. Households have their sitting-room rules and regularities, of course: fathers and sons rule the channel-hopper; the men watch the politics and the women watch the soaps; the VCR stops the family row about what to watch; mothers use TV as a sanction for small children ('if you aren't good, you can't watch'). Audiences hold a veering, equivocal balance between fantasy and action. They give caustic room to reflection, and to conversation about what they watch and read; they also give way uninhibitedly to the imaginary joys of fantasy life.

Sorting out the varieties of human response to the mass media is like reading the encyclopedia. It's all bits and pieces. The media theorist might try to get two things clear. First, he wants to discover, if he can, what the balance is between manipulation and expression. To what extent do people make their narratives for themselves, and to what extent are they pushed about by the producers of narratives for their own ends? Secondly, our theorist could do with a more workmanlike, less mystifying account of the imagination and what to do with it in practical life.

Notes

1 William Wordsworth, Preface to *Lyrical Ballads* (1800), (Oxford, 1953).
2 See C. H. Rolph, *The Trial of 'Lady Chatterley'* (Penguin, 1961).

3 *Report of the Committee on Obscenity and Film Censorhip*, Chairman, Bernard Williams, Command. 7772 (HMSO, 1979). 'The Williams Report'.

4 Notably, Karl Popper in *The Logic of Scientific Inquiry* (Routledge & Kegan Paul, 1961).

5 Stuart Hall, 'Encoding/decoding', in *Culture, Media, Language*, ed. Stuart Hall, D. Hobson, A. Lowe and P. Willis (Hutchinson, 1980).

6 The phrase and method are taken from the philosopher R. G. Collingwood in his *an Autobiography* (Clarendon Press, 1939).

7 Joseph Klapper, *The Effects of Mass Communication* (New York Free Press, 1960).

8 Harold Lasswell, 'The structure and function of communication in society', in *Mass Communication* ed. Wilbur Schramm (University of Illinois Press, 1960).

9 Paul Lazarsfeld, B. Berelson and H. Gander, *The People's Choice*, (Columbia University Press, 1948).

10 Elihu Katz and Paul Lazarsfeld, *Personal Influence: the Part Played by People in the Flow of Mass Communications* (Free Press of Glencoe, 1955).

11 Jay Blumler and Elihu Katz, *The Uses of Mass Communications* (Sage Publications, 1974). See also J. G. Blumler and D. McQuail, *Television in Politics, Its Uses and Influence* (Faber & Faber, 1968).

12 Denis McQuail, *Mass Communication Theory: an Introduction* (Sage Publications, 1983).

13 See n. 5 to this chapter.

14 Nicholas Garnham, 'The strange case of Dr Blumler', *Media, Culture and Society*, vol. 1 No. 2 (1979).

15 Jay Blumler, Michael Gurevitch and J. Ires, *The Challenge of Election Broadcasting* (Leeds University Press, 1978).

16 Colin Seymour-Ure, *The Political Impact of the Mass Media* (Constable, 1974.)

17 Graham Murdock with James Halloran and Phillip Elliott, *Demonstrations and Communication: a Case Study* (Penguin, 1971).

18 The treatment of publicity and glamour is stirringly handled by John Berger in *Ways of Seeing* (BBC with Penguin, 1972). See also my *The Imagery of Power* (Heinemann, 1972).

19 Graham Murdock, 'Large corporations and the control of the communications industry', in *Culture, Society and the Media*, ed. Michael Gurevitch, James Curran, Tony Bennett and Janet Woollacott (Methuen, 1982).

20 David Morley, *Family Television* (Comedia, 1986).

8

Making and Thinking:
Practice with Cameras

I

I have stressed a strong anti-passivity thesis in the last chapter, and throughout the book. Communication systems are public and purposeful (you couldn't have a private language – the very idea of language is communal). They do not make up meanings from scratch, but rather come along replete with meanings from which we have to select what seem to us the most sensible, while we discard the rest. And when we reply to a communication, we draw easily upon the great stock of meanings conserved in language, and just as easily speak sentences which embody radically new meanings. Language, like mind, is of its structure and nature a creative action.

My attention in this chapter is on the creative nature of all our signification or sign-making. We *make* the signs yield up the many meanings they carry. This is the way of speech and thought, and it connects naturally with practical action. In all acts of signification, we are doing something by meaning it. Put in homelier words and on a good day, we mean what we say and we do what we intend.

This little homily is less footling than it sounds. The lethal tendency of theoretic reason is for those who have mastered it to talk like the Mock Turtle, and for nobody to know what to *do* with their theories. A classroom example will bring out my point.

Most of the countries with nationally established systems of primary education start children off by tying the connection between making and thinking quite tightly in all classroom activity. Small children learn, as part of their daily routine, that making things as well as they can is where schooling begins. In such a way, aesthetics is placed where it belongs at the foundation of education. Story-making and -telling, which has featured so largely in this book, is part of the same process. In all this busy classroom life, aesthetic thought is seen as intrinsic to the business of making things, stories, poems, pictures, music, models. There is no boundary between making and thinking.

This custom ratifies the ancient tradition of the arts as the most practical and everyday means we have of theorizing and modelling. A story, as I said in the first two chapters, is a simple theory: it explains actions by placing them in a narrative. A child's picture of a house in a landscape is a little model of its geography, just as, on a grander scale, Turner's late, majestic paintings are models of colour and form, place and passion, all at once. Small children would not put things to themselves like this, of course, but this is how they use art and aesthetic thought. It is functional: they can use it to interpret the world; it is usable and useful.

Gradually, however, shades of the prison-house close in. As pupils become older, and as certain of them are picked out as bright, so they are taught the dominance of a different tradition. Art becomes not a practical and useful activity, but a formal one. The students are taught formalism, which is to say to identify form before content, properties and attributes before their sense of the work in their own lives. So, 'This is the form of a sonata', 'This poem is a Shakespearian sonnet. It has fourteen lines divided into the rhyme scheme as follows: abab cdcd efef gg.' At the same time, the students learn the tradition of a particular art as fixed and given. They do not study the making of the new, only the finished product of the old. This is canonical study, which originally referred to the purely formal study of sacred texts. The ancient privilege of industrial society handed to mental over manual forms of labour also leads gradually to academic study of the canon which is so wholly divorced from making that there are separate colleges of art, music, drama and so forth, whose primary purpose is making art. Universities, on the other hand, study its formal properties.

These divisions of labour go deep in industrial society. Naturally, people ignore them, but it isn't easy. They also, and sensibly, try to have things both ways. That is to say, they argue that without study of the formal properties of a work of art, we can attain no hold on it at all. We cannot think about it, or hold it away a little with the detachment necessary for any kind of critical reflection. They also argue, rightly, that unless a student of the arts is capable of that surrender of the self to the experience and its uncontrollable pleasures which is ecstasy in art, then the formal study is stone dead, like doing skeletons instead of patients in medicine.

In so much of our education, in Europe and in the English-speaking societies, formalism rules. Its cast of mind is judicious and objective. It teaches the withholding of oneself from passion and commitment. This is the demeanour of the impartial observer-scientist, and his forbidding features carry enormous authority in our culture. Oddly enough, even the spankingly up-to-date and fashionable new theories of semiotics and discourses look the same way. Semiotics broke with judiciousness in a moral sense; it offered a route into the analysis of culture without getting tangled up in what's good and what's bad. But it simply denied the facts of local human nature in doing so. We *live* by definitions of worth, and these inform and shape our deepest feelings. Those feelings are the occasion of our final values – happiness, trust, lovingness, to travel no further along a big list. To ignore the definitions of what matters, as much latter-day media theory does with such sanctimoniousness,[1] is simply to make the theory irrelevant to those it was designed to liberate. It is to situate mass media study alongside all the other grim disciplines which subjugate the practical, local usefulness of culture, its lived content, and offer as their ideal spokesman the detached, objective, observer-scientist.

I don't intend by this yet another version of contemporary irrationalism. Modern society can hardly do without science, though its record, what with nuclear and chemical weapons and such, should surely make it a bit less pleased with itself than is usual. But the ordinary uses and experiences of the sort of culture usually referred to as popular might teach us, not only much about all that good media theory needs to reckon with, but also something about the connections between pleasure and education.

II

Much popular culture gives pleasure simply because it is not education. Indeed, some of it is defined by its deliberately anti-educational stance. The success of some of the ghastlier quiz shows and party game shows on TV, the more studiedly repulsive of the video nasties, is due in large part to their deliberately turning upside-down the standards of good taste and respect for other individuals' bodies and minds which official education rightly upholds.

But its strident anti-respectability is not all that popular culture has. Certainly there is nothing to prevent its best values being those which will ground our media theory and teaching in the practice of local and historical experience. Those best values and moments seek to turn the narratives of culture back to practical use. Gossip and the folklore of political history are alike ways of interpreting the world around us. Such history, of course, may be wildly inaccurate, which is where the judicious detachment of traditional education must come in and insist on truthfulness as a test of *all* experience. (No one would deny that they want to get at the truth of things.)

The best example I know of a history written deliberately on the side of the oppressed, condescended-to, and forgotten-about is Edward Thompson's famous study, *The Making of the English Working Class.*[2] It illustrates my argument perfectly. Thompson set himself to show that this class came to a consciousness of itself and its power during the key period for British parliamentary democracy of 1790 to 1832. It is a tale told from a huge welter of historical documents – newspapers, magazines, police reports, courtroom records, books of the time. It is, in other words, faithful to the facts. It is also a tale full of heroes forgotten by official history – heroic journalists, people's leaders and preachers, and martyrs of class injustice who died on a public gallows in a spirit of fine defiance.

It is the grandest instance of history from below, sweeping, gripping, passionate. Such a history brings to fulfilment the best marriage of theory and experience we can look for. It is a study of mass communication in the action of popular political culture. It is a terrific read.

Thompson's book gives us one lead. He works in the grain of the best of popular culture: its localness, its free, noisy exchange, of which the best examples in leisure life are festivals, fairgrounds, sporting arenas, ice-rinks, music-halls. Its dominant music is laughter, and however much laughter may be cruel, it is still the uncontrollable expression of freedom. Totalitarianism must regulate laughter: you mustn't laugh at a policeman.[3] A laughing woman is a free woman.

There are excellently comic figures in Thompson's book, and a proper gravity as well. Working with the stuff of popular culture, particularly its typical media, mass communications, we can see how to follow such a lead. The readiest way is through the practice of photography.

Photography does not attract a lot of notice in the media literature.[4] It is, however, the nearest thing we have to a universal popular art, cherished in official culture by museums and coffee table books, but placed within easy, everyday reach by the cheap availability of the technology. Surely almost every household in the rich west owns a camera? Surely, also, it keeps its archive in snapshot albums, now so easy to fill with their large sheets of adhesive transparency (none of that antique fiddling about with sticky corners). The snapshot album stands to the framed family portraits of weddings and golden weddings as the night-school water-colour does to the framed souvenir oil-painting bought on holiday along the *Costa del Sol*. There is no break enforced by formalist aesthetics between my snapshot of my much-loved family larking about at the seaside and grinning at the camera, and this posed, correct but entirely familiar framed photograph of the daughter, then a little girl, now a grown woman and away from home.

The aesthetics of these relations is both practical and utterly non-philistine. The subjects and their representations in the photographs are both crucial. These people are members of my family. Their presence in the picture reminds me, perhaps, of their absence from home. The picture restores them to me by recalling (fondly) the happiness of that moment. Domestic photography has to be fairly selective. People like a good photograph of themselves, looking their best, smiling. The balance of a precious photograph is between its expressive capacity (how good a photograph, including formally good, well composed, clean definition and so forth) and the importance of its subject to the person looking at it (me).

Let me try to put that crucial point again. It is at the heart of the popular aesthetics I profess here, and therefore an essential component of our theory. But theory just at this moment is too pompous a word to be tolerated. The balance under discussion is the balancing everyone aims for between reflective thought and the vivid life of action. The loved snapshot brings together the way things were represented at that moment and my keen thought about and valuing of it now. In such aesthetics, the experience and the art-object carry an equal charge. The things of art and the things of life are equivalent (as when the marvellous piece of Mozart and my feelings chime together). It will be the ethical significance of either that decides which is to come first in any dispute. Sometimes Mozart will matter more than me; sometimes (not usually), the reverse.

Photography as presently practised is a good place to learn this new aesthetics. It is, as I keep saying, a local, practical aesthetics, but by this I don't mean that it refuses serious thought. Even less do I mean that 'practical' equals 'intuitive', and that that in turn is summed up in the grisly phrase, gut-reaction. Your guts are changeable sources of feeling as any sailor knows, and no guide to anything much except the size of the waves.

The guide we shall rely on is, once again, Roland Barthes, in his meditation *Camera Lucida*.[5] But this is a rather different Barthes from the one we met in chapter 5. Both authors are witty, even quirky, but as Barthes developed towards elderliness (he died, most unluckily, in a road accident at the age of 65), he brought together the formalism we criticized in chapter 5 with a much more direct, wide-open appeal to the felt truths of experience.

Photography, and one photograph in particular, was his cue for this synthesis.

> From the beginning, I had determined on a principle to myself: never to reduce myself-as-subject, confronting certain photographs, to the disincarnated, disaffected *socius* which science is concerned with. (p. 74)

[By *socius* I think he means the judicious objectivist, the social-scientist-in-a-white-coat I sketched out a few pages ago.] The photograph which effected the union between the particular and the universal, as Aristotle puts it, or between experience and theory, as I put it, was of his recently dead mother as a five-year-old.

Before Barthes comes to this moment, however, he turns to his structuralist-formalist origins, and comes up with a second heuristic instrument paralleling the earlier meaning–form distinction (quick thinkers will notice how both devices are similar to the Gestalt psychologist's perceptual distinction between figure and ground). He asserts that photographs come with a content which arouses what he calls, from Latin, *studium*.

> What I feel about these photographs derives from an *average* affect, almost from a certain training. I did not know a French word which might account for this kind of human interest, but I believe this word exists in Latin: it is *studium*, which doesn't mean, at least not immediately, 'study', but application to a thing, taste for someone, a kind of general, enthusiastic commitment, of course, but without special acuity. It is by *studium* that I am interested in so many photographs, whether I receive them as political testimony or enjoy them as good historical scenes: for it is culturally (this connotation is present in *studium*) that I participate in the figures, the faces, the gestures, the settings, the actions. (p. 20)

This general ground of our interest is split by what Barthes names the *punctum*, literally a small wound or puncture, which sharpens general attention into human connection. One could say it turns the calm surface of sympathy into a momentum with a clear current. 'A photograph's punctum is that accident which pricks me (but also bruises me, is poignant to me).' *Poignant* in French, we should recall, means piercing. The moment of *punctum* is not the same as a shock. News photographs may shock us by the horror of their content, but they largely alert our *studium*, our generalized concern to know the world (we would hardly *love* them). As Barthes puts it, such a photograph can shout but not wound. Similarly, a pornographic photo arouses the *studium*. 'It is always a naive photograph, without intention and without calculation.' The girl stares out of the photograph with an entirely unspecific meltingness. Her hair is disarranged for the studio, not by a lover's hand. Her lips are unsmudged, her dentition gleaming, fearsomely white. Her body is hard and round; it has none of the softness and creases of experience.

The girlie photo turns into an erotic photo by virtue of the *punctum* (Barthes' subdued sexual imagery is gently explicit). The *punctum* may be brought into being by the placing of her wraps or a change in her look which blurs the hard naivety of pornography. All great portraits have the *punctum*, of course. Rembrandt stares at us and at himself in the mirror morosely, certain of his own genius, profound and unassuageable in the depth of his seeing; into us, into himself.

Rembrandt, however, belongs to the metropolitan gallery. Barthes's mother with whom he, a bachelor, lived most of his life, belonged to Barthes.

He searched among all the family photographs after her death, looking for her.

> ... I would have recognised her among thousands of other women, yet I did not 'find' her. I recognised her differentially, not essentially. Photography thereby compelled me to perform a painful labor; straining toward the essence of her identity, I was struggling among images partially true, and therefore totally false. To say, confronted with a certain photograph, 'That's *almost* the way she was' was more distressing than to say, confronted with another, 'That's not the way she was at all.' The *almost*: love's dreadful regime, but also the dream's disappointing status – which is why I hate dreams. For I often dream about her (I dream only about her), but it is never quite my mother ... There I was, alone in the apartment where she had died, looking at these pictures of my mother, one by one, under the lamp, gradually moving back in time with her, looking for the truth of the face I had loved. And I found it.
>
> The photograph was very old. The corners were blunted from

having been pasted into an album, the sepia print had faded, and the picture just managed to show two children standing together at the end of a little wooden bridge in a glassed-in conservatory, what was called a Winter Garden in those days. My mother was five at the time (1898), her brother seven. He was leaning against the bridge railing, along which he had extended one arm; she, shorter than he, was standing a little back, facing the camera; you could tell that the photographer had said, 'Step forward a little so we can see you'. (pp. 66–7)

He studied the little girl, and could discern in her 'the kindness which had formed her being immediately and forever'. It is a surprising discovery, of the mother in a snapshot of her as so small, so long before her son was born.

I join Barthes in his search, hunting for a photograph of my beloved mother, now dead, which will re-present all I loved in her and now miss so painfully and continuously. This one won't do, she's become (by then) too old and frail. This other one won't do, it's too posed, or too badly printed, or 'not a bit like her'. And so on. I look for her, perhaps, as Rembrandt looked for himself. But I find her, if I do, in a photograph anybody could have taken. Such a snapshot, Barthes says, achieves 'the impossible science of the unique being' (p. 71).

This treatment of the photograph, at once casual and intense, is, I believe, a common thing. That is why I offer photography as *the* type of popular culture, which brings together our creative practice and our aesthetics. Comparatively speaking, there is no division in the world of photography into high and low culture. People readily make judgements about the quality of photos and photographers ('you take it, I'm no good'). But the practice is not divided up by class and money. People practise it by doing it, and they make an aesthetics as they go.

III

This is a bit rough-and-ready for our purposes, but it returns us to the central place that doing has in thinking. But of course thinking *is* a kind of doing, and imagining an even more elusive kind. Barthes speaks of photography as incorrigibly connected to the 'necessarily real thing which has been placed before the lens' (p. 76). In spite of misgivings about cameras and lies having been much expressed in law courts and elsewhere, one sees what he means. 'In photography, I can never deny that *the thing has been there*' (Barthes's italics, p. 76). On the other hand, seeing a snapshot and recognizing it, like seeing any other image (including print), is an imaginative business. Those shapes out there have to be matched to these schemes in my brain until one fits the other, and I see what I have created.

In another seminal work for our purposes, Ernst Gombrich's *Art and Illusion*,[6] Gombrich assigns a large part of what has to happen for a painting to become a painting, to 'the beholder's share' (and 'beholder', however archaic, is a more illuminating word than 'spectator'). Throughout the book he has insisted on the inevitable blend of creativity and conventionality in all representation. We can only learn to see muddy smudges on canvas as trees and fields and sky because of known conventions. When a painter (or a photographer or film-maker) comes along who flouts the conventions, we don't know how to see him.

Gombrich speaks of schemata shaped, learned and laid up in the cortex, animated by percepts (seeing) and so matched to the world-out-there that we recognize what we see. Sometimes we do this involuntarily, because the schemata we store up for matching to the human face, for instance, are so manifold and learned so young, we can see faces everywhere. We can see them in a fold in the curtain (especially when we're little) or in a circle containing two half-moons for eyes, and a half-moon below them for a smile. When we see a picture, our conventional schema in the brain and the schema in the painting or photograph come together in the clarity of what Gombrich calls matching-and-making. He writes:

> In our study of the language of art we have come increasingly to stress one fact – the power of interpretation. We saw it at work in the last three chapters, which probed the beholder's share in the readings of images, his capacity, that is, to collaborate with the artist and to transform a piece of coloured canvas into a likeness of the visible world. We had seen it in earlier chapters, where is was the artist who interpreted the world in terms of the schemata he made and knew. (p. 246)

I think it is probably true to claim, after Gombrich, that the history of the representation of stories in *words* can also only be understood 'by considering the psychological aspects of image-making and image-reading', as long as we follow Gombrich in grounding that psychology deep in the culture and its practical contexts which make meaning possible. But his point is obviously true about films and television. Style and meaning in the film narrative depend on our creatively 'matching and making' correspondences between the image and the world, which in turn express meaning. This matching and making, the powers of classification and consistency which these practices demand, our acute and natural 'self-centredness', the interplay of schema and correction (or formula and experience), are all parts of the common grammar which makes perception possible. Encoding and decoding alike call for the creativeness Gombrich has analysed.

The source of power in Gombrich's analysis lies in his combination of conceptual inventiveness and practical criticism. He takes Gestalt psychology, and paraphrases and assimilates it until he can make it describe how to behold (*sic*) a painting. A film demands perhaps even greater address – certainly *faster* decoding movements – than a painting, but the practical criticism of decoding looks easy enough. First you check up on the peculiarities of the technology, then on the peculiarities of the imagination. Stuart Hall will help us in a moment with the stages of such analysis; we have already noted some of the oddities of representation in all media (nothing, really, could be odder than that print can prefigure sound).

Take the example always to hand: television, the people's medium. We are apt to think of it as completely natural – 'naturalizing the sign' as the semioticians say – and therefore as representing reality with a one-to-one fidelity. But the first thing to notice in comparison with either paintings or films is television's extreme crudeness of technology. Even with the introduction of 625 lines (replacing 405) in 1964, the definition of images is still poor and blurred. Similarly, although the full dress advent of colour technology in 1969 (in Britain; it was generally available in the USA from 1962) was a notable advance, for the reasons given in chapter 2, colour transmission can only be done in primary colours, and the combination controls are very approximate (particularly with cable television) as everyone knows from adjusting their own sets.

These technical conditions have, as they always do, specific consequences for television conventions, schemata, and effects. Most obviously, the decision to create a television set small enough and portable enough to sit in the corner of a living room meant giving up some of the most powerful of the cinema's effects: the companionship of audience, the effectiveness of the cinema's sheer size of images and bulk of sound, as well as clarity of definition and accuracy of colour. A wide-open western, for instance, famously depends upon the huge expanses of mountain, scrub and desert for a proper understanding of its political geography. Even on a 22-inch screen, and with our most imaginative effort to reconstruct the big image, the results are rather puny.

In response to these limits, new schemata and their conventions have developed for television. At their simplest, these represent action much less by the careful watching-from-a-distance (a distance constantly varied, but rarely very close) of the film camera, and much more by abrupt cross-cutting of sudden movement, often with a sharp juxtaposition of contrasting scales – something of what Hall indicates when writing of 'technical infrastructure and meaning structure'. Above all, television drama is carried on with faces in close-up – often taken so very close as to cut off jaw and forehead. In addition, as Raymond Williams points out, there is the convention of its speech patterns:

> The voices were no longer speaking to or at each other; were speaking with each other perhaps, with themselves in the presence of others. But there was a new composition, in which a group was speaking, yet a strange negative group; no individual ever quite finishing what he had begun to say, but intersecting, being intersected by the words of others, casual and distracted, words in their turn unfinished: a weaving of voices in which though still negatively, the group was speaking and yet no single person was ever finally articulate. It is by now so normal a process, in writing dramatic speech, that it can be heard, any night, in a television serial, and this is not just imitation. It is a way of speaking and of listening, a specific rhythm of a particular consciousness; in the end a form of unfinished, transient, anxious relationship, which is there on the stage or in the text but which is also, pervasively, a structure of feeling in a precise contemporary world.[7]

Those faces and half-faces, that texture of interwoven but always unfinished speech, compose our present schemes of representation. Williams gives us the form of the conversation of our culture. It is in relation to that conversation that, in both directions, art and reality at once, we say 'that's true' or 'that's good', or, even, 'that's beautiful'. The constructs of imagination are made out of the traffic between life and fiction.

Smallness of size, indistinctness of definition, domesticity of context, these technical limits pull television towards all that is familiar, homely, even boring. Something else, however, makes it magic. Mostly this is the magic of stardom which has such a central position in the political economy of mass communications. The subordination of citizens to stars is one theme in my closing chapter, and one way into the sacred mystery of film and television. We have to answer the question, why is this system so magical and mysterious? Why do we pay people these ridiculous sums of money to tell us what we can see is happening anyway, or to read aloud very easy prose from the autocue at news-time? How *can* these things be normal?

These are large, blunt and disobliging questions about the way we are. They begin to gather up all the threads of this book. But there is one strictly technical condenser of magic on television. The transmission of only primary colours on such broad rows of dots means that colour itself is made very high and crude; it tends therefore to dazzle (quite literally; the dots vibrate intensely). Dazzle, as any painter knows, glamorizes the subject. Glamour, in an aphorism, is the aura radiated by a subject-matter (person or place) which is enviable. Envy is the unfulfillable longing to own what is owned by others (including themselves), and which is unattainable. The dazzle of colour television adds volume to the structure of glamour which is in any case given by television's own political economy.

IV

These ruminations about the way technology interacts with culture to emerge as the particular forms of television, film, radio programme or anything else, need to be made more methodical. I have several times mentioned Hall's short paper 'Encoding/decoding'[8] and here cite it as one of the set texts for the devout media theorist. Although I have set my face resolutely against diagrams in a book on a subject fatally liable to break out into diagrams which are only helpful on rare occasions, Hall's diagram of analysis really is useful because brief, neat and surprising (p. 130).

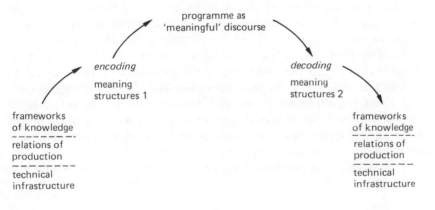

The paper itself is a bit too heavily laden with the more cumbrous end of Marxist linguistics as well as with inverted commas, but it is far richer and more human than the communication models squeezed into their diagrams by the regular trade.

Hall's argument is that the moment of the message – in his diagram, the programme [or film or novel] as meaningful discourse – needs to be dismantled into its constituents on *both* sides of its exchange. He contends that the production and the reproduction of meaning go through the same four stages in order to be encoded and decoded; encoding carries the meaning to be given, decoding the meaning to be taken.

The four stages are unlikely to be symmetrical. The 'technical infrastructure' of the studio is very different from that of the living room. What does Hall mean by the phrase? First, it announces the materialist-Marxist ground on which experience stands. We live within the scenery our culture makes out of its technology. The messages we receive are its products in a very obvious way: a film in the cinema is not just any old story, it is a story told (encoded) by the huge effort of technical organization, starting from the conditions imposed by contemporary film cameras and proceeding by way of the extraordinary team of people whose names appear on the interminable, unread list of credits at the beginning or the end of a movie, a list which presents (very directly) to us the relations of its production.

It is, then, a story watched and listened to (decoded) by you and me, sitting, say, in the dark of the immense and splendid auditorium of the Leicester Square Odeon, with its grand façade, its Royal Opera House sweep of seats and flights of stairs, its brilliantly illuminated drapes, and smart girls with trays of ices. Our evening out at this great occasion has cost us, well, ten quid, but what the hell, look at the technical infrastructure we have enjoyed, the relations of production which fix us as audience and ensure that we go to the movie (decode it) in the right clothes, paying the right money, spending our leisure time in the profitable fields of consumption.

Starting from the bottom of Hall's diagram, and working up in parallel is not quite the right way to go about it. It is more logical to follow the arrows up through encoding and down through decoding. In each case, however, the real foundations are the relations of production and the technical infrastructure. (I would myself find it hard to separate these two procedurally, as will come out in a moment when discussing practical work.)

Technology and productive relations are in turn transformed and mediated by our frameworks of knowledge. Hall reminds us that 'there is no intelligible discourse without the operation of a code'. Eco defines a code (according to my paraphrase) as the mechanism of translation from out-there to in-here. Like the matching-and-making in our perceptual system which we looked at a page or two ago, the working of the code connects word and object, sign and thing, so that they light up and mean something. Frameworks of knowledge are not, however, just mediating the stuff from downstairs – transforming, as vulgar Marxists might say, base into superstructure or economics into ideology. If knowledge *is* a product, someone said, it is more like a work of art than a pair of shoes. It is made, worked over, created, until something knowable is known. Thus the frameworks of knowledge organize but also create the message of the film, the book, the TV programme.

This is obvious if we simply look at the TV schedules for the week. The frameworks of knowledge are busily at work classifying programmes so that decoding is possible. This programme is natural history (*Life on Earth*), that one economics (*The Money Programme*), a third political history (*World at War*), a fourth high literature (*King Lear*) and so on. The editor and programme head have to do a very brisk job allocating their materials according to these classifications. The audience uses the same ones in decoding what to watch and how to watch it.

It isn't just a matter of the kind of slot a programme occupies on the timetable, however. The frameworks of knowledge also operate *within* the encoding and decoding processes to organize such aspects of knowledge into its structure, whose components include evidence, authority, what is reasonable and rational (not the same thing), what is proof and conjecture. This way knowledge is created and built, as well as framed. (To understand this, the word mediation is not much help.)

Finally, as the message is embodied, so the meaning structures do their work. The numerals 1 and 2 in the diagram serve to remind us that here asymmetry between the encoding and decoding is most likely. There will be misunderstandings. A meaning structure, let us say, is the grammar whose rules generate meaning in the language we share. It is also the convention which makes it possible for us to understand the wide penumbra of meanings which comes along surrounding the plain and simple kernel we look for at the heart of all utterances. Denotation is the core meaning of a sign, connotation all the associations round it. (Think of the connotations of such magic words as 'rose' or 'gold' or 'charity'.)

Our meaning structures obviously depend on our education as well as our more general experience and dispositions. So there is a struggle in society – a class struggle, if you like – over meanings. This is the ideological struggle, and I have already referred to Hall's three types of meaning structures which operate in that first stage of the deconstruction of our decoding. His first type was 'the dominant-hegemonic' according to which, as we watch television, we see exactly what hegemony wants us to see. The second type was 'negotiated', where we see the messages slightly less obligingly, agreeing with the general approach but making important personal reservations – a two- or three-tier kind of response. The third type was 'oppositional', where we won't have it at all, and shout at the set.

Obviously the devout theorist will want to extend and ramify this short list. Many more possibilities on both sides of encoding/ decoding need to be thought up. It is my concluding contention in this chapter that such inquiry – inquiry into the weight and volume of the stages in Stuart Hall's diagram – will itself only be given due weight and volume by some elementary practice with technology.

That is one reason why I gave pride of place to photography at the start. It is, as they say, common practice. No doubt, like writing a novel on a typewriter, it looks like old-fashioned artisanal production, rather than anything tasting headily of high technology. The relations of production between camera, family subject, the local developing shop, and the snapshot album are pretty clear. So is the technical infrastructure, so long as you know how a camera really works, and why photographic film holds an image. The frameworks of its knowledge and its meaning structures are given us as plain as day by the cultural habits which put photographs in their right place – a handsome portrait in the living-room, a prize-winning landscape at the local club's annual competition, a colour transparency of a rare find by the amateur birdwatcher.

Even with the common practice of home photography, however, we are more than slightly awed by what Hall calls 'the professional code'. Len Masterman also has sensible things to say[9] about our overdone humility before the sheer technical mastery, brilliance and finish of the professional photograph, film or video-broadcast. But as it has been one point of this chapter to show, artificial, natural-seeming high polish is itself the subject of our theory, and we can only understand its construction if we try for ourselves. Training of this kind, just like learning to paint water-colours or to write short stories, is a training in respect, certainly, for workmanship, design and, when things are good enough, for art. Great movies, in the cinema or on the television screen, arc great art, and there is no problem about saying so.

Aesthetics, in its turn, is a theory of art. Media theory must take art seriously, as the coda to this book declares. Art, however, is a practical because a creative matter, not a worshipful one. It holds a balance between making and thinking which is exactly on the fulcrum of human sanity. We learn to keep steady the claims of vividly lived life and reflective detachment from it. Messing about in a properly self-conscious way with cameras is the best place nowadays to learn how to keep that balance.

Notes

1   There are some gruesome examples in *Screen*, otherwise such a trail-blazing magazine. See, e.g. vol. 16 no. 3, 1975, and vol. 23 nos. 3–4, 1982.

2   E. P. Thompson, *The Making of the English Working Class* (Gollancz, 1963; Penguin, 1968).

3   I am quoting directly here and later from my *Popular Culture and Political Power* (Harvester Wheatsheaf, 1988).

4   But see Susan Sontag, *On Photography* (Penguin, 1977), and John Berger with Jean Mohr, *Another Way of Telling* (Readers and Writers Collective, 1982).

5   Roland Barthes, *Camera Lucida: Reflections on Photography* (Fontana Flamingo, 1984).

6   E. H. Gombrich, *Art and Illusion: A Study in the Psychology of Pictorial Representation* (Phaidon Books, 1960).

7   Raymond Williams, 'Drama in the dramatised society', in his *Writing in Society* (Verso, 1983).

8   Stuart Hall, 'Encoding/decoding', in *Culture, Media, Language*, ed. Stuart Hall, D. Hobson, A. Lowe and P. Willis (Hutchinson, 1980).

9   Len Masterman, *Teaching about the Media* (Comedia, 1985), especially chapter 2.

9

The Narratives of Culture and the Education of the Citizen

I

I have made so much of practice and the practical usefulness of theory because, after all, the title of this book is *Media Theory*. As we began by noting, the divisions of labour in our societies mark a deep cleft between theory and practice, which the over-theoretical keep wide open by talking at such an abstract height that the air is too thin to breathe, while the over-practical do worse by insisting on themselves as plain, blunt, uncomplicated folk who just get on with the job.

For our homely purposes, I have several times suggested that a theory is *like* a narrative (it is not always the same). It is like a narrative in that it permits us to understand and explain what people are doing by situating their actions in a continuing story. To repeat the well-known, useful example: if I see you at a meeting and you raise your hand, the more fully I know the story of the occasion, the more precisely I can interpret your hand in the air (or, decode the sign you are making) as attracting the chairman's attention, waving to a friend, voting, or just stretching because you're fed up. To make such interpretation I need a sufficient amount of historical information of an everyday sort. I need to know the kind of meeting it is and a little of the kind of person you are.

This humdrum example could come from the processes of anybody's social thought. No one would think of calling it theoretical, but only, if they thought about it at all, normal and reasonable. We work out what it seems reasonable and rational for others to be doing from the stories we have always by us about human life, and the particular history of the lives in question. One way of seeing the topics dealt with in each of the preceding chapters is as a series of explanatory narratives, each with its own specialized vocabulary, which allows us to interpret and understand the actions relevant to each topic. Thus, the chapter on audiences provides some domestic tales which give a rather richer picture of television-watching folk than is provided by the short straight line from stimulus to response. The chapter on ideology, by the same token, tells a newish tale about the story hidden underneath the one you are listening to. Its hero is the person who blows the gaff on the sinister, shadowy character who is putting things over us with a tale to fuddle our wits. The chapter on political economy – a stiffer narrative this, with unfamiliar characters like capital accumulation, a recalcitrant mob of consumers, and a difficult plot to its mergers – can still be given the old, satisfying silhouettes of hard-faced and grasping entrepreneurs, exploited Third World receiving stations, seedy shops selling run-down old movies to the poor, and gallant English public schoolboys fighting to defend the BBC.

Each of these aspects of theory translates into a narrative. The simpler the narrative, no doubt, the more breezily confident the theory. But this book has no wish to raise the ghost of Dave Spart, *Private Eye*'s dementedly sloganeering and infantile Leftist from the dead of 1968. Over-confident media theory is too much for our stomach. The more disobliging the facts, the more intense and close our practical reading, the more provisional the theory. And as to its structure, well, models of the social world are not usually the clean, complex, hard-edged and beautiful models of the natural sciences. Nature is lawfully elegant, culture is conventionally messy. An adequate theory of public communications (as I agree with Raymond Williams that the mass media would be better named) must at least match its form to the forms of life themselves. Human theory has to stay near enough to the messiness of human life to take account of time and chance, death and passion, war and money.

It follows that the theory each of us will come up with is likely to be a rather lumpy, home-made and awkward creature altogether, with all the signs of having been some years in the making. It will be, in the first place, a historical product, some bits of which will be older than others (and none the worse for that). It will be, in the aphorism we encountered earlier, more like a work of art than a piece of cast-iron machinery. Like a novel, or a long symphony, it will have been worked out and worked on for quite a while, and it will have rather unfinished or roughed-in areas, and joins or fittings which the maker will be dissatisfied with.

No one, therefore, should reach this stage in my handbook of theory-making, and expect to have everything straight. Some areas of inquiry are simply more appealing than others, and some refuse to fit in comfortably. The only thing to do is to allow your intellectual construction to settle into its place in your mind, always to prevent its merely becoming a theory-machine into which you pump the data, crank the handle, and turn out neat, pat conclusions and explanations. Theories are themselves historical and have to adapt to a changing history, or they are left washed up on the beach as the tide goes out.

Hegel was the first great philosopher of this process.[1] He saw that ideas arrived with an explosion of novelty, blowing apart previous ideas and rousing men and women to action with their new thrust and energy. Gradually, however, those same ideas cooled and became hard and rigid until a new liberation occurred. Hegel, however, believed that this motion of ideas was always progressive, and that although we leave old ideas behind, they have played their part in impelling us forward to new freedom, always nearer to the attainment of reason.

Hegel was also committed to the argument that the attainment of reason by the human spirit would ultimately be achieved, and that this achievement would have a sort of absolute end, embodied in an ideal state. In other words, his vision of progress involved a final unity of the human spirit and the culture which expressed it. Men and women would be members one of another in the good society.

It is a stirring vision, even if we are very much more sceptical of its feasibility today. It teased a number of nineteenth-century philosophers, most notably Marx, with its power and horizons. While we would reject the notion of finality explicit in both Hegel and Marx, however, the dream of a perfect culture continues to haunt all cultural theory and much ordinary expression. In the small corners of domestic television, pulp fiction, popular sport, children's comics, and even Government policy documents, we can regularly detect an ideal picture of happy, productive, non-exploitative relations between all men and women.

Let me repeat Clifford Geertz's definition of culture as 'an ensemble of stories we tell ourselves about ourselves'.[2] The idea of a story has been made much of in these pages. Once again, it figures here as the classic form of explanation in the human sciences, but also – to repeat myself – the form we all use in everyday life by which to understand what people, ourselves and others, are doing. The substance of our subject-matter – 'stories we tell ourselves about ourselves' – is, therefore, at the same time the instrument we have for understanding and analysing those stories. The descriptions and explanations of the media theorist may be no more practical, critic-al, and useful than the descriptions and explanations of a man arguing in a pub. They *ought* to be, of course, because we, as media theorists, have put a lot more reflection into our account of things. But we are using the same form as the man in the pub, and with the same view in mind: to understand what is going on for the sake of our own freedom and empowerment.

That is what a theory is for. The illumination that comes when we truly understand something which was earlier a deep puzzle to us is like coming out of a dark, twisting path in the woods where we are anxiously afraid we are lost, into the wide space and bright light of a clearing which leads us out into the open. The relief of such a moment and the exhilarated surge of the sense of freedom and happy self-possession which goes with it is at the heart of education. It is for this that we use a theory.

II

To define culture as 'the ensemble of stories we tell ourselves about ourselves' is, at first sight, to make culture sound static. But, as I have insisted time and again in these pages, our first narrative is historical, and the quickest early route to the moment of illumina-tion is to discover what the history of the puzzle was. Understanding the present muddle of the BBC or Hollywood, for instance, is first of all a matter of knowing how they got to be that shape, who decided upon it, and then trying to work out all the *un*intended consequences for ourselves.

In studying the making of culture, therefore, we are studying the making of ourselves, and that is something to which, naturally enough, people give binding allegiance. If the cultural theorist points out the history of the making of culture, its arbitrary nature perhaps, its injustice maybe, those faithful to the culture become angry and upset and accuse the theorist of faithlessness, a lust for power, or worse. Arguments over culture are inherent to its nature, and are then compounded by the conflicts of class, generation, gender, race, and so forth. Making a culture produces the great human benefits of identity, membership, mutuality, patriotism, loyalty. These values entail by definition exclusion, enemies, rejection, quarrels, betrayal, warfare.

Culture, it must be said again, is competitive. We tell ourselves our stories, some true, some false, some ennobling, some degrading, in order to win the moment of illumination, the freedom and empowerment that go with it. Walter Benjamin[3] has a very sympathetic if rather compact description of how generations imagine their cultural inventions not only in competition with one another, but also *on behalf of* the future. In an essay on the importance of the great new metropolis of Paris to the sort of lyric poetry the French dandy-Bohemian Baudelaire was writing in the 1850s, Benjamin said that 'each generation imagines the epoch which is to succeed it', and does so by seeking in such images 'to transcend the immaturity of the social product' (p. 159). In less Frankfurter diction, we might put it that the culture of an epoch tries to imagine a better world for its beloved children, in which the obviously unequal and inadequate goods of the present will provide more sensibly and creatively for human happiness in the future. Such goods include, no doubt, consumer appliances: in the good society, everyone will have a decent washing machine; awful drudgery will be gone. But the goods of the social product will also include health, education, contented labour, access to beautiful objects which are good for the spirit, objects which might range from music or paintings to stretches of landscape.

One testimony to this imagining may be seen along any big shopping mall or high street in those shop windows which prefigure for our envy and admiration ideal kitchens, or other rooms in the house. For Benjamin goes on to note that, in imagining the ideal future free of inequalities, abundant and contented, the 'collective consciousness' of a society turns back in order to find such images towards an idealized past, 'which is to say, the classless society' (p. 159). In some version of classlessness, where no obstacles of wealth or origin obtrude between equal citizens, we shall find the pastoral paradise. Hence, he says, the future is imagined out of the bits and pieces of the past which the imagination at work prefers for its vision. This is the invention of culture and the traditions it builds. Thus, the ideal kitchen embodies a space capsule future, in which dirt, grease, burned hands, smoke, are all things of the past, but in which the ideal farmhouse of that past is reproduced to restore the grand comforts of oak settle and plank table, wooden cupboards and the plenty, not of deep-freeze, but of a well-husbanded kitchen garden, hen-coop, and orchards. The dream kitchen is space-capsule white at one end, Devon farmhouse wood at the other.

We can see Benjamin's sequence at work in many tales of the day, and one example I am particularly fond of.[4] The BBC has broadcast for over 20 years a series of tales for five-year-olds about three imaginary villages, Chigley, Trumpton, and Camberwick Green. The villages are not so much tim*cless*, as assembled from the best moments of European political and technological history of the last century and a half. Thus, the high streets and marketplaces of the three villages are made out of a pastel-painted plasti-version of the street: an irregular but graceful roofline of gable, balustrade and pediment quoting that ideal Marlborough and Yarm whose echoes are audible in Nantucket or Fremantle. The centre of Trumpton has a cobbled square, a fountain and a diminutively handsome Victorian town hall, all more than a little reminiscent of north-western France and the Third Republic, but set about by arcaded shops with old-fashioned craftsmen: a clockmaker's, a carpenter's, a confectioner's. In one episode, a journeyman painter with a wide hat and smock, a mixture of pre-Raphaelite and Courbet, comes to paint the riverscape to everyone's admiration. The only emblems and officers of state are the endearing fire leader and crew (Captain Flack and his men) and a troop of redcoat soldiers, dressed in the apparel and equipment of the Crimea. But their authority is never exerted; they are only there to be *helpful*, to rescue stranded cows and retrieve paintpots from the clock tower.

Social authority is vested only in the mayor, a French–American figure who addresses the people of Trumpton on high days and holidays, and ceremoniously thanks the firemen. There is a titled lordship, Lord Barleycorn, who lives in a Palladian house with his butler, but whose place in the egalitarian politics favoured in Utopia is so accessible that the engine driver, who with his friend the fireman drives, of course, a brass and blackleaded steam train from about 1900, can ask Lord Barleycorn to take over delivery of some freight when the driver goes on holiday. By the same token, Windy Miller, whose business is indeed the windmill, shares his passion for natural history with the general practitioner Dr Mopp, who carries a Gladstone bag and drives a stately 1906 vintage car.

Technology and economics yield the secret of this series (not an animated cartoon, but filmed in three dimensions on a miniature set with puppets). Each instrument or vehicle is taken from a tamed and beatified moment in the history of technology: the vintage car, the electric milk float, the fire engine with a brass bell *and* an automatically extending ladder, the steam train, the helicopter (but not the 747), the tricycle, the fork-lift truck. These are the standard toys of the pre-space-invader toyshop. They occupy a genteel, cleanly museum of industrial revolution; they fill an undamaged model landscape of hedges, trees, ponds and village greens. The only primary production is eggs and milk and flour; there is no money. The modes of address are those of a sort of Quaker politeness: always 'Mr' or 'Mrs', 'Mayor' or 'Farmer'. Courtesy moves from manners to action as unfailing kindliness and helpfulness.

The class relations are fixed but inoffensive. They don't matter, because everyone is nice and friendly, and shares the same ceremonies and tradition. Culture and nature work in perfect harmony. It is an excellent tale to tell to five-year-olds, and only the very silly would want to tell them how impossible it all is in real life. The programme is a careful sample from a range of social orders, intelligible to the very small, and critically using the past to prefigure Utopia.

The ideal street is a familiar story. *Sesame Street* similarly unifies people, animals (Big Bird and Kermit) and a happy range of slightly dotty science fiction characters who promise the future as colourful, weird, but safe. It is the same transformation of the best past into a plentiful, happily educated future (all those pecan pies). These serene streets are small pictures of an ideal social order, 'transcending present immaturity' in Benjamin's cumbrous phrase, imagining the good society as we might better put it.

Imagining the good society is *the* most typically human activity of mind. Implicit in the phrase itself is a critical stance towards the present. You look at the present and see all that's wrong with it; you imagine an alternative, necessarily in terms derived from the present, but coming up with different results. You try to take the measure of the gap between the two. Such criticism, however, is conducted very differently according to different positions in the social structure, and this commonplace brings out something curiously missing from Benjamin's benign picture of the making of popular culture out of the shiny bits of debris from the past. It is that culture and art are *fought over*. Wherever there is a struggle over art there is a struggle over the arts of living, and never more than now.

In this book I have consistently spoken up for the progressive values. There is no need to ratify Hegel's optimism about the inevitability of progress, to believe that for many of the oppressed and wretched of the world things have got much better since Hegel's day, and that although this has been a murderously dreadful century, it is well within human capacity to maintain such advances for everyone, even if that means cutting sharply back the advantages of the impossibly rich classes of the world (in Britain and the USA for a start). Speaking in these terms of progressive values, of the still strong promise in the project of modernization, I align this current in human thought with the great tradition of socialism, and roundly declare that the moral criticism socialism makes of the evils of the world is still far and away the most comprehensive and clinching call to high ideals which can plausibly be made in the world as it is. But this is not a sermon intended to enlist supporters or new converts to a political church. Appalling cruelties have been performed in the name of socialism: it has to say so if it is to clear the truth of its own name, and its claim to speak for human community, equality and justice. The point, however, is that *any* theory of the world makes certain deep commitments to value. A critical theory of public communications has to stand on the ground it chooses as being worth something (Taylor's 'distinctions of worth' which we met in chapter 1) in order to talk about its subject at all.

I labour the point about the value-assumptions of theory because on the one hand, some empiricists, as we saw in chapter 3, believe that you can keep values and facts apart, and on the other hand, some Marxists simply equate the truth of their theory with universal values. Neither position will hold. Values impregnate inquiry. Inquiry and experience change true values. Or rather, the texture of experience is shot through with the threads of value. The pattern you see in it is really there, no doubt, even though someone else could see the same texture with different lines and patches gleaming. The pattern you see, and invite others to see, is the pattern of your values. Learning to see the pattern is the course of the education of a citizen.

III

Defining culture as the stories we tell ourselves about ourselves is a reminder that media theory, or the study of public communications, just *is* the study of the making of culture itself. As we heard Ricoeur remind us also in chapter 1, History with a capital H is written about the history which was once life-in-earnest. So, too, media theory is a critical narrative about the many narratives which compose a culture. That it is, by and large, now become critical in a progressive sense is a product of its peculiar birth and growth as we have chronicled them here. It might have turned out to be reactionary, anti-modern, and conservative, if it had a different history of its own. The present crisis in English studies,[5] related as it has to be to a deeper crisis of identity and affiliation in the societies who study English literature, is torn, by contrast, between its progressive and traditionalist factions.

Media theory, pushy, avant-garde, newly arrived as it is, is generally brisk with the idea of tradition. As I say, its genesis has given it a frame of mind which is innately anti-conservative. It is dismissive of *memory* as a dominant faculty of mind; it largely rejects the idea of a canon, which is to say, a relatively fixed assembly of great works by which all newcomer works must be judged. Like so much modern thought, especially in managerial studies, it prefers process to product, form to content, structure to practical experience. It wants to dissolve the categories of art and aesthetics into the systems of production and their organizing discourses.

This is media theory in its shiny, high-technology gear, gibbering fluently about the latest name to become à la mode. As we have gradually assembled our picture of the subject, we certainly need some of this equipment. But in these concluding sections, I want to recast it in a rather different idiom. For a subject to *be* a subject in the curriculum, it has to have a structure of typifying concepts which may be borrowed from all over the place, indeed usually are, but are put to specific uses in the field. 'Cultural industries', 'leisure time', 'encoding/decoding', 'uses and gratifications' are all examples of such concepts in media theory.

A subject also has to have a few sacred texts and leading intellectual heroes. Our texts, or some of them, are listed in the notes to the various chapters, and in a more official list at the end. A few of the heroes have been named, chapter by chapter, once or twice borrowed from other disciplines. The subject has also to have a more or less recognizable subject-matter, although there is no need to go round beating its boundaries and warning off interlopers. Media theory has recruited a very mixed bunch of contributors from politics, literature, sociology, art, psychology and elsewhere. There is no call now for it to become supercilious. Its subject-matter is too blurred and scattered for it to insist on purity of selection. It is, as I say, no less than the sum of narratives as circulated by the media of public communication: print, film, television.

This being so, the most audible and important characterizing feature of a subject is its *idiom*, its habits of conversation and thought. How should it sound to talk about media theory? What is its voice in the conversation of humankind?[6]

The best way of answering this question is to point to the voices of one's masters and friends, and say, 'talk like that'. One reason I have quoted from many sacred texts has been in order to offer up their cadences for imitation. Richard Hoggart in *The Uses of Literacy*, Roland Barthes in *Camera Lucida*, Krishan Kumar in 'Holding the middle ground', Raymond Williams in 'Drama in the dramatised society', are all admirable examples of our best idiom, what W. H. Auden called ' a sane, affirmative speech'. But in any case, although it is right that media theory should have a few pieties and a company of saints, it ought also to be a gregarious and democratic subject. Its subject-matter is no less than the people's stories, and it should therefore be open and intelligible to any citizen who wants to join in.

If it is so open, then we shall need to recall that culture is not only the collective and mutual creation of societies, it is competitive and quarrelsome about who will do the job best. Its creators quarrel over who is right and who is wrong, and never more so than in questions of allegiance to tradition. It is here, if anywhere, that the careful student of media must indeed mediate between the claims of truth and the claims of invention in establishing the meaning which it is his or her business to analyse, criticize, and celebrate.

Consider the creation of culture which is going on when traditions are invented. We see people busiest at the making of tradition when other, taken-for-granted traditions and their narratives are beginning to falter badly. It may be a moment of decline or of buoyant new social energy, but either way classes and nations will be repositioning themselves in an unusually fluid social structure and gluing together new ceremonies and customs in order to lay claim to a long-standing tradition which justifies their changing circumstance, whatever it is. In a celebrated collection of historical essays, *The Invention of Tradition*,[7] Hugh Trevor-Roper tells the tale about the invention of Scottishness in the years between 1780 and 1840.

The story begins a generation after the last and most brutal putting-down of Bonnie Prince Charlie's hopes for the English crown. Edinburgh was by then a thinning metropolis, and a host of Scotsmen had gone south to make their fortune. They coincided with the vast surge of production, repopulation, mechanization and money-making now generalized as the industrial revolution. Expatriate and successful, they invented Scottishness out of a remarkably sparse recipe. Using a volume of phoney folk-poems known as 'Ossian', the novels of Walter Scott, the new woollen looms of Yorkshire, and the tribal names of the Highlands, they brewed up a thick, intoxicating punch concocted of tartans, reels, golf, clans, chieftains, thistles, dirks, and the Gaelic whiskies, which now adorns the international rituals of Burns night.

No Scotsmen will believe Trevor-Roper, of course. They will hang on in the teeth of historical scholarship to the whole mad, necessary cavalcade. For that was and is the point: when nationalism really

got going in the nineteenth century all across Europe, then to establish new traditions which defined that nationalism was the way one
had of finding membership, allegiance, identity. Within nations, the
new classes, with new strengths won from industrialization and the
great dynamo of capitalism, battled to gain status and power. The
new traditions were one key ideological weapon.

This summary is not, however, another essay on ideology; it is not
a running through of chapter 4. Ideology is a useful, two-pronged
concept with which to understand the creation of culture, but it is
only one such instrument. Readers will remember the three realms
of inquiry which I suggested as shaping the field of media theory:
signification, power, production. We can now gather them under
one heading, a heading which could cover all the best work in the
human sciences. I take the heading from an essay by Clifford
Geertz,[8] 'The social history of the moral imagination'.

Geertz is an anthropologist, and the stuff of his subject is the
pre-industrial society, in his case Bali and Morocco. But as he says,
such societies insist on progressing out of the exotic into the everyday. Are they then no longer to be his concern but that, say, of
sociology, which does for modern society? So too with media
theory: its field of work looks at first sight comprehensive but
clearly bounded: it is the field of public communications. And so it
is. But as I have been at pains to show, that takes us back beyond
the advent of the book to the discovery of the alphabet, takes us
world-wide in the search to comprehend the spread of global and
galactic electronics, brings us back abruptly to the details of home
photography. So whose subject is it?

This crossing of the boundaries is also a mark of our times. The
invention of a subject is just the same as the invention of tradition.[9]
It battles for its class position, claims a long family history, pretends
to great ceremonies of learning and antique customs of scholarship.
All subjects overlap. None is fixed either by method or content.
The human point of any subject in the human sciences, whether
philosophy, French, linguistics, economics, anthropology, art history
or media, is to write the social history of the moral imagination.
Furthermore, it should be written in an idiom at once sociable,
conversable, and democratic.

Geertz compares his own efforts to describe and understand the
ghastly, beautiful ceremony of widow-immolation (*suttee*) in nineteenth-century Bali with the efforts of literary critics to understand
no less peculiar stories in novels. Both, he says,

pursue their vocations haunted by a riddle quite as irresolvable as it is fundamental: namely, that the significant works of the human imagination . . . speak with equal power to the consoling piety that we are all like to one another and to the worrying suspicion that we are not. (p. 42)

And he goes on to locate a trembling point of balance in the most unsettling position of his fearsome tale of 'high artistry and high cruelty'. His conclusion, both aesthetic and moral, is that such a contrary difficulty is essential to taking the study of human beings seriously. That study is bound to be contrary and contradictory. And so, if we take as our subject the stories of human lives for the sake of understanding and of edification, for a degree certainly and for a job if possible, but also in order to live a decent enough life and a rational, educated one as well, then the best we can do is catch human lives in action in the traffic between imagination and memory. That traffic escorts our social and moral theme.

This is a more slippery, as well as a more urgent, business than it looks. The point of my brief summary from *The Invention of Tradition* was to show what creative havoc the imagination wreaks with memory. Walter Benjamin tells us that writing history is not a question of trying to tell things the way they really were, as some of the nineteenth-century historians believed they could do if only they could set down enough of the facts. Instead, 'to articulate the past historically . . . means to seize hold of a memory as it flashes up at a moment of danger'. We might put Benjamin's aphorism beside one of the philosopher A. N. Whitehead's, who defined the present, this very moment now, as 'memory tinged with anticipation'. Both observations serve to emphasize that, however vivid and spontaneous life may seem at every second, it is the product of the past. Memory works with what happened; imagination works with what might have happened. The two together are what we think with, and what we think about.

One last set text for this handbook will demonstrate what I mean, and provide readers with an example to follow. Paul Fussell's social history of the moral imagination takes on a very large segment of both. He calls it *The Great War and Modern Memory*,[10] and in the book he documents from a great stock of sources – letters, poems, diaries, autobiographies, novels, newspapers, military records – the shaping of modern memory by the irresistible images of the 1914–18 war. To begin with, it looks an easy game to play. Just list a few such images, and let your memory and imagination rip. Trenches, barbed wire, shell-holes, torrential rain, gun-horses hauling field guns through the mud, Verey lights, machine-guns, stand-to, rats, decaying corpses, waterproof capes and tin hats, the bombardments, the ruined French and Flemish market towns. That excellent movie by Richard Attenborough of Joan Littlewood's stage show, *Oh What a Lovely War*, whipped up these same images in a deliciously kitsch mixture.

Fussell takes this pile of images and shows, first, how the writers of all kinds, poets or not, subverted the classical imagery of heroism and gallant soldiery in a series of bitter ironies made from the experience of trench life, its pointless slaughter, efficiency, and incompetence. Different individuals found different ways of expressing the bitterness, horror, irony, madness and unbelief which were the states of mind in which they survived or died. Fussell then contends that their successor-writers in the Second World War such as Norman Mailer in *The Naked and the Dead* or Joseph Heller in *Catch 22* picked up and made grotesque these visions and the form which contained them. As a result, all of us have had our vision of life in the present mis-shaped profoundly by these memories and metaphors.

It is an enormous claim to make, but we need not worry here about its truth. Fussell's importance for us is that he takes a whole range of historical narratives and analyses their shaping power in the making of memory and the directing of imagination.

It is also noticeable to the media theorist that he respects the canon of art but is not hemmed in by it. That is, he treats seriously as objects of art the poems of Sassoon or Wilfred Owen, the novels of Henry Williamson, while he also includes as being perfectly suitable for his treatment a large anthology of non-artistic writing of all sorts. In this way, he admits a canon of war books – the canon being the classics whose imaginative power gives them claims to special attention – but also finds singular and significant writing in many other places. He does not follow a fixed scheme – poems this side, diaries and letters over there – but *uses* them all for his purposes, and on their merits.

This egalitarian lesson is particularly good for media folk. It is plain silly or plain malignant to pretend, as some radical freebooters do, that nothing cultural is of superior value to anything else. Turner's great paintings are obviously much better than my lousy ones. They *mean* more, move us more, look more like their subject than mine do, are much more beautiful. But the absolute egalitarians are really objecting to the ideological and snobbish use by different elites of their taste and judgement to set themselves up as superior to other people. So the egalitarians argue for the tearing down of all monuments and icons. This is absolute iconoclasm.

One sees what they mean.[11] Literature with a capital L has frozen many classrooms stiff with boredom. Throw away the category, Literature, and set the books free, by all means. Then a new canon will emerge, answering the historical needs of new classes, nations, and generations. This is the invention of tradition, and unstoppable. Our business is never to use a technical language, or the special weaponry of education and learning, in order to dominate those without such protection. This moral duty returns us to the question of idiom, and the question of *what to do* with our studies, their methods and mania. Fussell lights a lamp to follow because he starts without a canon, and devises for himself a method to sort out the countless narratives in front of him. He takes a humanly colossal subject – the making of modern sensibility out of modern war – and works out what is telling in its memory and powerful in its imagining as he goes along. Finally, he follows the precept I set up in chapter 8: a Second World War combat soldier himself, he always balances experience against form, life against art. Neither is allowed to win outright. He uses the material in front of him to determine why we now imagine (and live) as we do, and what we should do about it.

IV

We have discussed the limits of formalism, in semiotics and elsewhere. We have affirmed that ethical and political questions cannot be excluded from the human sciences. We propose that all academic subjects are ways of seeing and criticizing the historical narratives of the day. We nominate aesthetics as our best candidate for everyday theory-making. This is a rather manifesto-like summary of this finale. It is, however, very general. How do we now bring together our different sorts of inquiry so that they are recognizably of a piece? Is media theory just a convenient name for a family of more or less related studies, or is it something more coherent, close, and articulated?

The answer is that it's probably a bit of both, and that that is how it should be. In the first place, no one person could seriously pursue everything in the media studies curriculum. A historically grounded political economy is no doubt the most powerful engine in the team, but not everyone will want to drive it. If it leads off into audience research, as it reasonably might, then other kinds of inquiry have to wait. If the political economy of media sends someone off to collect the constantly changing and vast amounts of investment, takeover, and new technology data, then such research cannot also take in the detailed analysis of political partisanship in election programmes on television. Even less can an interest in, say, the semiotics of popular culture during the Middle Ages go easily along with a cultural history like Paul Fussell's or Edward Said's.

Yet all these studies could legitimately be called media studies, and each would draw upon one of the methodologies as they are aligned here, chapter by chapter. The same family variety and disagreements would be apparent in the English, Music, Physics or Geography departments. Just as the natural scientist has a controlling method, a subject-matter, and a theoretic model, so too the human scientist, amongst whom we easily count ourselves. The human scientist takes culture, not nature, for subject-matter. His method is practical and historical, rather than empirical and hypothetical. For the natural scientist, criticism arises from observation. For the human scientist, criticism is inscribed in the practice of inquiry. That is to say, he and she, studying human action-in-history, can only interpret what they find in terms of their sympathies, assumptions and commitments. They are as aware of these as possible, but they cannot keep them out of things. Valid interpretation *turns on* a strong and capacious range of feelings which we are always revising and reconstituting.

This is not, absolutely not, a doctrine for what philosophers call emotivism in one version, intuitionism in another. Either way, these doctrines teach that feelings dominate values and supersede reason. They also imply, in their sillier versions, that spontaneous, unchecked intuitions ('gut-reactions') are better and truer than ones you have thought about. Without going into a very long disquisition on a very tricky subject, let us say that the movement of our feeling is the same thing as the movement of interpretation, and that this is naturally a conscious and a verbal experience.[12] Indeed, it is the standard form of all experience. We feel an emotion. We give it a name (joy, love, misery, remorse). This gives a form to what is happening. We think (and feel) again. We give it a slightly different name (not joy, but quiet happiness, not misery but sullen defeat). We reinterpret feeling and experience in terms of each other. This is the spiral of self-interpretation. It is how we make our cognitions stick, and decide what action to take about them.

Within the human sciences in general and media theory in particular, there can be no question of trying to keep away from this human, natural and essential self-interpretation. There is only the effort to make such interpretation larger, more understanding, better in every sense including the moral one. We cannot stay away from ethical questions without lapsing into stupidity or nihilism.

Knowledge motivates action. There is no saying in what direction, of course. But as we ask questions of experience, and discover facts which are the answers, our stance towards the experience is altered. This is in parallel to the movement of feeling I have just described. The facts are themselves 'distinctions of worth'. We have looked for those facts, not for others. Or they have turned up unexpectedly (the teacher has only just told them to us). There is a shock. Then our feelings, momentarily recoiled, come forward to comprehend (which in origin means 'en-fold') the facts and take an attitude towards them.

Then we wonder what to do about it. Knowledge leads to decision (including the decision to do nothing). This is the model of thought and action which is equivalent to the natural scientist's model of hypothesis-plus-verification. It explains the heading of this chapter a little more. Self-interpretation is just a synonym for the interplay of the narratives of culture. The educated citizen acquires these narratives and, as a result of a decent education, knows what they mean. Since citizenship is defined by its being a common membership with duties towards others to match the rights for oneself, there is then action to take.

Citizenship has become a rather comical word in English recently. Consumer culture drives us so exclusively into the small rooms and gardens of private life, that we lose its power and its vision of us as members of the *polity*, the old Greek word for the common state. Yet national education carries within it a definition of citizenship, and it is the drive and meaning of the studies outlined in this book that they push their students towards recognition of that citizenship.

I don't imply that media theory will necessarily make you free or virtuous. But you cannot practise it without having, at some level, to take decisions *about* freedom and virtue. I shall end with a short account of a media project, well within the scope of any citizen-student, which leads in its small way to such a moment.

A very terse example might be given by studying the British tabloid press, and asking what picture of human behaviour is presented and endorsed there. We would go on (encoding/decoding) to ask what ideal reader that press presupposes. Any answers, taking in the raucous cruelty and lying, the appalling sentimentality and crude nationalism of these newspapers, would have to be bleak. We could only salvage the ideal reader by marking a big space between his real attitudes and the trivial satisfactions of girlie photos and bullying pub-slogans.

Well, the bleak picture might be a true one. How could we know? The answer can only be, in academic study, by trying to find out more about production and consumption. And if that led our virtuous student to think that the owners and producers of such newspapers must be cynical, money-lustful bigots who ought to be expropriated, well, that's where it led.

The moral of such a terse tale can go two ways, no doubt. The student might rush off to become an advertising agent. (She might come to the right conclusion *and* have to take the wrong job.) But let us try something a bit harder. Let us follow Raymond Williams[13] (and Inglis[14]) in seeing our society as 'the society of the spectacle', a world at a great distance from our real life. That is to say, apart from a tiny elite in power, all the rest of us can do is sit in small rooms and watch the window or the television for something menacing to turn up. The spectacle of society is drawn past the screen at a *distance* for us to watch and to envy, but we sit powerless. If anything important happens, it will happen *to* us. Our powerlessness makes it impossible for us to *make* things happen. Citizenship is worn out.

There is an echo here of what Garnham said about empirical research in chapter 7, that the best explanation of people's use of electronic television is that they feel powerless in private. So they vote crudely for the money, and leave the world as a spectacle.

This would account for television's magic power, and the weird exaltation of the star, the celebrity, and the personality as enshrined in 625 lines of shimmering dots and primary colours. We can only watch the screen (we can't get into it). They can embody power on it. Then there is not much difference between Terry Wogan and the President, Barbara Walters and the Prime Minister. Their magic is that they appear on the screen, and are recognized worldwide. Nothing we can do will make any difference.

To understand this process would take us off in many directions: finding out how much they're all paid would be a start, and then how they live and how what they say squares up with what they do. We might go on to study the framing and manners of stardom by the screen and by all the supporting magazines. Beyond that we could follow the fate of the spectacle into the looking glass, and study how extremely ordinary neighbours in the East End, in

Coronation Street, in Melbourne and Dallas and Miami, are represented to us ordinary neighbours by figures of international celebrity and El Dorado riches.

All these disciplined inquiries could only bring us, as students, back to deep, lived and committed questions of freedom and power, of truthfulness to life and treatment of other people. We may shrug or we may be angry; we may be amused or bemused. But the study of the enigmatic narratives of our culture is the study of the news of the world. It is the study of what to make of it all.

Notes

1 For a valuable, plainly written guide to Hegel's present relevance, see Charles Taylor, *Hegel and Modern Society* (Cambridge University Press, 1979).
2 Clifford Geertz, *The Interpretation of Cultures* (Hutchinson, 1975), p. 448.
3 Walter Benjamin, *Charles Baudelaire: the Lyric Poet in the Era of High Capitalism* (New Left Books, 1974).
4 I am following myself here, in my *Popular Culture and Political Power* (Harvester Wheatsheaf, 1988), chapter 6.
5 The best summary of the state of English is, by a long chalk, Terry Eagleton's *Literary Theory* (Basil Blackwell, 1983).
6 This is a reference to an essay by Michael Oakeshott called 'The language of poetry in the conversation of mankind', from his *Rationalism in Politics* (Methuen, 1962).
7 *The Invention of Tradition*, ed. Eric Hobsbawm and Terence Ranger (Cambridge University Press, 1983).
8 In Clifford Geertz, *Local Knowledge: Further Essays in Interpretive Anthropology* (Basic Books, 1983), chapter 2.
9 In this argument, I am summarizing my *The Management of Ignorance: a Political Theory of the Curriculum* (Basil Blackwell, 1985).
10 Paul Fussell, *The Great War and Modern Memory* (Oxford University Press, 1975).
11 We are uncompromisingly told so by Terry Eagleton (1983); see n. 5 above.
12 For the refinements of the argument, see Charles Taylor's essay, 'Self-interpreting animals' in his *Philosophical Papers Vol II: Human Agency and Language* (Cambridge University Press, 1985).
13 See Raymond Williams's essay, 'Drama in the dramatised society', in his *Writing in Society* (Verso Books, 1983). See also his brief article 'Distance', about TV and the Falklands adventure, *London Review of Books*, 17–30 June (1982).
14 In my *Popular Culture and Political Power* (1988) (n. 4 above).

Question Time: How to Make Theory out of Practice

I

I shall not provide a huge bibliography. In introductory textbooks like this, and indeed on the matching courses in college and in Higher Education, there is a fatal tendency on the part of author or tutor to hand out a ludicrously comprehensive bibliography headed 'Further Reading'. I propose two more modest and more manageable forms of student help; the first is simply a list, as short as possible, of the readings which, if you take the argument of this book seriously, you really must go on to read. The second is a short sequence of representative student projects, of varying difficulty but all roughly of the sort media students are asked to do as part of the assessment by course work for their degree or qualification. In each case, the suggested project takes its point of departure from the approach outlined in this book. In each case, also, I suggest relevant reading which can be reduced or amplified according to the level of difficulty at which the student is working.

The fullest bibliography of the whole subject in an easily available text is by Denis McQuail in his *Mass Communication Theory* (Sage Publications, 1983). Obviously, in this field there are new books coming out the whole time, but for anyone looking for the most comprehensive list from which to begin research, McQuail can't be beaten.

The immediate essential reading upon which this book is based and which, in my judgement, the virtuous media student-theorist should have read by the day the degrees are awarded, is as follows:

Adorno, Theodor W. and Max Horkheimer, 'The culture industries', chapter 2 of *The Dialectic of the Enlightenment*, Allen Lane, The Penguin Press, 1973. Also collected in Curran et al., 1977, as cited.

Barthes, Roland, *Mythologies* (1957) Jonathan Cape, 1972; Paladin, 1973.

——, *Camera Lucida: Reflections on Photography*, Fontana Flamingo, 1984.

Benjamin, Walter, the two essays, 'The storyteller' and 'The work of art in the age of mechanical reproduction', in *Illuminations*, Jonathan Cape, 1970.

——, *Charles Baudelaire: The Lyric Poet in the Era of High Capitalism*, New Left Books, 1974.

Blumler, Jay and Elihu Katz, *The Uses of Mass Communication*, Sage publications, 1974.

Collins, Richard, James Curran, Nicholas Garnham and Colin Sparks (eds) *Media, Culture and Society: a Critical Reader*, Sage Publications, 1986.

Curran, James, 'Capitalism and control of the press 1800–1975', in James Curran et al., as cited, 1977.

Curran, James, Michael Gurevitch and Janet Woollacott (eds), *Mass Communication and Society*, Edward Arnold and Open University Press, 1977.

Curran, James and Jean Seaton, *Power Without Responsibility*, Sage Publications, rev. ed. 1988.

Eagleton, Terry, *Literary Theory*, Basil Blackwell, 1983.

Eco, Umberto, *Essays in Hyper-reality*, Picador Books, 1987.

Febvre, Lucien and Henri-Jean Martin, *The Coming of the Book: the Impact of Printing 1450–1800*, New Left Books, 1976.

Fussell, Paul, *The Great War and Modern Memory*, Oxford University Press, 1975.

Garnham, Nicholas, 'Contribution to a political economy of mass communication', in Richard Collins et al. (eds), as cited, 1986.

——, *Structures of Television*, BFI monograph, rev. edn, 1979.

——, 'Concepts of culture, public policy and the cultural industries', GLC Economic Policy Group, 1983. A version of this appears in Garnham's selection of his essays, forthcoming from Sage Publications in 1990 as *Communications and Capitalism*.

Geertz, Clifford, 'Ideology as a cultural system', in *The Interpretation of Cultures*, Basic Books, 1973; Hutchinson, 1975.

——, 'The social history of the moral imagination', in *Local Knowledge: Further Essays in Interpretive Anthropology*, Basic Books, 1983.

Goody, Jack and Ian Watt, 'The consequences of literacy' in J. Goody (ed.), *Literacy in Traditional Societies*, Cambridge University Press, 1972. Several other papers in this collection are of great interest.

Gurevitch, Michael, James Curran, Tony Bennett and Janet Woolla-cott (eds), *Culture, Society and the Media*, Methuen, 1982.

Hall, Stuart, 'Encoding/decoding', in Stuart Hall, D. Hobson, A. Lowe and P. Willis (eds), *Culture, Media, Language*, Hutchinson, 1980.

HMSO (Government publications), *Social Trends*, annually.

Hodge, Bob and David Tripp, *Children and Television*, Polity Press, 1986.

Hoggart, Richard, *The Uses of Literacy*, Chatto & Windus with Penguin, 1957.

Katz, Elihu and Paul Lazarsfeld, *Personal Influence: the Part Played by People in the Flow of Mass Communications*, Free Press of Glencoe, 1955.

Kumar, Krishan, 'Holding the middle ground', in James Curran et al., as cited, 1977.

——, 'Public service broadcasting and its public', in Colin McCabe and Olivia Stewart (eds), *The Future of Public Service Broadcasting*, Manchester University Press, 1986.

Leavis, F. R., 'Mass civilisation and minority culture', in Leavis's *Education and the University*, Chatto & Windus, 1943.

—— with Denys Thompson, *Culture and Environment*, Chatto & Windus, 1932.

Leavis, Q. D., *Fiction and the Reading Public*, Chatto & Windus, 1932.

McLuhan, Marshall, *The Gutenberg Galaxy*, Routledge & Kegan Paul, 1962, especially the last chapter, 'The plight of mass man in an individualist society'.

Marx, Karl and Friedrich Engels, *The German Ideology*, C. J. Arthur (ed.), Lawrence and Wishart, 1970.

——, *The Thought of Karl Marx*, David McLellan (ed.), Macmillan, 1977.

Masterman, Len, *Teaching about Television*, Macmillan, 1980.

——, *Teaching About the Media*, Comedia, 1985.

Morley, David, *Family Television*, Comedia, 1986.

Murdock, Graham, 'Capitalism, communication and class relations' (with Peter Golding), in Curran et al., as cited, 1977.

——, 'Large corporations and the control of the communications industry', in Michael Gurevitch et al., as cited, 1982.

Said, Edward, *Orientalism*, Vintage Books, 1979; Penguin, 1987.

Schramm, Wilbur, Jack Lyle and Edwin Parker, *Television in the Lives of our Children*, Stanford University Press, 1961.

Sontag, Susan, *On Photography*, Penguin, 1977.

Williams, Bernard, *Obscenity and Censorship: a Shortened Version of the Report of the Committee on Obscenity and Film Censorship*, originally Cmnd. 7772, HMSO, 1979, now Cambridge University Press, 1981.

Williams, Raymond, *Television: Technology and Cultural Form*, Fontana Collins, 1974.

——, *Communications*, rev. ed, Penguin, 1979.

——, 'Drama in the dramatised society', in Williams's collection, *Writing in Society*, Verso, 1983.

——, 'Distance', *London Review of Books*, 17–30 June, 1982.

——, *Williams on Television*, Routledge, 1989.

Wollen, Peter, *Sign and Meaning in the Cinema*, Secker & Warburg, 1969.

II

The best way to make theory out of practice is, of course, to practise. We turn to the experience and the facts which interest us, and look for the patterns which give experience its meaning. The following brief research projects are offered as illustrating the sort of inquiry prompted by the various chapters of this book. They are also intended to be similar to the sort of pieces of personal research undertaken by degree students of mass media and public communications during the more sensible kinds of course-work assessment now common in further and higher education.

Each inquiry may be pursued to a level suitable to the student in question: simpler inquiries will take fewer books, and briefer treatment. In each case I attempt very succinctly to show how to pursue the topics identified in the argument of this book and in such a way that the student will discover for himself the theoretic patterns of his understanding. As I said in chapter 1, 'theory' is a name for the sense we can make of different parts of the world. No theory can get everything in. Some theories are just vacuous: that is, it is never clear what would count as evidence *against* them. Plenty of students will also find, as we all do, that their theoretic understanding, even after plenty of practice, remains murky. They can see the form of the thing, but obscurely and in a bad light. The vivid excitement of thought itself is then to struggle to see better, to make sense of what looms through the dense fog, the thickly crowded trees, the chaos of the traffic. In this connection it is worth insisting on a respect for facts. Obviously the naked fact by itself is pretty useless. It can't mean anything alone. We have to be interested in it. But the patient collection of facts that *are* interesting or significant is itself illuminating, both to the fact-collector and his or her readers. The theory may still be murky but the facts are bound to bring a bit of light.

As I stressed in the body of the book, facts and values, like practice and theory, cannot ever be simply separated one from another. My remarks are intended to be mildly encouraging to students whose research hasn't led them into the well-lit place of theory, but in which they have succeeded in describing faithfully for themselves and others the nature and appearance of one small corner of the media world.

1 The social meanings of the photograph album

This first project begins from the familiar facts and local knowledge provided by the family photograph album. The researcher would start from the meditation suggested by chapter 8, and drawing in detail upon the commonplace materials of snapshots at home, at parental and grandparental houses, ask what these photographs mean to those who took and cherish them. 'Meaning' here is a manifold word but not a difficult one: we say (with Barthes) 'this picture of my mother means a lot to me', and if asked to explain, we would develop the remark in terms of our feelings and memories.

Asking the same question of photographs whose origins we know less about, let us say Walker Evans's famous photographs of the poor farmers of the Western dustbowl in the 1930s, we treat the photographer's intentions, for their human meaning, for their historical resonance and context, for their ideological significance ('meaning-form'), for their composition, and above all, for the balance of their aesthetic and their experienced life. Photography, as it was the business of chapter 8 to bring out, is the homeliest medium. We can deal with it in a perfectly unafraid way.

The books which would help include:

Agee, James and Walker Evans, *Let Us Now Praise Famous Men*, Houghton Mifflin, 1980.
Barthes, Roland, as cited, 1984.
Berger, John, *About Looking*, Readers and Writers, 1978.
——, *Ways of Seeing*, BBC with Penguin, 1972.
Berger, John with Jean Mohr, *Another Way of Telling*, Readers and Writers Collective, 1982.
——, *A Fortunate Man*, Penguin, 1968.

Burgin, Victor (ed.), *Thinking Photography*, Macmillan, 1982.
Hall, Stuart, 'The social eye of Picture Post', *Working Papers in Cultural Studies*, 2, 1972.
Sontag, Susan, *On Photography*, Penguin, 1979.
Tagg, John, *The Burden of Representation: Essays on Photographies and Histories*, Macmillan, 1988.

2   The spectacle of power

This topic would turn on the treatment of ideology and semiotics in chapters 4 and 5, as well as on the suggestions made in chapter 9 about the drastic limits set on present-day definitions of citizenship, our increasingly general sense of our powerlessness in public affairs, and the pushing back by the forces of both politics and the media of all individuals into the position of spectators, generally sitting at home and watching or listening to the powerful telling them what. Such a study would invite discussion of the semiotics of power: how do presidents, prime ministers or monarchs present themselves to the people? It would go on, no doubt, to analyse how they talk to those people, whether directly, or via our so-called representatives in interviews. It could include such state and party occasions as Inaugurations, openings of Parliament, and elections. It would take in the relations of the press to power (fawning, critical, toadying, distant, respectful; what else?), and it might, if it were *very* ambitious, include historical comparisons with the spectacle of power in remote times or places. Interested students might start with:

Anglo, S., *Spectacle, Pageantry and Early Tudor Policy*, Oxford University Press, 1969.
Boorstin, Daniel, *The Image*, Penguin, 1963.
Chaney, David, 'Civic ritual in mass society', in Richard Collins et al. as cited., 1986.
Debord, Gary, *The Society of the Spectacle*, Black and Red Press, 1970.
Geertz, Clifford, 'Centers, kings and charisma: reflections on the Symbolics of power', in his *Local Knowledge*, 1983, as cited.
Goffman, Erving, *The Presentation of Self in Everyday Life*, Penguin, 1968.
Halloran, James, Graham Murdock and Phillip Elliott, *Demonstrations and Communication: a Case Study*, Penguin, 1970.
Inglis, Fred, 'Spectacle and domesticity', in his *Popular Culture and Political Power*, Harvester Wheatsheaf, 1988.

Mailer, Norman, *Miami and the Siege of Chicago*, Penguin, 1968.
Novak, Michael, *Choosing our King*, Doubleday, 1974.
Scribner, R. W., *For the Sake of Simple Folk*, Cambridge University Press, 1981.
Thompson, Hunter, *Fear and Loathing on the Campaign Trail*, Paladin, 1974.
Williams, Raymond, 'Drama in the dramatised society', as cited, 1974, 1983.

3   Ideology and hegemony at work

Such an undertaking tackles two of the largest and most problematic concepts in social and political theory (of which, as I said, media studies are part), and tries to catch them in action. Antonio Gramsci, first coiner and then analyst of the term hegemony, insists on the sheer difficulty of stepping outside our taken-for-granted frames of reference in order to see who constructed them for us, without our noticing or with our complicity. Hegemony, as he says, soaks deep into the grain of our common sense, and finding it out means doing a bit of violence to our most everyday assumptions.

So, too, with ideology: ideology, as I suggested (following Geertz), may be interpreted either as an attempt to fool people into assuming values and believing ideas which are against their real interests (the fix theory), or as the system of ideas with which they more or less arbitrarily take the weight of an alien world (the strain theory). Either way, it is here strongly advocated that in the study of ideology *and* of hegemony, we should try simply to treat all such manifestations as *texts* of a kind. That is, we should analyse social action as part of a continuing, always historical set of narratives, and see people's behaviour as taking its meaning from their place in the story of the times. If we do so, we will then be awake to the sheer variety of human performances, their *symbolic* purposes and declarations.

Examples in our field are legion. Most of them are narratives in the most literal sense. So one could chart the narrative of television soap opera or situation comedy for its ideological meanings, taking care not to be crass about it. It's no good calling a programme sexist (say), if when you look closely at it you find that objections to sexism are the subject-matter of the joke. In other words, what is called for in the study of ideology is at least the same degree of careful attention as we would give to the study of a work of art.

This, however, turns out to be truistic as well as circular. For we understand *any* text, work of art or daily newspaper, as potentially ideological or, in the mouth-filling adjective, hegemonic. The two terms are useful instruments of analysis to determine the meaning of what is in front of us. They are important – vital, even – but not by any means all that has to be said. However priggish it is to say so, goodness, truth, and beauty are every bit as central. A movie may be beautiful as well as hegemonic (the two are connected); a newspaper report may be merely ideological, and to that extent untruthful.

The student will mark out her own field of examples amongst the torrent of narratives of the day. The books and essays that follow will be useful in the analysis, for its ideological or hegemonic meaning, of *any* text in whatever medium, including such commonplace social actions-considered-as-a-test as sport, hobbies, wedding-days, funerals, strikes, or going to posh restaurants.

Geertz, Clifford, 'Ideology as a cultural system', as cited, 1975.

Glasgow University Media Group, *Bad News*, Routledge, 1976; also catalogued under Philo, Greg.

——, *More Bad News*, Routledge, 1980.

——, *Really Bad News*, Writers and Readers, 1982.

Gramsci, Antonio, on hegemony (see index), in *Selections from the Prison Notebooks*, Cr, and ed. Quentin Hoare and Geoffrey Nowell-Smith, Lawrence & Wishart, 1971.

Hall, Stuart, 'Culture, the media and the ideological effect', in Curran et al., as cited, 1977.

Kumar, Krishan, 'Holding the middle ground', as cited, 1977.

McLellan, David, *Ideology*, Macmillan, 1984.

Marx, Karl and Friedrich Engels, as cited, 1970.

Masterman, Len, as cited, 1985.

4   The tyranny of discourse

Discourse, it will be remembered, is the concept whereby theorists try to trap a whole field of, as they say, social practices, within a single topic. It isn't a very secure term once it is in operation because it proves so hard to decide what to include and what to exclude. But it is made more precise by writers such as Foucault when he documents the rules and conventions which, to use his term, inscribe the discourse in the lives of those who speak, read and write it. In particular, he follows those rules into the legislation which, in the most exact sense, inscribes the systems of society on our minds and bodies. Hence, a student wanting to pursue such a lead might indeed follow Foucault himself into analysis of the discourse of sexuality, noting how its rules, categories, imperatives and structures organize and evaluate our emotions and sensations even at those moments we most confidently think of as being our absolute and intimate own.

Discourse, however, need not designate quite such a heavily per-spiring field of discursive practices as sex, and its cognate, gender. In Paul Fussell's book *Abroad*, listed below, the author plots the man-ners and mechanisms of travel-writing in the twenties and thirties and in a more or less traditionally literary-critical way. By this token, discourse designates little more than the subject of a wide-spread cultural conversation, but it is none the worse for that. In the first, more severe sense of discourse, students could take up either Foucault's lead in charting sexuality and its linguistic structures, or Said's and the forms of racism, or Michele Barrett's and Juliet Mitchell's and the many stereotypes of modern women. In the weaker sense of discourse, they could bring Fussell up to date with contemporary tourism (asking when and why tourism replaced travelling), or could independently launch upon such vast subject-matters as the imagery and semantics of citizenship, political resist-ance, countryside (and landscape), childhood, illness, or such great moral names as heroism, duty, loving-kindness.

A warning about the use of the word 'stereotype'. Stereotypes in the literature of discourse are invariably a bad thing. I can't see why. On some showings, a stereotype is simply a synonym for a category, and without fairly secure categories nobody can think at all. Stereo-typing, I suppose, obstructs our thought and feeling when it blinds us to relevant human detail. But as Barthes' use of the meaning–form distinction brings out, and my criticism of him further qual-ifies, to *have* meaning, you must have form. The great thing is to hold the two in balance, meaning against form, living experience and fixed category.

This list of books includes several which are not easy, but each tries to make discourse analysis historical and specific. Each is, therefore, an example of how to conduct this sort of inquiry; no-body would need to read each one in order to follow any.

Aries, Phillippe, *Centuries of Childhood*, Penguin, 1979.
Barrett, Michele, *Women's Oppression Today*, Verso, 1988.
Clark, T. J., *The Painting of Modern Life*, Thames and Hudson, 1985.
Eagleton, Terry, as cited, 1983.
Foucault, Michel, *Discipline and Punish*, Penguin, 1977.

———, *A History of Sexuality*, vol. I, Penguin, 1979.

Fussell, Paul, as cited, 1975.

———, *Abroad: British Literary Travelling Between the Wars*, Oxford University Press, 1980.

Goffmann, Erving, *Asylums: the Social Situations of Mental Patients and other Inmates*, Anchor Books, 1961.

———, *Stigma: Notes on the Management of Spoiled Identity*, Simon and Schuster, rev. ed. 1986.

Mitchell, Juliet, *Women's Estate*, Penguin, 1977.

Said, Edward, *Orientalism*, Penguin, 1987.

Sontag, Susan, *Illness as Metaphor*, Random House, 1979.

5   Outline of a research topic in the political economy of media

I put this heading in an elementary way because this is the area of inquiry people regard as the most fearsome. In point of fact, all that is really needed is a grasp on the simple economic model outlined in chapter 6. So long as you understand the very broad features of capitalist production systems – its mass production and distribution, its managerial hierarchy, its cost-effective criteria and its drive for new markets – you can't go far wrong.

Such details ought to be standard currency in the educated citizen's vocabulary. Add to them the only slightly more technical notions of economies of scale, unit costs, the falling rate of all profits over time (merely a historical and statistical fact), and the margin set between manufacturing costs and selling price in which profit is made, and there you are. It is then only important to recognize that economic production in general and capitalism in particular is fraught with inherent contradictions, and to look out for them, and research into the facts of economic life can begin.

Certain kinds of topic are easy, and the most obvious is ownership. Take James Curran's and Graham Murdock's research as outlined in chapter 6, and as the ghost in *All the President's Men* advises, 'follow the money'. The mergers and takeovers reported in *The Financial Times* or *The Economist* will provide a fat dossier in no time with which, say, to bring up to date Curran's essay on 'Capitalism and control of the Press, 1800–1975', cited above. Similarly, to plot the ownership of 'vertical control' whereby the conglomerates try to buy up the whole sequence of production in software (film-making, for instance), distribution (cinemas) *and* hardware (rented video-recorders) is to grasp in as full and concrete a version as possible the concept of verticality. The crucial position of the editor can be plainly understood if we set side by side the balance sheet or annual report of a big publishing house with its catalogue of titles. We can see what specialist market they have identified, what new range of titles, what kind of investment and profit. Sometimes, in such work, it is hard to get, for example, sales figures from an individual firm; but even then, much can be done with, in the case of books, the trade's monthly journal, *The Bookseller*, the HMSO record *Social Trends* (as cited), and National Book Committee reports (sure to be in the public library). For the economics of the BBC and IBA in Britain, consult the two authorities' annual *Handbooks* in which the virulently competitive audience figures may be studied, and thereby the relative success of the programme planners who backed them.

In a political economy as ebullient and unpredictable as that of public communications, the researcher has to live day by day. The subject is inherently unstable and explosive, and a bracing reminder that media theory cannot of its nature and history be fixed and dogmatic. The most ambitious topic would be to guess at the future of the broadcasting industries world-wide, as cable, satellite and deregulation (in the fatuous term) start to move faster towards the year 2000. For such inquiry, only tentative conclusions will do, and the journal *Media, Culture and Society* (since 1979) will be a tough but indispensable ally. Otherwise, these few references will provide a grounding:

Beesley, Michael, *Liberalisation of the Use of British Telecommunications Network*: Report to the Secretary of State, HMSO, 1981.

Bell, Daniel, *The Coming of the Post-Industrial Society*, Penguin, 1976.

Collins, Richard et al. as cited.

Curran, James, as cited, 1977, 1986, 1988.

Garnham, Nicholas, as cited, 1979, 1983, (chapter 6, n. 4), 1986, 1990.

HMSO, *The Development of Cable Systems and Services*, Command 8866 (British Government White Paper), 1983.

Mattelart, Armand, *Multinational Corporations and the Control of Culture*, Humanities Press, 1979.

Milman, Seymour, *Pentagon Capitalism*, McGraw-Hill, 1970.

Murdock, Graham, as cited, 1977, 1982.

Schiller, Herbert, *Mass Communications and American Empire*, Kelley, 1970.

Whale, John, *The Politics of the Media*, Fontana Collins, 1977.
In addition, the BBC publishes regularly, through its Broadcasting Research Department, a variety of papers relevant to this area, as do the journals *Media World* and *Telematics* (USA).

6   Institutional history in the mass media

This sort of work announces its own method. Throughout this book I have said that if in doubt or difficulty about what is going on in any section of the cultural industries, the way to clarity is by doing history. Find out how things got to be the way they are. Probably this is also the straightest way into political economy. Certainly history explains much of ideological tendencies in any sphere of cultural production, although we should remind ourselves that to pick out and accurately to describe ideological tendencies does not somehow explain away the artistic power of film, novel or television programme. There is an awful tendency to think that blowing the gaff on ideology does down the narrative in question, as though saying that the BBC is the product of the social class formations, Lord Reith and the Universities of Oxford and Cambridge, as it undoubtedly is, somehow puts us in an ineffably superior position as knowing what's what, and how things in the great world really work.

What really is the case is that knowing the history of the BBC, the ABC, CBS, US public broadcasting, Hollywood, or the *Daily Mail*, will go a long way to explain the present world, and bolt together our theories about it a lot tighter. I shall stay with the example of the BBC, not only because it has been, and remains for a doubtless short season, so influential world-wide, but also because its sheer size and its internal contradictions make its history fascinating to write and always open to new disclosures and interpretations. But, of course, the history of other such institutions as Hollywood, and within Hollywood, individual companies, or of the new organizations of cultural production constantly springing up (Channel Four, pirate radio, new newspapers), make the field one without boundaries. There is everything to do.

If we stick, as an instance, with the BBC, then we have to start from Asa Briggs's monumental history, and go on from there.

Briggs, Asa, *The History of Broadcasting in the United Kingdom*, 4 vols, Oxford University Press, 1961–79:

I: *The Birth of Broadcasting,*
II: *The Golden Age of Wireless,*
III: *The War of Words.*
IV: *Sound and Vision.*

Burns, Tom, *The BBC: Public Institution and Private World*, Macmillan, 1977.

HMSO, *The Future of Broadcasting: Report of the Royal Commission on Broadcasting* ('The Annan Report'), HMSO, 1977. See also its predecessor, 'The Pilkington Report', HMSO, 1963, in which Richard Hoggart had a main hand. The most recent Government report on the future of the BBC is the more informal 'Peacock Report' of 1987. It recommended against the BBC's taking advertising and left its licence in place. Many people now (1990) think, however, that Peacock will be very quickly superannuated. Certainly, it gives little evidence of such careful thought as Annan or Pilkington.

Kumar, Krishan, as cited, 1977, 1986.

Leapman, Michael, *The Last Days of the Beeb*, Allen & Unwin, 1986.

McCabe, Colin and Olivia Stewart (eds), *The Future of Public Service Broadcasting*, Manchester University Press, 1986.

Milne, Alasdair, *DG: the Memoirs of a British Broadcaster*, Hodder & Stoughton, 1988.

Smith, Anthony, *The Shadow in the Cave: Broadcasting and its Public*, Quartet Books, 1976.

Wyndham Goldie, Grace, *Facing the Nation: Television and Politics 1936–1976*, Bodley Head, 1977.

Finally, the BBC weekly, *The Listener*, used to be a source of continuing and informed debate about the Corporation. Researchers should pay particular attention, there and elsewhere, to the contributions of Phillip Whitehead.

7   Encoding and decoding the cultural product

This project is the one most fully to engage with the tradition of practical criticism in literature. It cannot escape questions and judgements of value. Who, indeed, would want to? We all start in cultural life from our preferences ('I like that') and our judgements ('That's lovely; this is very good'). The problem is the connection between the two kinds of observation.

The terms encoding and decoding have become jargon words for putting meaning into a message, and taking a meaning out of it. But as both Umberto Eco and Roland Barthes remind us, the word 'code' itself indicates a *system* of meaning whose structures precede our intentions and whose rules cannot be broken without our lapsing into nonsense. In his key paper for this project, Stuart Hall (1980, as cited) emphasizes four stages on each side of the duo encoding-decoding, and further shows how far these determine the frames and contexts of our meanings, irrespective of our intentions. That is, in using a camera, you are (obviously) directed by the limits and scope of the technology. You can't write a novel with it, although some films are much more like novels than others. (John Houston and John Schlesinger make films like novels; Ingmar Bergman and Werner Fassbinder don't.)

The point is much less obvious than it sounds. Hall pushes us to think hard about how the technical infrastructure and the relations of production, the frameworks of knowledge and the structures which give and yield meaning (like a grammar), all work to decide *for* us what we have to say. Moreover, these work on both sides; we are as deeply settled in these structures, relations and frameworks reading a novel at home as we are making a movie on location.

This is the point of using the fearsome phrase 'cultural product' in the title of this section. Media messages are produced by the cultural industries for our leisure consumption. This was as true of Shakespeare's plays for the Globe theatre (although all the structures of production would, naturally, have been very different then) as it is true now for a Promenade concert broadcast from the Lincoln Centre. Mention of the Shakespeare play and the concert, however, poses the question, what is art? (and does it matter?).

It is my view as voiced in this book that art matters a lot. This project could easily take its main point from the distinction. A student could choose any sheaf of texts – whether films, novels, magazines, pub chat, children's picture books, or an evening's television – and while following Hall's four-step analysis up to encoding and down through decoding, decide whether and where definitions of art need and must apply. Such an inquiry would take the argument to the heart of what we believe, according to our priorities, to be precious about our narratives: how much money do they make? (and for whom?), how much pleasure do they give? (and of what sort?), how much truth do they tell (and what is a lie in a story, in any case?). Are they beautiful? Are they good for us? And if they *are* art, who says so?

The problem of art is not the only way into the analysis of

encoding and decoding, but it has a long and absorbing debate behind it, and it is the best way I know with which to distinguish between merely snobbish claims about taste and connoisseurship, and about the mightiest and most enduring matters of human life, of birth and death, and good and evil.

A booklist on this debate would go back to the Greeks. These few titles make a beginning.

Barthes, Roland, as cited, 1973.

Geertz, Clifford, 'Art as a Cultural System', in Geertz, 1983, as cited.

Hebdige, Dick, *Subculture: the Meaning of Style*, Methuen, 1977.

Hirsch, E. D., *Validity in Interpretation*, Yale University Press, 1976.

Hoggart, Richard, 1957, as cited.

Holub, Miloslav, *Reception Theory*, Methuen, 1980.

Leavis, F. R., 'Literature and Criticism' and 'Literature and Sociology', in *The Common Pursuit*, Chatto & Windus, 1952.

Lowenthal, Leo, *Literature, Popular Culture, and Society*, Doubleday Anchor, 1961.

Murdoch, Iris, *The Sovereignty of Good*, Routledge & Kegan Paul, 1970.

——, *The Fire and the Sun: Plato and the Artists*, Oxford University Press, 1977.

Sartre, Jean-Paul, *What is Literature?*, Methuen, 1968.

Taylor, R. L., *Art: an Enemy of the People*, Harvester, 1978.

Wollheim, Richard, *Art and its Objects*, Penguin, rev. ed, 1985.

8   The varieties of audience experience

This is the only project suggested in this chapter which directly invites the brave, or foolhardy, student into quantitative field-work. Work in political economy certainly turns on figures, but it is likely that, for our purposes, such research will be done in the pages of annual reports, of *The Economist*, and of the newspapers as well as of *Media, Culture and Society*, rather than on the ground. Audience research, however, generally indicates empirical inquiry, and any newcomer to such work is apt to think of it as broadly *easier* than thought about theory.

It is to be hoped that chapter 7 will prevent any too great naivety of this kind, but in the case of those researchers who are really determined to go and find out what people do with their systems of public communications, they should be advised to start from a full-blown television market research questionnaire obtainable from any big agency. Student theses at all levels have for years been disfigured by questionnaires whose content has been entirely vacuous and whose purported findings, often solemnly followed up by our old friend, the so-called structured interview, have been the rehearsal of utter banalities. Questionnaires absolutely demand intelligent collaboration in the first place – collaboration which entails going through the questions endlessly to sharpen, simplify and refine them, remove ambiguities, include lie-detectors or checks on mistakes, cut down the time taken to fill them in. In the second place, questionnaires must be tested in at least one pilot experiment before they are trusted on the main inquiry.

These demands are minimal if students are to learn some respect for the instruments of survey research. (I say nothing here about the logic of statistical inference, which is the title of a handbook in itself.) Nevertheless, the work is undoubtedly fascinating: to quarry raw data of the sort sampled in chapter 3 is to dig out weird and absorbing truths about human behaviour. For those set on such a project, the great thing to hang on to is the *reciprocal* nature of audience response. People are active and passive in their uses of all media; the researcher must be exceptionally agile in the devising of many interpretations of people's actions, observations and immobility. Ingenuity and strong human sympathy are the first qualities called for.

The books which will encourage these attributes include:

Blumler, Jay and D. McQuail, *Television in Politics: Its Uses and Influence*, Faber & Faber, 1968.
Blumler, Jay and Elihu Katz, as cited, 1974.
Halloran, J. D. (ed.), *The Effects of Television*, Granada, 1970.
Himmelweit, Hilde, P. Vince and A. N. Oppenheim, *Television and the Child*, Oxford University Press, 1958.
Hodge, Bob and David Tripp, as cited, 1986.
Holub, Miloslav, *Reception Theory*, Methuen, 1980.
Leavis, Q. D., as cited, 1932.
McLuhan, Marshall, *Understanding Media*, Routledge & Kegan Paul, 1964.
Masterman, Len, as cited, 1985, chapter 7.
Morley, David, as cited, 1986.
Seymour-Ure, Colin, *The Political Impact of the Mass Media*, Constable, 1974.
Williams, Bernard as cited, 1981.

9   *Literate, oral and electronic cultures*

This final project recapitulates the first moral of the whole book: that the media did not arrive all of a sudden in the 1960s, but that media itself is a plural noun, that each medium has a singular as well as an interwoven history, and that, finally, the straightest, most comprehensible road to theory (and therefore to reasonable under-standing) is by way of that history.

The history implied here is, like all other history, a matter of intelligent speculation shaping such facts and reports as we have. The invitation held out by the project is to reconstruct, from both imagination and experience, the frames of mind peculiar to those societies in which oral, written or electronic communication has the most visible power.

In the first instance, this is straightforwardly a matter of reviewing the records we have of non-literate, oral societies, a few of which are listed below (such an essay would have to start from Jack Goody's classic collection). It is then a matter of trying to catch societies as they become literate, and by way of identifying literacy's conse-quences, trying to imagine what difference it would make to its frames of mind. After the moment of conversion to literacy, things become more complicated. Before the advent of printing, books make an enormous difference only to the clerical elite; even after 1460, universal literacy is a long time coming (it isn't here yet). And now, as it is almost achieved, at least in the first and second worlds, this coming-to-literacy coincides with the present uncontrollable expan-sion of electronic communications, such that the whole world can get close to a radio, if not a television, and learn what the powerful decide to tell them about the whole of the rest of the world.

Clearly, our project has many dimensions, and a speculating stu-dent could only take one corner of it, such as these: the first consequences of literacy, perhaps; the change of mind brought by print; the effect on social relations of the radio or the telephone; the struggle for dominance between the book and the film; the persist-ence (for example, amongst school children) of oral, unofficial cul-ture alongside the formal culture of the book. All these constitute inquiries of themselves, and each suggests a way of discovering the shaping presence of each distinct medium.

These books hint at our approach to several of the sub-topics. I would myself counsel that a student in this area select a fairly limited historical period (only a few years), or as it may be a mo-ment of change or overlap between one system of communication and another.

Anderson, Benedict, *Imagined Communities: Reflections on the Origins and Spread of Nationalism*, Verso, 1983.

Benjamin, Walter as cited, 1970 on p.243.

Diringer, David, *Writing*, Thames & Hudson, 1962.

Eco, Umberto, *The Name of the Rose*, Secker & Warburg, 1984.

Evans-Pritchard, E. E., *Death and Witchcraft among the Azande*, Oxford University Press, 1946.

Febvre, Lucien and H. J. Martin, *The Coming of the Book: the Impact of Printing 1450–1800*, New Left Books, 1976.

Goody, Jack (ed.), as cited, 1972.

McLuhan, Marshall as cited, 1962.

Opie, Peter and Iona, *The Lore and Language of Schoolchildren*, Oxford University Press, 1954.

Owst, G. R., *Literature and Pulpit in Medieval England*, Cambridge University Press, 1951.

Scribner, R. W., *For the Sake of Simple Folk*, Cambridge University Press, 1981.

Watt, Ian, *The Rise of the Novel*, Chatto & Windus, 1957.

Weber, Max, *The Theory of Social and Economic Organisations* (final section on the mandarin Chinese), New York Free Press, 1947.

Worsley, Peter, *The Trumpet shall Sound*, Paladin, 1967.

Yeats, W. B., *Essays on Good and Evil* ('Popular Poetry'), Macmillan, 1924.

Index